Praise for *Outwitting History*

"It's a marvelous yarn, loaded with near-calamitous adventures and characters as memorable as Singer creations." —*New York Post*

"Anyone who loves books—not just reading, but books themselves . . . will love *Outwitting History*." —MSNBC.com

"Book lovers of all linguistic persuasions will find it as stirring as it is *geshmak* (delectable!)." —Cynthia Ozick

"Incredible. . . . Inspiring. . . . Important." —*Library Journal*, starred review

"The real reason to read the book is to remind yourself of the value of a great idea, Jewish or otherwise, (even if you are the only person who has it or believes in it) and the impact of enthusiasm on productivity. . . . The stories here fill up your spirit." —*Minneapolis Star Tribune*

"Both hilarious and moving, filled with Jewish humor, conversations with elderly Jewish immigrants for whom the books evoke memories of a faraway past, stories of desperate midnight rescues from rain-soaked Dumpsters, and touching accounts of Lansky's trips to what were once thriving Jewish communities in Europe. The book is a testimony to his love of Judaism and literature and his desire to make a difference in the world." —*Publishers Weekly*, starred review

"Every now and again a book with near-universal appeal comes along: *Outwitting History* is just such a book. . . . An unpretentious, entertaining account." —*The Portland Oregonian*

"A tale of triumph over tragedy. . . . Mr. Lansky tells his story and that of the Book Center with remarkable brio and cheer." —*The New York Sun*

"A rollicking, readable account of one man's passion and the difference it made."   —Rabbi Harold Kushner, author of
When Bad Things Happen to Good People

"What began as a quixotic journey was also a picaresque romp, a detective story, a profound history lesson, and a poignant evocation of a bygone world. Lansky's extraordinary storytelling conveys the daunting task he set for himself."   —*The Boston Globe*

"On one delightful level, *Outwitting History* is a litany of East European gastronomy and of young, more assimilated stomachs attempting to absorb it. . . . The best part of *Outwitting History* is Lansky's accounts of the elderly Jews he meets. He has a wonderful ear for Yiddish and (fractured) English dialogue, and for the many layers of humor, disappointment, irony, etc., those words sometimes reveal."   —*Cleveland Jewish News*

"Upbeat and profoundly moving."   —*Booklist,* starred review

"Any book lover will enjoy Lansky's story about how he got involved in creating the National Yiddish Book Center. . . . Lansky brings to life the people behind the Yiddish books he has saved, telling their stories as well as his own in this heartwarming volume."
—*The Southern Pines (North Carolina) Pilot*

"Lansky's memoir fascinates as it recounts how his relatively simple quest for books . . . turned into a rescue mission of historic proportions. . . . One comes away from this memoir with a sense of the panorama of history through which even the most common Yiddish book has passed."   —*Jewish Book World*

"Highly readable and entertaining as it tells the history of the *mame loshn*, the mother tongue, of these Jews."—*Los Angeles Times Book Review*

"[An] inspiring chronicle."   —*BookPage*

"More than a fascinating account of how an institution can rise from the ruins. It is a love story about a man smitten with a whole culture, an inspiring tale." —Jonathan Rosen, author of *Joy Comes in the Morning* and *The Talmud and the Internet*

"Despite seemingly insurmountable financial obstacles, *Outwitting History* is a feel-good saga." —*The Cleveland Plain Dealer*

"[An] engaging first-person account of how some committed young people rescued from history's dustbin more than a million books published in Yiddish. . . . Lansky unfolds a tale of rare emotion and devotion. . . . A rollicking ride in company with a man who has performed an enormously important public service." —*Kirkus Reviews*, starred review

"At times laugh-out-loud funny, at times poignantly sad." —*The Jerusalem Post*

"I loved Lansky's book. It's full of unforgettable characters and hilarious, affecting anecdotes." —*New York Newsday*

"The anecdotes of *Outwitting History* are so numerous and tasty (in Yiddish, *geshmak*) that no review can begin to do them justice." —*San Francisco Chronicle*

"I have been inspired by Aaron Lansky's work since I first learned of it, twenty-five years ago. He is, quite simply, a hero." —Anita Diamant, author of *The Red Tent*

"[A] haunted but stubbornly hopeful book." —*The Kansas City Star*

"In a breezy style, the author takes readers on his quarter-century quest inside Dumpsters and moldy basements in search of books and best of all, their owners' personal stories. I was hooked." —*The Rockville (Maryland) Gazette*

"Lansky's prodigious anecdotes recounting his book-rescue mission alternate between the achingly poignant and knee-slapping hilarious. . . . In a life story as improbable as any of those chronicled in the beloved Yiddish tales of our ancestors, Lansky has become an integral part of the history and Jewish civilization that he succeeded in saving—one book at a time." —*The Jewish Ledger* (Western Massachusetts)

"Fascinating." —*The Sanford (North Carolina) Herald*

"A lively, engaging, often moving and sometimes humorous account." —*The Hamilton (Ontario) Spectator*

"Yiddish never looked so intriguing. With all the enthusiasm and creative energy of a man who's found his true calling, Lansky takes us along for an enjoyable quest that helps us bridge between the old world and the new." —*Jewsweek*

"Mr. Lansky captures it all in this compelling memoir." —*The Wall Street Journal*

"What Aaron Lansky has accomplished . . . is nothing short of miraculous. *Outwitting History* is a must read for bibliophiles." —Nicholas A. Basbanes, author of *A Gentle Madness, Patience and Fortitude*, and *A Splendor of Letters*

"A truly interesting and unique book. . . . Lansky also does a magnificent job of relating to the general public how alive the Yiddish culture was. . . . A great book about books, and should be enjoyed by all." —*Framingham (Massachusetts) Metro West Daily News*

"This against-all-odds story is engaging and surprising, culturally significant and a whole lot of fun. Aaron Lansky, who lived it, tells it beautifully." —Kenneth Turan, film critic for the *Los Angeles Times* and NPR's *Morning Edition*

Outwitting History

Outwitting History

THE AMAZING ADVENTURES OF A MAN WHO RESCUED A MILLION YIDDISH BOOKS

—◆—

by Aaron Lansky

ALGONQUIN BOOKS OF CHAPEL HILL
2005

for Gail

Author's Note

Because I was a participant in the events that follow and not a reporter, most of the people who appear in this book did not know I would write about them one day. To protect their privacy, I have changed certain names, places of residence, and other identifying characteristics. The rest of their stories are accurate within the limits of memory, both theirs and mine.

Published by
ALGONQUIN BOOKS OF CHAPEL HILL
Post Office Box 2225
Chapel Hill, North Carolina 27515-2225

a division of
Workman Publishing
225 Varick Street
New York, New York 10014

First paperback edition, Algonquin Books of Chapel Hill, September 2005.
Originally published by Algonquin Books of Chapel Hill in 2004.
Printed in the United States of America.
Published simultaneously in Canada by Thomas Allen & Son Limited.
Design by Anne Winslow.

Excerpt reprinted with the permission of Simon & Schuster Adult Publishing Group from *Patrimony* by Philip Roth. Copyright © 1991 by Philip Roth. Excerpt from *Tevye's Daughters* by Sholom Aleichem, copyright © 1949 by the Children of Sholom Aleichem and Crown Publishers, a division of Random House, Inc. Used by permission of Crown Publishers, a division of Random House, Inc.

Library of Congress Cataloging-in-Publication Data
Lansky, Aaron, 1955–
    Outwitting history : the amazing adventures of a man who rescued a million Yiddish books / by Aaron Lansky.—1st ed.
       p. cm.
    Includes bibliographical references.
    ISBN-13: 978-1-56512-429-5 (HC)
       1. Book collecting.   2. Yiddish imprints.   3. Lansky, Aaron, 1955—Contributions in Yiddish language.   4. Language revival.   5. Yiddish language—Revival.   6. National Yiddish Book Center (U.S.)—History.   I. Title.
    Z987.L25 2004
    002'.075—dc22   2004051587
    ISBN-13: 978-1-56512-513-1 (paper)

10 9 8 7 6 5 4 3

CONTENTS

FOREWORD

AX WEINREICH, the greatest Yiddish scholar of his generation, was delivering a lecture in Finland when the Nazis invaded Poland on September 1, 1939. The lecture saved his life. Unable to return to his home in Vilna, he made his way to New York, where he opened his doors to American students. Few came. Although many thought his work here was hopeless, Weinreich persevered. When a student asked him why, he answered simply: "Because Yiddish has magic, it will outwit history."

And so it has. Not long ago, I met under an apple tree with a group of very bright college students. "Why are you interested in Yiddish?" I asked. They laughed. "Don't you understand," one young woman explained, the sun glinting off a diamond stud in her bellybutton, "nowadays Yiddish is *hip!*"

Just how hip is something I've had a chance to gauge for myself over the past twenty-five years. In 1980, at the age of twenty-four, I decided to save the world's Yiddish books. At the time scholars believed 70,000 volumes remained; today, my colleagues and I have collected more than one and one-half *million*—many of them at the last minute from attics and basements, demolition sites and Dumpsters. Most Jewish leaders dismissed my plans by saying that Yiddish was dead; today the organization I founded, the National Yiddish Book Center, has thirty-five thousand members, making it one of the largest Jewish cultural organizations in the United States.

This book is an adventure story: It tells how a small group of young people saved Yiddish books from extinction. It's also the story of the Yiddish-speaking immigrants who owned and read those books—how they sat us down at their kitchen tables, plied us with tea and cakes, and handed us their personal libraries, one volume at a time. The encounters were almost always emotional: People cried and poured out their hearts, often with a candor that surprised us all.

At the time, my coworkers and I were still in our early twenties. We drove dented trucks and wore sweatshirts and faded jeans. Yet whether out of hope or desperation, people trusted us with their *yerushe,* their inheritance—their books and stories. For us it was a huge and sometimes overwhelming responsibility: How could we take care of so many books, remember so many stories, preserve so much history?

I am now forty-nine years old, and with few exceptions the people who entrusted me with their books in those early years are gone, and their world with them. Even as I write, despite the growing curiosity of scholars and the enthusiasm of young people, within the Jewish mainstream the story of Yiddish culture continues to be erased, our history rewritten, our sensibility recast, our identity redefined. More and more, as memory fades, the books we collected are all that remain. For that reason, the time has now come to tell this tale. It's sad, and funny, too. It's the best way I know to identify what's missing from contemporary Jewish life—and to begin to reclaim what we've lost.

PART ONE

Learning Yiddish

1 . Out of the Dumpster

The phone rang at midnight. That wasn't unusual: Older Jews often waited until the rates went down before phoning me about their Yiddish books. But tonight I had just returned from a long collection trip, it was snowing outside, our house was cold, the phone was in the kitchen, and I had no intention of crawling out from under the covers to answer it.

Brinnnnng! Brinnnnng!

My girlfriend, Laura Nelson, covered my ears. "It can wait," she hushed.

Apparently it couldn't. Five, ten, fifteen rings and finally my housemate, Scott Bolotin, went bounding downstairs to answer it himself. Thirty seconds later he was pounding on my bedroom door. "Aaron! Quick! Get up! It's for you! It sounds really important this time!"

I wrapped myself in a blanket and stumbled to the phone.

"Aaron, is that you?" I recognized the voice at once: It was Sheva Zucker, a young woman who had taught me Yiddish at a summer program in New York four years before. "I'm sorry to call so late," she said, "but this is an emergency! There are thousands of Yiddish books in a garbage Dumpster on Sixteenth Street and it looks like it's going to rain. How soon can you be here?"

There was only one train a day from Northampton, Massachusetts, near where I lived, to New York City, but fortuitously it came through at 2 A.M. If I hurried I could make it. I phoned my old college friend Roger Mummert in New York and told him to expect me at 6:45. Laura stuffed a sleeping bag, work gloves, and a loaf of bread into my rucksack. Scott raided our communal food kitty and the *tsedoke* jar, the shared charity fund we kept hidden in the freezer, and handed me a paper bag filled with $60 in loose bills and change. All I had to do was figure out how to get to the train station, eight miles away.

The roads were too slippery to go by bike. The local cab company was closed for the night. "What about your pickup?" Scott asked. He meant my '63 Ford, a vehicle so unroadworthy, so full of rust and holes, it had stood abandoned under a pine tree in the backyard since failing the state inspection six months before. But there was no other choice. Scott, Laura, and I rushed outside and brushed off the snow. I pulled out the choke, turned the key, and somehow the old engine shuddered to life. With a lot of pushing we managed to rock it out of the ruts where it had frozen in place. I plastered a clump of snow and pine needles to the windshield to cover the expired inspection sticker and made it to the train station with ten minutes to spare.

"*LAAAADIES AND GENTLEMENNNN,* the station stop is Pennsylvania Station, New York City. Please watch your step while leaving the train. *Pennnnnnn* Station . . ." I was out the door and running through the station before the conductor could finish. On Eighth Avenue I looked up and noticed the inscription chiseled on the post office across the street: "Neither Rain Nor Snow Nor Heat Nor Gloom of Night Stays These Couriers from the Swift Completion of Their Appointed Rounds." The sky was dark and spitting sleet. The clock read 6:37. I hailed a cab and picked up Roger, and together we raced over to Sixth and Sixteenth to find the Dumpster.

It wasn't hard to see. Standing on the street, the size of a tractor-trailer, it was literally overflowing with Yiddish books. The volumes at the top were already wet. A few dozen lay splayed on the street, run over by passing cars. The sleet had turned to rain, which showed no sign of letting up anytime soon.

Roger and I climbed into the Dumpster, where a few minutes later we were joined by Sheva and her friend Eric Byron, the young man who had discovered the scene the night before. By this point they had managed to figure out where the books came from. It seems an old Yiddish organization had once occupied offices in a nearby building. As their membership dwindled they could no longer afford the rent, so they moved out, consigning their large Yiddish library to a basement storeroom for safekeeping. Now the building was being made over into condos. When workmen found the forgotten books in the cellar, they began hauling them out to the Dumpster. It was only last night, when the pile got high enough for books to spill over the sides, that Eric noticed them and phoned Sheva, who in turn phoned me.

There was no time to lose. Roger went to the nearest pay phone and called the Dumpster company; their number was emblazoned on the side. They agreed not to pick up the bin until evening. He also called every friend the four of us could think of, looking for reinforcements. Meanwhile I was on the adjacent phone, trying to scare up a truck. After several calls I found a U-Haul dealer on Eleventh Avenue willing to rent without a credit card—none of us had one—provided we could come up with a cash deposit of $350.

For a motley crew like ours, $350 was a fortune, but luckily Sheva had money that she was saving to pay her taxes. As soon as the bank branch opened, she made the withdrawal. While Roger and Eric stayed with the books, Sheva and I took a cab over to Eleventh Avenue—with a Yiddish-speaking cab driver, no less!—and rented a twenty-four-foot truck, the biggest they had. By the time we made it back, a half dozen people, all under the age of twenty-five, had responded to Roger's call and were huddled on the corner, ready to help. I backed up to the Dumpster, turned on the emergency flashers, and then organized a "bucket brigade" so we could pass books into the truck. It was raining hard now, and within minutes all of us were soaked. Worse still, our clothes were turning colors: red, yellow, blue, and green, splotched by the book covers' dyes running in the rain.

At about 9:30, in response to an urgent phone call, our board member, Sidney Berg, arrived from Long Island with enough cash to reimburse Sheva. He also brought his handyman, Joe, a seasoned worker who seemed to double our speed single-handedly. We stayed in that Dumpster all day, racing the rain for every book. Many people stopped to watch. Some shrugged; others cried. A reporter for the *New York Times,* a young black woman in the process of converting to Judaism, told me it was the saddest sight she'd ever seen. Another reporter, for one of the tabloids, was less sympathetic. "I don't get it," he yelled up from under his umbrella. "I mean, these books are in *Yiddish.* Who's gonna read 'em? What is this for you kids, some kind of nostalgia trip?"

Shivering, half numb with fatigue and cold, I doubt I managed much of a response. And it probably didn't matter—the question was rhetorical, his stereotypes about Yiddish set long since. We continued working until dark. By that time our volunteers had gone home, leaving just Joe, Roger, and me in the Dumpster, with Sidney Berg, under an umbrella, standing vigil on the street. All told, we had saved almost five thousand volumes; the rest, probably another three thousand, were soaked beyond any hope of salvage, floating in a fetid, dye-stained pool at the bottom of the Dumpster. Roger and I said good-bye to Joe and Sidney, climbed into the cab of the U-Haul, turned the key . . . and nothing. The emergency flashers, blinking since morning, had drained the battery, and the truck wouldn't start.

I might have dissolved into tears right then and there had I not spied a gas station across the street. The burly mechanic on duty wasn't much help. "I ain't gonna leave the station to go work in the middle of no street," he said. "I'll tow you over here if you want, but that's gonna cost ya."

"How much?"

"Hundred bucks for the tow and five bucks to charge the battery."

"How about if we bring the battery to you?"

"In that case just five bucks. But how you gonna get that battery over here?"

After what we had been through that day, I was sure we could find a way. I asked the attendant if we could borrow a wrench, but he said it was against the rules. I handed him a soggy five-dollar bill and the rules changed. Roger and I walked back across the street, managed to disconnect the cables and lift the battery out of the truck. It was a heavy-duty truck battery, weighing a good fifty pounds. Since Roger is considerably taller than I, the battery listed precipitously as we walked. By the time we put it down on the oily floor of the garage, I realized the acid had leaked out and burned a hole right through my wet canvas parka.

We waited for the battery to charge, then drove back to Roger's apartment. I took a hot bath, ate supper, drank four cups of hot tea with honey, and fell sound asleep. At two o'clock the next afternoon I was back in Massachusetts, where a large crew of volunteers was waiting for me. Without a functional elevator it took us the rest of the afternoon and well into the evening to pass five thousand books from the back of the truck, up the stairs, and into our second-story loft, where we spread them on pallets to dry.

What had we saved? Almost two-thirds were "new": unread publishers' remainders printed in the 1930s and 1940s, including works on Zionist theory, history, memoirs, and at least five hundred copies of a large-format Yiddish translation of the Torah. The rest came from the organization's library: a solid assortment of Yiddish titles, most published in New York. Almost all of these books ended up in libraries or in the hands of students around the world.

Before I went home that night I returned the U-Haul and retrieved my unregistered pickup from the Northampton train station. Then I collapsed. For the next three days I remained in bed, my temperature spiking to 104. As I lay there, drifting in and out of fevered sleep, my thoughts turned to the tabloid reporter in the rain. Why *was* I doing this? Was it really just a matter of nostalgia? What did I hope to accomplish? And how had it all begun?

2. Bread and Wine

Well, it definitely wasn't nostalgia: I was too young to have much to be nostalgic about. Born in New Bedford, Massachusetts, in 1955, I heard Yiddish when my grandparents spoke to one another or when my American-born parents, whose Yiddish was imperfect but serviceable, wanted to discuss our bedtime or allowance. No one ever spoke Yiddish to me, to my brothers, or to anyone else our age. We were, after all, American kids, and there was no reason to weigh us down with the past.

As with so much else, it wasn't until I went off to college that all this began to change. In the fall of 1973, during my first semester at Hampshire College, I enrolled more or less by chance in a course called Thinking about the Unthinkable: An Encounter with the Holocaust. Organized the year before by a group of Hampshire students, it was, we were told, the first time a course on the Holocaust had ever been offered on an American campus. Our teachers, mostly visiting scholars, were the best in the field: Raul Hilberg, George Mosse, Eric Goldhagen, Yuri Suhl, Isaiah Trunk, and Zosa Szajkowski. As the semester progressed I found myself less interested in the Holocaust per se, in how the Germans went about murdering the Jews of Europe, and more in the people whom they sought to destroy. If, as the historian Salo Baron once argued, anti-Semitism resulted from the "dislike of the unlike," then in what way were the Jews of Europe "unlike," in what way were they so different, so utterly antithetical to fascist ideology, as to seal their destruction?

I shared these questions with Leonard Glick, a physician and professor of cultural anthropology who served as the course's faculty adviser. He told me he was becoming interested in similar questions himself, and he invited me to learn by his side. For the next three years my education progressed in exactly the way Hampshire's founders intended: days of discovery in the library, followed by lively discussion in Len's office or at his kitchen table. What I could not fully appreciate at the time was how revolutionary all this was, not only pedagogically but historiographically. In 1973 the field of Jewish scholarship was still called *Judaic* Studies, implying an emphasis on Judaism as a religion, as opposed to *Jewish* Studies, as the field is now widely called, the study of Jews as a people. The die was first cast in France almost two hundred years before, when Jews were permitted religious differences so long as they downplayed social, cultural, and above all, national specificity. With notable exceptions, mainstream Jewish historiography restricted itself to *Geistesgeschichte und Leidensgeschichte,* the history of spirituality and the history of suffering.

As an anthropologist, Len instinctively rejected this narrow view. "Jews must have been doing something more for the past two thousand years than writing books and getting killed," he insisted. "How did they make a living? What did they teach their children? What did they eat? What did they read? What stories did they tell? What songs did they sing? What was the relationship between men and women? How did they interact with their non-Jewish neighbors?" In short, Len was interested in *culture,* the full constellation of human experience, and he intuitively embraced what the pioneering Russian Jewish historian

Simon Dubnow had characterized as "the *sociological* view of Jewish history," the study not of Judaism but of *Jews.*

Knowing that I would need to learn languages in order to handle primary historical sources, I dutifully enrolled in courses in Hebrew and German, then the prescribed curriculum for aspiring Judaic-studies students. Those languages, together with Aramaic, may have sufficed had I limited myself to the study of theology, philosophy, and sacred texts. But as I quickly discovered, for much of the last millennium Jews in central and eastern Europe had spoken not Hebrew, not German, but Yiddish. If I wanted to understand their lives, I had no choice but to learn their language.

Yiddish (the word means "Jewish") first emerged in the tenth or eleventh century among Jews living along the banks of the Rhine River. The more distinct their communities became, the more their spoken language differentiated itself from that of their non-Jewish German-speaking neighbors. Not unlike Black English, it became the "in" language of a people on the outs, except that in the case of Yiddish, Jews brought with them a core culture rooted in Hebrew (the language of the Torah) and Aramaic (the language of the later sections of the Talmud). As a result, Yiddish, like other Jewish vernaculars—there were more than a dozen, including Ladino, Judeo-Arabic, Judeo-Greek, Judeo-Persian, and Judeo-Provençal—was written in the Hebrew alphabet and derived as much as 20 percent of its vocabulary from Hebrew and Aramaic. There were also words from Latin, French, and Italian, picked up in the course of earlier Jewish migrations. By the fourteenth and fifteenth centuries, when Jews were expelled from many of the duchies and counties of western Europe, opportunity beckoned in the huge, undeveloped Polish empire. Many Jews emigrated eastward, just as they were to move westward to America centuries later. They carried Yiddish with them, picking up new influences from local Slavic languages, including Polish, Ukrainian, White Russian, and Slovak. The East European "New World" was so welcoming that, especially at first, the Jewish population there expanded exponentially, until it comprised 75 percent of the world's Jewish population. These Yiddish-speaking settlers are the ancestors of most of today's American Jews.

As Max Weinreich observed, "a language is a dialect with an army." Of course, Yiddish never had a country of its own, let alone an army or navy, and this may be one reason people have sometimes wondered whether it's a language at all. For most of its history, Yiddish existed primarily as a spoken language, with only limited literary expression. Beginning in the second half of the nineteenth century, though, when Enlightenment ideas and economic modernization began to shake the foundations of the traditional Jewish world, Yiddish gave rise to a vibrant modern culture. By the early twentieth century there were Yiddish newspapers and magazines, films and plays, politics, art, music—and a free-wheeling literature that marked one of the most concentrated outpourings of literary creativity in all of Jewish history.

Today Yiddish language is taught at scores of major colleges and universities throughout North America; twenty-five years ago it was taught only at Brandeis, Columbia, and perhaps a handful of others. This dearth of instruction was indicative of long-standing prejudice in mainstream Jewish scholarship, where for the most part the Jewish vernacular was either denigrated or ignored. Yiddish-speakers themselves, including some of the most prominent Yiddish writers of the late nineteenth and early twentieth centuries, routinely referred to their language as *Zhargon*—Jargon. It was a bastard tongue, bad German, a linguistic *mishmash,* hardly a language at all. Jews intent on assimilation found it particularly odious. In Germany, for example, Jews tried to reduce Jewishness to a *Konfession,* a religion divorced from culture, insisting that they weren't Jews at all, but rather "Germans of the Mosaic persuasion." Go make the case in Yiddish, where every word, every linguistic tic, is a reminder of peoplehood. Consider, for example, Max Weinreich's example of a more or less random Yiddish sentence: *Di bobe est tsholent af Shabes* — The grandmother eats warmed-over bean stew on the Sabbath. *Bobe,* "grandmother," is a Slavic word that entered Yiddish in the thirteenth or fourteenth century. *Est* was adopted a thousand years ago, from Middle High German. *Tsholent,* bean stew, came from Old French more than a thousand years ago, probably from *chaud,* "hot," and *lent,* "slow"—a fitting name for a dish that Jews keep warm on the Sabbath, when cooking is not allowed. And *Shabes,* "Sabbath," is a Hebrew word that dates back several thousand years. Quite literally, Yiddish is a living chronicle of Jews' historical experience, proof of their peoplehood, and it therefore spills the beans on assimilationist aspirations. No wonder bourgeois Jews hated it; no wonder scholars ignored it. In 1873, for example, the German Jewish historian Heinrich Graetz afforded Yiddish just two paragraphs in his magisterial six-volume *History of the Jews.* Never mind that Yiddish was then the first or only language of 80 percent of the world's Jews; for Graetz, it was *"eine halbtierische Sprache,"* a half-bestial tongue.

However, half bestial or not, Yiddish was a language I needed to know, and since no courses were offered, I set off in the spring of 1974 in search of a teacher. Hampshire College is part of a five-college consortium with Amherst, Mount Holyoke, and Smith Colleges and the University of Massachusetts. I went from school to school until I finally came to Jules Piccus, a professor of medieval Spanish literature at the University of Massachusetts. A man in his early sixties with a head of snow-white hair and a full white beard, he bore an uncanny resemblance to Karl Marx—and in certain circles was almost as famous. Posted on his office wall was the front page of a 1960s Spanish newspaper with the headline PICCUS IS IN MADRID!—an alarm precipitated by his having discovered and removed long-forgotten, misplaced manuscripts by Leonardo da Vinci from the Spanish National Library. Jules was not only a bibliographic sleuth but an accomplished scholar and a genuine polyglot, familiar with twenty languages. But his first love remained Yiddish, which he had spoken growing up in Brooklyn. He told me that he had taught the language from time to time in the past, and he planned to teach it again the following semester. In September of 1974 I joined twenty other students for the first day of Elementary Yiddish 110.

Our text, *College Yiddish,* was a systematic introduction to Yiddish grammar written by Max Weinreich's son Uriel, a leading light in general linguistics until his untimely death in 1967. Jules was a demanding teacher. He gave lengthy homework assignments and was not much interested in excuses when students came to class unprepared. Most of the students, for their part, were dismayed at their teacher's zeal: They had signed up for Yiddish because it sounded easy, and they were shocked to discover that it was as much a language as any other, with its own vocabulary, phonology, and rules of grammar.

"Just because your grandmothers spoke Yiddish, don't think you're going to learn the goddamned language through osmosis!" Jules warned on the first day of class. But few took his admonitions seriously, fewer still did the homework, and at the end of the first semester I was one of just two students who passed.

Clearly exasperated, Jules decided to call it quits. "If you kids don't want to learn, then the hell with it!" he announced while handing back the final exams. Except that the two students still standing, Jack Jacobson and I, were not ready to give up so soon. Together with Roger Mummert and Kathy Singer, two friends from Hampshire College who had been studying Yiddish on their own, we went to see Jules in his office during the January intersession to ask if he'd continue to teach us privately. Jules agreed, under three conditions: We had to promise to "work like hell," to come to class prepared, and, since Jules would be teaching us on his own time at the end of the regular school day, to bring with us a suitable snack to tide us all over until dinner. We soon settled upon a regular menu: Roger provided a warm loaf of home-made whole wheat bread that he baked the morning of each class, and the rest of us took turns providing cheese, butter, occasional home-made cake or cookies, and, always, a bottle of red wine.

And so we began. Every Wednesday at 5 P.M., when the academic buildings at UMass emptied out, we would file into Jules's cramped office, slice the bread, uncork the wine, and set to work. Jules was an old-fashioned teacher: There were no games, no overhead projectors, no language labs. He believed that the only way to learn a language such as Yiddish, in which immersion was no longer practical, was by reading. We spent four weeks racing through the remaining chapters of *College Yiddish*—twice as much as we had covered during the whole previous semester. Fortunately, the task was not as difficult as it sounds, since Yiddish possesses only three tenses, three cases, and a fluid syntax that allows for remarkable subtlety of expression. Better yet, because it is, like English, a Germanic language, much of its vocabulary is sufficiently cognate to provide ready mnemonics. (For example, *unter* is "under," *bukh* is "book," *vaser* is "water," and so forth.) What *was* difficult to learn was the cultural context, the specifically Jewish concepts that infuse so much of the language—and make it so worth learning in the first place.

After completing Weinreich, Jules decided to jump right into a full-length novel. We protested that we didn't know enough yet, but he was insistent: "Do you want to spend your lives reading textbooks or do you want to read Yiddish?" He selected "the hardest goddamned book I could find": *Der Sotn in Goray (Satan in Goray)* by Isaac Bashevis Singer. The 1935 novel was written in a somewhat arcane Yiddish, intended to evoke the language of the seventeenth century, the period in which the story took place—even though its deeper meaning, the repudiation of redemptive ideology, could not have been more current. For the next year and a half we lived and breathed Bashevis Singer's story about the aftermath of the Chmielnicki massacres and the failure of false messiahs in the shtetl of Goray, "the little town at the end of the world." We worked *khevruse* style, meeting together during the week to prepare an assigned portion of text. At the beginning we had to look up every word in the dictionary, which was no small trick since modern Yiddish literature had emerged so recently—and its writers and publishers were so famously contentious—that standardized orthography was still not universally accepted, and we had to figure out for ourselves the spelling variant under which a given word could be found in the dictionary. Moreover, the newest dictionary at our disposal, the 1968 *Modern English–Yiddish Yiddish–English Dictionary* by Uriel Weinreich, included only words that Weinreich believed were appropriate for *modern* Yiddish; words that he felt were archaic, *daytshmerish* (excessively derivative from modern German), colloquial, vulgar, or otherwise inappropriate were left out—thus eliminating a significant percentage of Singer's lexicon.

When we couldn't find a word in Weinreich, we turned to Alexander Harkavy's *Jewish–English English–Jewish Dictionary,* a work first compiled in 1898. Here the problem was not so much Harkavy's Yiddish as his English. An immigrant from Russia, Harkavy had been somewhat overzealous in his embrace of the Queen's English, and not infrequently his English definitions sent us scurrying to an *English* dictionary to understand what he was trying to say. Here, for example, is a string of purportedly English words that appear under the letter "M" in the "English–Jewish" side of the dictionary: moxa, muchwat, mucid, mucidness, mucilage, mucilaginous, muciperous, mucours, mucus, mucusness. . . . And so forth. This was one Jewish immigrant who could give the *OED* a run for its money.

We persevered. On Wednesday morning we'd get together to review the week's text while Roger kneaded dough and kept an eye on the oven. Late in the afternoon we'd take a bus to the university, open our books, and begin.

"*Nu, Yankl, leyen a bisl!* (Nu, Jack, read a little!)" Jules began each class, addressing Jack Jacobson, who invariably sat to the teacher's right. We enjoyed this opening line so much that it became Jack's nickname. Even outside of class, we took to calling him Yankl Leyenabisl.

We proceeded word by word, sentence by sentence, taking turns reading out loud and translating as we went. At Jules's suggestion, we'd underline a word in the dictionary each time we looked it up, and it was seldom that we had to look up a word more than twice. It was an old-fashioned method, but it worked. After two years of kneading dough, sipping wine, and flipping through dictionaries, we not only finished *Sotn in Goray* but were able to make our way, slowly but surely, through almost any Yiddish text we could find.

If only we could find them.

AMONG THE FIVE colleges in and around Amherst, Massachusetts, only the library at the University of Massachusetts possessed any Yiddish books at all, and its holdings were eclectic at best. By the mid-1970s virtually the whole of Yiddish literature was out of print. The *Complete Works* of Sholem Aleichem, for example, the most popular and arguably the greatest work of Yiddish literature, was last published in the United States in 1928; The *Complete Works* of I. L. Peretz, consisting of plays, poems, essays, and stories by one of the most profound Jewish thinkers of the twentieth century, last appeared in 1948. My fellow students and I tried ordering used books by mail from an old Yiddish publisher and book distributor in New York, but its selection was small, its business practices arcane, and more often than not the books never arrived. Occasionally we'd see a Yiddish title listed at an exorbitant price in the catalog of a rare book dealer in Amsterdam; otherwise we had no idea where else to turn.

I tried. I scoured the used book stores of Cambridge; I got up at dawn to be first in line at the annual League of Women Voters' book sale under a tent on the Amherst Common. But to no avail. Finally it was Jules Piccus who suggested a solution. "Don't think the books are going to come to you," he said. "If you want Yiddish books you've got to go to them. Drive down to New York, to the Lower East Side. That's where Yiddish-readers used to live, that's where you'll find Yiddish books!" He paused for a moment, then, smiling through his white beard, he added, "And while you're there you can stop at Guss's Pickles on Hester Street and bring me back a gallon of half-sours."

3. "Come Back after *Yontef*!"

Dishes were clanging, trays banging, old people pushing, and just about everyone was yelling at once, the servers in Spanish and the customers in Yiddish. Roger, Kathy, and I had been studying Yiddish with Professor Piccus for almost a year now, and this, in the late spring of 1975, was the latest step in our determined but until now fruitless search for Yiddish books. Together with my friends Paul Novak and Laurie Radovsky, we had borrowed a van from Hampshire College and arrived in New York at about eleven o'clock on a beautiful April morning. I had been to New York just once before, to visit the World's Fair in 1964, and never to the Lower East Side. Stepping out of the van I was amazed at how Jewish it still seemed. Guss's was just one of several pickle emporia where workers in dirty aprons and rolled-up sleeves plunged their bare hands into big barrels of brine, coming up with half- and full-sour pickles, bright red peppers, fistfuls of sauerkraut, and heads of pickled cauliflower. Open barrels covered the sidewalk for half a block, and the entire street reeked of garlic, dill, and vinegar. Several blocks away the air turned heavy and sweet as we passed Shapiro's House of Kosher Wines, whose startling logo featured a knife standing upright in a glass of wine, topped by the dubious claim

"The Wine So Thick You Can Almost Cut It with a Knife!" On still other streets we passed fading, peeling signs in Hebrew and Yiddish, advertising tiny basement stores where dusty old men sold *taleysim,* mezuzahs, and other religious articles. In some storefronts one could watch *soyfrim* at work: ancient scribes with long gray beards who used quill pens to hand letter the parchment scrolls of the Torah. On every block were synagogues and the one-room Hasidic prayer houses known as *shtiblekh.* At the end of East Broadway, towering above the entire neighborhood, was the headquarters of the *Jewish Daily Forward,* the socialist Yiddish newspaper that had dominated immigrant Jewish life in America for more than eighty years. And right next to the ten-story *Forward* building was the Garden Cafeteria, a culinary landmark where Yiddish writers, intellectuals, shopkeepers, and workers had been coming for years to *farbrengen*—to eat, talk, and argue. It was almost noontime, and we could see through the steamy windows that the place was full. Figuring that someone among all those elderly Jews would know where we could find Yiddish books, we opened the door and stepped inside.

"Tickets!" the cashier yelled as we entered, forcing little printed cards into our hands. The system, it appeared, was that every time you ordered a dish, you presented the card to the server, who punched a hole in a box for the appropriate amount. You kept amassing holes until, after a full afternoon of shmoozing and eating, you were finally ready to settle accounts on your way out the door.

We, for our part, were having trouble just getting *in* the door. While the cashier impatiently explained the system, other patrons were already pushing from behind. By the time we made it to the cafeteria line, we were being jostled from all sides at once:

"Hurry up! What's the matter *mit* you?"

"Can't you see you got hungry people here?"

"*Nu* already, for what are you dillydallying?"

The Spanish-speaking servers were holding their own in the multi-lingual shouting match. A bit unnerved, we ordered as best we could, piling our trays high with blintzes and sour cream, kasha varnishkes and mushroom gravy, varenikes with fried onions, matzo brei and several other *milkhig* (dairy) specials. Then we tried to find a table. It goes without saying that none of the five of us looked like your typical Garden Cafeteria customer: We were fifty years too young, we spoke English, and every one of us sported long hair and jeans. But no one seemed to notice. In fact, as we squeezed ourselves into five empty seats at one of the cafeteria's long communal tables, the people already sitting there didn't even look up: They were far too busy arguing, engaged in a passionate discussion of some heated subject beyond our linguistic reach, which is to say that they were all speaking in Yiddish and all speaking at once. Hands were waving, fingers pointing, sentences punctuated with heaping spoonfuls of sour cream. It was only when one particularly vociferous old man banged his cup on his tray in a dramatic bid for attention and sent hot coffee splashing in every direction that someone finally noticed the five young newcomers in their midst. The argument came to a sudden halt.

"Um, *sholem aleykhem,*" I said in tentative greeting, taking advantage of the silence to address the whole table at once. These were the first Yiddish words I had ever spoken outside of a university setting, and I could feel myself blushing.

"*Aleykhem sholem,*" answered the woman closest to me, putting on her eyeglasses and looking me over from head to toe. Apart from the Hispanic servers and busboys, we appeared to be the only people in the restaurant under seventy-five.

"*Zogt mir,*" said the man with the coffee cup, looking at the five of us in our best post-hippie finery, "*ir zent yidishe kinder?* (Tell me, are you Jewish children?)"

"*Vu den?* (What else?)" We then explained, half in English, half in

Yiddish, that we were college students studying Yiddish who had come all the way from Massachusetts to look for Yiddish books. As might be expected, this news elicited considerable excitement.

"Hey, *Moyshe, kum aher un ze vos tut zikh bay di hayntike kinder!* —Hey, Moyshe, come over here and see what the kids these days are up to!" We were scrunched together as the news spread and more and more elderly Jews sat down at the table or leaned over our shoulders, asking us a hundred questions that, in their impatience, they then answered themselves. There was a widespread tone of disbelief: Jewish children going to university to study Yiddish! Who ever heard of such a thing? By the time we finished our meal (no small accomplishment, given the size of the portions and the crowd at the table), we had been examined, cross-examined, hugged, kissed, smeared with lipstick, pinched, and blessed more times than any of us thought healthy. We were also given the names of three nearby booksellers who, we were told, were likely to have Yiddish books.

THE FIRST WAS Rabinowitz's, just a block away on Canal Street. This was a relatively modern establishment with a large stock of English Judaica. The store did most of its business on Sunday, when second- and third-generation Jews came in from the suburbs to buy gifts for weddings and bar mitzvahs. When we asked the Israeli clerk for used Yiddish books he gave us a blank look and called the boss. The boss, a much older man, explained that he hadn't stocked Yiddish books for twenty years. He suggested we try Gottlieb just up the street, which happened to be the second name on our list. "Gottlieb's got a whole attic full of Yiddish books!" the man at Rabinowitz's assured us. "He's bound to have what you're looking for."

We walked the few blocks up Canal Street. From the outside Gottlieb's did not look promising. The building was old and decrepit, the display windows so caked with dust and grime we couldn't see inside. We opened the door with trepidation, stepped over the threshold, and were immediately swallowed up by must and gloom on that beautiful spring day. Packed from floor to ceiling were tottering shelves of *sforim,* weighty religious tomes in Hebrew and Aramaic. In the maze of narrow passageways between the shelves, bare lightbulbs hung from frayed cotton cords. The air was stale. As our eyes slowly adjusted to the dark, we could make out a half dozen black-coated Hasidim with long beards and *peyes,* ritual earlocks, rocking back and forth between the stacks as they leafed through their religious texts.

I, for one, was not eager to venture farther. Paul, Roger, and I were wearing neither hats nor yarmulkes. Kathy and Laurie were in jeans, young, pretty, and braless, their waist-length hair flowing free.

"This must be the wrong place," I whispered over my shoulder. "Let's get out of here!"

But my companions were either more oblivious or more determined than I. "We've come all this way, let's give it a try," said Paul, pushing me deeper into the store. Fortunately, the Hasidic customers were too engrossed in their reading to notice us. We remembered what the man at Rabinowitz's had said, that Gottlieb had an *attic* full of Yiddish books. To the right of the front door was a rickety staircase, and so, without asking questions, the five of us just walked on up.

The stairs creaked and groaned, but none of the Hasidim looked up from their *sforim.* The second-floor "attic" was brighter than downstairs, its green window shades so torn and tattered that they let ample light filter through. There, in the center of the room, were piled *thousands* of Yiddish books covered with several inches of dust. They were tossed this way and that, one atop the other. The pile was so prodigious—and had apparently been there for so long—that the floor literally sagged beneath it, and we had to walk slightly downhill to get from the stairs to the books.

Certain that we had reached the end of the trail—all the Yiddish books we could ever want—we wasted no time in pulling out treasure after treasure, gleefully calling out the authors as we went: "Itzik Manger!" "Sholem Asch!" "Dovid Bergelson!" There was every manner of writing: short stories, novels, scholarly works on Jewish history, essays, polemics, political theory. We were each hoarding personal piles of the books we wanted to buy, hoping that they wouldn't be too expensive, when suddenly we looked up to see an imposing figure, with a full dark beard, black hat, and black coat, scowling at us from the doorway.

"Vos tut zikh do? (What's happening here?)" he demanded. "Who are you? What do you want? Who gave you permission to come upstairs?"

My friends and I looked at one another, not sure how to respond. Kathy, who was probably the most conciliatory among us, tried to say something, but she was a woman, so the man covered his eyes with his hand and turned away. Laurie, with her bright smile and long red hair, fared no better. Then Roger tried, explaining as best he could that we were college students who had come to New York in search of Yiddish books. "And," he added with a grin, indicating the pile with a sweep of his hand, "it looks like we've found them!"

The old Jew was not amused. *"Shkotsim! Apikorsim!* (Non-Jews! Heretics!)" he cursed. "What do you want with *Yiddish* books? Better you should study *Toyre,* study *Gemore! Far vos zolt ir avekpatern di tsayt mit mayselekh?* (Why waste your time with stories?)"

This abrupt attack was our first introduction to one of the great ironies of contemporary Jewish life: Hasidic and extreme orthodox Jews, the only demographically significant segment of the Jewish population who continue to speak Yiddish and teach the language to their children, are completely hostile to modern Yiddish literature. For them, most Yiddish books are *treyf posl,* forbidden, unkosher. Works by a writer such as Sholem Aleichem would be as unwelcome in their homes as a slab of bacon. That's because Yiddish is an inherently *modern* literature, the product of intellectuals who had broken from the constraints of halakha—Talmudic law. Yiddish writers, almost by definition, embraced worldly knowledge, seeking to reinterpret and reconstruct Jewish tradition in a modern context—an endeavor that, while not without precedent in Jewish history, was nonetheless anathema to the black-coated defenders of tradition. Even when modern Yiddish books were not explicitly antireligious, they were still forbidden, since observant Jews were supposed to spend their time studying legal and religious texts in Hebrew and Aramaic, not reading "frivolous" works such as novels, stories, and poetry.

What, then, were thousands of Yiddish books doing in a religious bookstore? After the man calmed down a bit he explained that people often came to him with boxes of old books to sell, usually after the death of a husband or parent. He would take the boxes, sell the Hebrew texts, and stash the Yiddish books out of sight in the attic. True, he considered the Yiddish books *treyf;* but as a Jew with an innate sense of respect for the written word, he could not bring himself to throw them out. And so the pile in his attic had grown larger with every passing year: He didn't want to throw the books out, but he didn't want to sell them, either.

We, for our part, desperately wanted the books, and we suggested what seemed to us a reasonable way out. "Look, *we're* not *frum*—we're not observant—so there's no way these books are going to corrupt us any more than we already are. We're studying Jewish history, the history of all Jews, secular and religious alike. You have no use for the books and we do. For you they're just taking up space. We have a van parked nearby. How about if we just take them off your hands?"

I thought I saw the man waver for a moment, but he did not relent. Perhaps he honestly believed that the books would contribute to our moral corruption and he didn't want the sin on his head. On the other hand, maybe it suddenly dawned on him that there was a commercial market for these old books after all, and he figured he could sell them for a greater profit somewhere else. Whatever the case, he said he needed time to think it over. *"Kumt nokh yontef . . . ,"* he said, dismissing us with a wave of the hand. "Come after the Jewish holidays—then we'll see."

It was two weeks after Pesakh. The next *yontef* was not until Shavues, four weeks away. But we agreed to wait. Two months later, in mid-June, Roger and I returned. The bookseller remembered us, but he wasn't ready to deal. "Not today," he said, "today we're too busy. I'll tell you what, *kumt nokh yontef*—come after the holidays. Maybe I'll have more time then."

Nokh yontef? Not counting a few odd fast days, it was three months until Rosh Hashanah, the next Jewish holiday. No matter, the owner was insistent. I went back alone after Yom Kippur, and then returned a few more times during the next few years. I went in the summer, I went in the winter; I went after Simkhes Torah, when it was more than five months till the next Jewish festival. It made no difference, the reply was always the same: *"Kumt nokh yontef."* I was still trying several years later when I found the building boarded up and abandoned. By then the Lower East Side was in precipitous decline as a Jewish neighborhood and many storekeepers were leaving. I never did discover the fate of the Yiddish books in Gottlieb's attic. As far as I know, he's *still* waiting for *yontef* to be over.

ALL WAS NOT LOST, though, on that first pilgrimage to the Lower East Side. There was still one more name on our list: J. Levine, on Eldridge Street. Levine's was altogether different from the two stores we had already visited. In fact, it wasn't really a store at all, but rather a wholesale house, distributing books, vestments, and other religious articles to Jewish bookstores and synagogue gift shops around the country. We rang the bell, stepped through a heavy steel door, and informed the owner, Mr. Levine, a dignified man with a kind face and reassuring smile, that we were students in search of Yiddish books.

"*Yiddish* books?" Mr. Levine smiled. "I think I can help you. Follow me, please."

He led us onto an old freight elevator, down into the basement, and past shelves and shelves of merchandise: a hundred kiddush cups wrapped in tissue paper, crates of tin-foil menorahs, rows of shofars. Finally, in the farthest corner of the basement, we came to an old-fashioned wooden bookcase packed with about one hundred Yiddish books, all of them in excellent condition.

"Well, here they are," said Mr. Levine with a smile.

"Wow!" was all we could manage; and then I got worried, because they were such important books in such fine condition and we didn't have a lot of money with us. "Er, how much are they?"

Mr. Levine looked offended. "Oh, no, you don't understand. We don't *sell* Yiddish books here. These books belonged to my father, *alev hasholem* (may he rest in peace). My father loved Yiddish, he loved to read Yiddish books. When he died I brought his library down here for safekeeping. I always knew that someday someone would come for it, and it looks like you're finally here. If you young people are interested in Yiddish, then the books are yours. There's no charge."

He asked us where we were parked. When we told him—in a garage twelve blocks away—he called over two of his warehousemen and had them pack the books into boxes and load them into the trunk of his car. Mr. Levine himself then drove us to our van. When we tried to thank him he cut us short. "All I want is that the books should be read," he said. "Continue with your studies. That will be thanks enough."

Before leaving the Lower East Side we stopped off at Guss's to pick up a gallon of half-sours for Professor Piccus, along with a few quarts for ourselves. It was late when we arrived home in Amherst, but we stayed up to unpack the boxes and divide the books among us. My share consisted of a beautiful, fourteen-volume "deluxe" edition of the complete works of Sholem Aleichem, its covers etched in gold. I returned to my dorm room, unpacked the books, and spent most of the night trying to read them. In the years since, I've collected almost 1.5 million Yiddish books; but those first volumes of Sholem Aleichem, now tattered and dog-eared from use, are, for me, still the most precious of all.

4. "What Is Mendele Doing in a Fruit Basket on the Floor?"

I finished college in December of 1976, planning to continue my studies the following fall as a graduate student in East European Jewish Studies at McGill University, in Montreal. But first, with eight months of freedom ahead of me, I decided to "split for the Coast," taking advantage of a $49 fare to ride the Greyhound to San Francisco. There I hooked up with my college friend Paul Novak, who had accompanied me on my first trip to the Lower East Side, and moved into a railroad flat in the Fillmore district. After a few false starts I landed a job at the Judah Magnes Museum in Berkeley, a converted mansion on a tree-lined street, that billed itself as the Jewish Museum of the West.

Chronically underfunded, the Jewish Museum of the West was in no position to hire additional staff—the curator, with a Ph.D. in art history, was making $7,000 a year—and it's unlikely the founder and director, an affable Jewish Community Federation official based in San Francisco named Seymour Fromer, would have agreed to interview me at all if he hadn't had a big problem on his hands. Several years before my arrival, the museum's small library had been overwhelmed by the donation of almost ten thousand Yiddish books from a declining commune of left-wing Jewish chicken farmers in nearby Petaluma. Having no room in the main building, Seymour consigned the Yiddish books to an old carriage house out back. Now he wanted to transform the carriage house into badly needed museum space, but first he had to do something with those books. As soon as he heard that I had studied Yiddish, he hired me on the spot for an effective salary of $1 an hour plus all the duplicate Yiddish books I could carry.

Talk about *hefkeyres* (disorder): The carriage house overflowed with books, and it was my job to sort them and weed out the duplicates. I loved every second of it. As word of my efforts spread, curious visitors began to show up. Kathryn Hellerstein, a graduate student of Yiddish poetry at Stanford, came looking for books for herself. Sometimes she brought with her Malka Heifetz Tussman, a distinguished Yiddish poet who seemed to have a personal story about every author I shelved— a remarkable number of whom she claimed had courted her in her youth. Another regular visitor was Dov Noy, head of the folklore department at the Hebrew University in Jerusalem, who was in town as a visiting professor at Berkeley. A native Yiddish-speaker, Dov had been the first professor to teach Yiddish literature in Israel, and he enjoyed regaling me for hours with stories about the books I was sorting and the people who wrote them.

Perhaps the most revealing visitor was an old man who showed up one day to "tell the truth about all these books." An early member of the Petaluma commune, he quit after Khrushchev's revelations of Stalin's crimes in 1956 and had been bitterly disillusioned ever since. "You want to know why these books are in such good condition?" he asked. "I'll tell you why. It's because nobody ever read them! The only reason the commune had Yiddish books at all was because the Party made them buy them!"

Be that as it may, the books *were* in uncommonly good condition. I remained at the carriage house for four months, until all the boxes were unpacked and the sorting complete. Between work and commuting, I had little time for reading, but a process of literary osmosis took place nonetheless. By the time I got to graduate school in Montreal I not only recognized most authors' names, but thanks to Malka Tussman and Dov Noy, I felt I knew many of them personally. And, what with all the duplicate books I received in lieu of salary, I arrived with the best personal Yiddish library of any student in my class.

WHEN I WAS growing up my mother used to call upstairs with the same question: "How would you like your sandwich today, dear, on rye bread or on *gayishe?*" *Gayishe* was her folksy Galitsianer pronunciation for *goyishe,* which, as I learned before I could walk, was synonymous in this context with white bread. Jewish or goyish was the grand bifurcation of the universe. If, on rare occasion, my parents uttered a sentence that did not contain the word "Jewish," odds were it contained "goyish" instead.

I learned other aspects of Yiddish sensibility at shul, in the Conservative synagogue we attended every Saturday morning. In the front rows, where my parents sat with other American-born professionals, the proceedings grew steadily more decorous with each passing year. In the back it was different. There the European-born immigrants davened (prayed): tough Jews in enormous wool *taleysim* (prayer shawls), bootleggers, peddlers, and junkmen, who drank *shnaps* (straight whiskey) out of water glasses, munched on herring and raw onions, spoke mostly in Yiddish, and almost never stopped talking. I was seven years old, with a clip-on tie, but instinctively I preferred the *heymish,* homegrown, back of the shul over the highbrow front, and I escaped there every chance I got. The old men greeted me in their heavy Yiddish accents, hugged me to their bristly cheeks (they never shaved on Shabbos) and let me sit with them while they told and retold their jokes and stories. They listened with one ear to the service and interrupted their kibbitzing only long enough to shout *"Omeyn!* (Amen!)"

I learned about Yiddish sensibility at Hebrew school, too—albeit inadvertently. Our teachers taught us to read siddur (the prayer book) and Torah in Ashkenazic Hebrew. There was something strange about these nervous men with their heavy accents. Mr. Asch used to smoke half a cigarette, pinch the end between his fingers, and save the rest for later. Dr. Gross once got so exasperated with a student that he threw the boy's public-school notebook out the second-story window. Only years later did I learn that most of these teachers were Holocaust survivors, philologists with Ph.D.s from Viennese universities. Not that it would have mattered. We were American kids and we tormented them mercilessly, imitating their accents, hiding their books, placing tacks and bubble gum on their chairs, barraging them with spit balls and paper airplanes. But at least they were colorful. And authentic.

A year before my bar mitzvah our synagogue, in concert with other Conservative congregations across the country, changed from Ashkenazic to Sephardic Hebrew. The ostensible reason was to bring liturgical Hebrew in line with the spoken language of the young State of Israel. Never mind that 99 percent of the congregants were Ashkenazic Jews with roots in central and eastern Europe. And never mind that the reason Zionist leaders insisted on the harsher, more "masculine"-sounding Sephardic pronunciation in the first place had more to do with ideology than linguistics: They wanted to purge the ancient Jewish language of its "Yiddish accent," of the slightest whiff of the European diaspora. To me, Sephardic Hebrew sounded more like a tonsil exam—*"BAAAH-rukh AHHHH-tah"*—than like the soulful prayers I had known, and the characters in our new Israeli textbooks—yu-ri, YA-el—sounded as though they'd be more at home in a Superman comic book. To this day I have a hard time substituting *mah-ZAHL TOVE* for *mazl tov, nah-khat* for *nakhes,* or *rahk-mah-NOOT* for *rakhmones.* It's as though the most intimate Jewish expressions of our parents and grandparents, the felicitations, endearments, and consolations used by Jews for countless generations, were somehow wrong, illegitimate, and in need of reinvention.

Pronunciation was hardly the only sphere where the past was recast. That same year, 1967, we returned from summer vacation to find that every one of our European teachers had been dismissed, replaced by young Israeli women, the wives of local doctors and lawyers, who spoke fluent Hebrew but had little or no knowledge of Jewish tradition. The course they taught in Jewish history began with Abraham and Moses and continued—if we were lucky—until the defeat of Bar Kokhba and the fall of Jerusalem in 135 CE. Then, in a single dizzying leap, they skipped over the next eighteen hundred years until—*whoosh!*—suddenly it was 1948 and we were all back in Israel. What happened during those intervening centuries—how Jews ended up in Europe; where my own grandparents came from; why they spoke with Yiddish accents; even what happened during the Holocaust—these were stories never told.

Like most of my classmates, I didn't take well to the new regime. One by one the noisy, *shnaps*-drinking old men disappeared from the back of the shul. What remained up front was stiff, formal, and boring. I celebrated my bar mitzvah in May of 1968—a year when it seemed the whole country was coming of age. Seven months later I aimed a snowball at a friend, missed, and hit my Israeli Hebrew school teacher instead, unseating her beehive hairdo. She sent me to the principal's office and I was summarily expelled. While my classmates looked on with silent envy, I gleefully scooped up my books and left Hebrew school for the last time, certain that my Jewish education had come to an end at last.

It was, appropriately enough, a book that finally brought me back, and that led me to study Yiddish literature in Montreal: a slim volume by Ruth R. Wisse called *The Schlemiel as Modern Hero*. I read it during the summer of 1976, when I was running a fruit juice cart in Copley Square, across the street from the Boston Public Library. Business was bad that summer but reading was good, which was lucky, because once I started the book I couldn't put it down.

Ruth's thesis was this: The schlemiel, the familiar protagonist of much of Yiddish and, later, American-Jewish fiction, appears foolish only insofar as he is out of place—a Jew who ventures into the mainstream world and asks "the wholly spontaneous questions of a different culture."

Outrageous and absurd as his innocence may be by the normal guidelines of political reality, the Jew is simply rational within the context of ideal humanism. He is a fool, seriously—maybe even fatally—out of step with the actual march of events. Yet the impulse . . . of schlemiel literature is generally to use this comic stance as a stage from which to challenge the political and philosophical status quo.

Born in the shadow of nuclear weapons, coming of age during Vietnam, I was all for changing the status quo. The book confirmed my conviction that culture—and in particular Yiddish culture—could undermine political policy and in so doing become a powerful tool for social change. It showed why Yiddish literature could still speak to modern readers (or at least to me). And, not incidentally, it was one of the few academic books I had encountered that was not only profound but beautifully written: clear, fresh, and fun to read. I didn't know at the time who Ruth Wisse was or whether she even offered a graduate course, but by the time I finished the book I knew for sure that there was no one else with whom I wanted to study.

Fortunately Ruth had just established a graduate program at McGill in East European Jewish studies, and when I arrived in the fall of 1977 I found my teacher every bit as brilliant, human, and down-to-earth as her book suggested. As I had guessed, she was plenty political: though in exactly the opposite direction from what I had assumed. She was, in fact, the most right-wing person—or at least the most right-wing rational person—I had ever met: an unyielding hawk on Israel; a critic of feminism who opposed the ordination of women rabbis; a fierce anti-Communist who championed American military strength to a degree that made Ronald Reagan look like a dove. One might think, given my Hampshire College education, where feminism, pacifism, and critical theory are imparted as revealed truth, that Ruth's stridency would prove a problem for me. And in a certain sense it did: She once handed back a paper, telling me it was an excellent effort, "even if it is inimical to everything I believe in." I was still too young to question my own politics, but thankfully she was too much of a *mentsh* to let political differences stand in our way. She had been a student of Max Weinreich's and she knew as much about Yiddish literature as any person alive. As a teacher she was unfailingly warm and generous. Her classes were intellectually exhilarating. And despite her literary acumen, despite her genius, she never lost sight of the fundamental humanity upon which Yiddish literature rests. One day, for example, we were pursuing a complex analysis of Sholem Aleichem's short story "Hodel" when Ruth decided to underscore her point by reading directly from the text; she read out loud, in Yiddish, with such empathy and feeling that before she was through she and all her students were in tears.

Did we ever read! Between Ruth and our other professor, Eugene Orenstein, we were often assigned two full-length novels a week. I still read relatively slowly in Yiddish, with frequent recourse to a dictionary, and my first year of graduate school found me at my desk till two or three in the morning every night but Shabbos.

Where did we find all the books our teachers assigned? Thanks to its native bilingualism and a large postwar Jewish immigrant population, Montreal was, at the time, remarkably hospitable to Yiddish. There were quadrilingual Jewish schools in the city: English, French, Hebrew, and Yiddish; a thriving Yiddish theater (where the laughter always came in two waves: once when the line was delivered, and again after the Yiddish-speaking members of the audience had a chance to whisper the translation to their neighbors); and the Jewish Public Library, a unique institution where several hundred people turned out every Saturday night—often braving biting winds and subzero temperatures—to hear scholarly talks on Yiddish literature. So when Ruth or Eugene assigned a given Yiddish book—inevitably out of print—the four or five students in our class knew exactly where to go. The fastest would claim the copy at the Jewish Public Library. If we were lucky, there might be another copy at the McGill library. The rest of us loaded up with change and resigned ourselves to hours at the coin-operated Xerox machine—a recourse so common it once caused Ruth's brother, David Roskies, a professor at the Jewish Theological Seminary in New York, to lament that "We are no longer *Am hasefer,* the People of the Book; we are now *Am ha-kseroks,* the People of the Xerox."

There was an alternative. There were still many individuals in Montreal with excellent Yiddish libraries of their own. As time went on, we figured out who they were and began ringing doorbells, asking to borrow the books we needed for class. People were remarkably forthcoming: They gladly provided them, as well as hot tea, cookies, and impromptu reviews. When we returned the books the following week we were served more tea and cookies and then examined on what we had read. The arrangement worked well enough in Montreal, with its large Yiddish-speaking population, but I couldn't imagine what students were doing in Austin, Madison, Berkeley, Ithaca, or other, more far-flung communities where Yiddish was by then being taught.

Then I received a letter from Kathryn Hellerstein, the graduate student who used to visit me with Malka Heifetz Tussman at the carriage house in California. She wrote that she had just returned from a visit to her home city in Ohio, where the local rabbi informed her that he had been given a nine-hundred-volume Yiddish library from the estate of a recently deceased congregant. He tried to donate the books to various schools and libraries, but no one wanted them, so, he told Kathryn, there was nothing else to do but send them to the junkyard to be sold as scrap.

I was incredulous. Dispersed and landless throughout most of our history, Jews venerated books as a "portable homeland," the repository of our collective memory and identity. As a child I had been taught that if a book fell on the floor—it didn't matter whether it was the Rambam or Norman Mailer—I was supposed to pick it up and kiss it. So how could a rabbi, of all people, throw books out?

A month later, while visiting my parents in New Bedford, I stopped by the local shul to chat with the rabbi, Bernard Glassman, a kind, scholarly man who had just published a work on the persistence of anti-Semitic stereotypes in England during the centuries of Jewish expulsion. I found the book intriguing, and was just settling down in his study for a leisurely conversation when, out of the corner of my eye, I spied a fruit basket filled to the brim with what appeared to be old Yiddish books! On the top of the pile I could make out the *Collected Works* of Mendele Moykher Seforim, about whom I was then writing my dissertation.

"Excuse me, Rabbi," I inquired, "but what is Mendele doing in a fruit basket on the floor?"

"Oh, we're going to bury him," the rabbi answered nonchalantly.

"You're gonna *what?*"

"Bury him. We bury all our old religious books when they're no longer of use. We have a bunch of old *siddurim* (prayer books) to bury, so we'll just throw these in at the same time."

I gasped. As a sign of respect it was traditional for Jews to bury *shames,* worn-out religious books that contained the name of God. But these were modern, secular *Yiddish* books. I jumped out of my chair and began rummaging through the basket.

"Look, Rabbi, here's Mendele!" I exclaimed. "And beneath him, here's . . . Avrom Reisen! And Karl Marx—*Karl Marx* in Yiddish translation! Do you really think the members of the congregation want you to be burying *Das Kapital* together with the old siddurim, *l'havdil* (you should make a distinction)?"

The rabbi could see the point.

"Listen," I said, still crouched beside the fruit basket and exaggerating slightly, "I know *millions* of people who are looking for Yiddish books! There are all sorts of students who could use them. . . ."

The rabbi was a scholar in his own right. He had tried to place the books at several university libraries but could find no takers. "Aaron," he sighed, "if you know someone who wants Yiddish books, then by all means, they're yours."

I thanked him profusely, repacked the fruit basket, propped it on my shoulder, and headed for the door before he could change his mind.

"We get Yiddish books here all the time," Rabbi Glassman called after me. "I'll tell you what. From now on I'll save them for you and give them to your parents. Just let me know when you've got enough."

I arranged things with my parents and returned to Montreal with my rucksack and two heavy shopping bags full of books. I was beginning to suspect that unwanted Yiddish books were a problem not only in Ohio and New Bedford, but in communities throughout North America. After all, immigrant Jews had been voracious readers. When they died, their treasured Yiddish libraries were left to children or grandchildren who couldn't read the language. In the best of cases books were preserved in synagogue libraries or stored in cellars or attics for safekeeping; more often, it seemed, they ended up shredded, buried, or thrown out with the trash.

Admittedly, at the time, I was looking for Yiddish books strictly for my own use, and I figured that if I could just walk into a synagogue and find them in a small city such as New Bedford, imagine what lay in store in a city as big as Montreal, with a Jewish population forty times as large! And so, as nonchalantly as I could manage, I let it be known in my own Montreal neighborhood that I personally, a young graduate student, was interested in Yiddish books.

Almost immediately people started calling: widows and widowers, children and grandchildren. Within days I was racing around the city on my bicycle, then on a moped with a milk crate bolted to the back, and finally in a borrowed station wagon. When the local Jewish high school decided to clear its shelves of "surplus" books, they offered me a two-thousand-volume Yiddish library. I rented a van, hired two neighborhood kids, and carried all the books up to my apartment. That night my fellow grad student Borukh Hill, Ruth Wisse, and I crouched on my living room floor and opened boxes, sorting through hundreds of dusty volumes and dividing the books among us. My share included two crucial reference works: a complete, ornately bound, four-volume set of Zalman Rejzen's *Leksikon fun der yidisher literatur, prese un filologye* *(Lexicon of Yiddish Literature, Press and Philology)*, a pioneering biograph-ical dictionary of Yiddish literature, published in Vilna between 1926 and 1929; and, a bit less practical but no less enjoyable, Nahum Stutchkoff's 35,000-word *Yidisher gramen-leksikon,* the first and only *Yid-dish Rhyming Dictionary,* published in New York in 1931. Both Ruth and Borukh went away with treasures of their own.

Meanwhile the calls continued. Before I knew it Yiddish books cov-ered every square inch of my living room floor, then the hallway and the kitchen. When the piles spilled over into the bedroom, my new girlfriend decided enough was enough. I responded by buying a big, colorful Guatemalan hammock, which I suspended high over the grow-ing mountain of books on the bedroom floor. That provided enough novelty to smooth things over for a while. But a week later my parents were on the phone from Massachusetts, and now *they* were issuing ul-timata: The rabbi had given them so many Yiddish books that they were afraid the second story of their house was about to collapse.

Even I had to admit the situation was getting out of control. The next day—I remember the exact moment—I was sitting in class at McGill. Sleet pounded against the window pane, the lecture droned, the radiator hissed, and suddenly, like that, the idea came to me: I would take a leave of absence to save the world's Yiddish books before it was too late. When I shared the idea with Ruth she could not have been more supportive. At the end of the semester I loaded my now for-midable personal library onto a U-Haul truck and headed south, where untold Yiddish books—and a very different sort of Yiddish educa-tion—awaited.

PART TWO

On the Road

5. A Ritual of Cultural Transmission

Dear Mr. Lansky,

I thank you for your interest in Yiddish books. I hope you are interested in Hebrew also as I have books in both languages to give away. I am a very old man and I am afraid that after I will be gone they may throw them in the trash. Please do help me out.

Your Respectfully,
Norman Temmelman

In late July of 1980, I emptied my bank account, packed my rucksack, rented a van, and set out on the road for the first time. My plan was to begin with Mr. Temmelman in Atlantic City, then make additional stops in Philadelphia and New York. I figured that if I left Amherst early enough, I could do it all in a single day.

As I soon discovered, just scheduling such a trip was a workout. My knowledge of East Coast geography was imperfect, and when I phoned people to get directions and set a time for pickup, they were often so eager to talk, they wouldn't let me off the phone.

All except Mr. Temmelman. He, it turned out, didn't have a phone.

So I sent him a telegram letting him know when I'd arrive. On the appointed day I left Amherst early and made it to Atlantic City by noon. Mr. Temmelman's address turned out to be a high-rise building for the Jewish elderly just off the boardwalk, a block from one of the city's sprawling new casinos.

I entered the lobby and was immediately approached by a very old man wearing a heavy, dark wool suit on this steaming summer day.

"Mr. Lahnsky?" he asked in an unmistakable Yiddish accent.

"Mr. Temmelman?"

He smiled and shook my hand. "I've been waiting here in the lobby since seven this morning, I didn't want I should miss you." He took me firmly by the arm and led me up the elevator to his fifth-floor apartment. He lived in a single room. In one corner were a narrow bed and a metal nightstand piled with bottles of pills, in the other were a sink, a hot plate, and a kitchen table covered with stacks of bills and papers. The rest of the room was taken up with bookcases and cardboard boxes filled with hundreds of Yiddish and Hebrew books.

Mr. Temmelman put a kettle on the hot plate and set out a bowl of sugar cubes and two glasses for tea.

"Have you lived here long?" I asked.

"Oh no, we had a regular house. But three years ago my wife, *olehasholem* (may she rest in peace), died, and I had to move here, for the elderly. I left the furniture behind, but the books I brought with me." He was eighty-seven years old, he told me, and was about to leave on a trip to visit relatives in Israel. At his age he might not return, and he wanted to make sure his books were taken care of before he left.

I had figured book collection meant picking up boxes, carrying them out to the truck, and *fartig*, you're done and it's time to move on to the next stop. Instead, Mr. Temmelman insisted I join him at the kitchen table, where, for what seemed like hours, we sipped tea, sucked on sugar cubes, and talked. When it came time to part with his books, his eyes welled with tears as he began handing them to me, one volume at a time.

"This book," he recalled, pulling a handsome volume of Zishe Landau's *Lider (Poems)* from a cardboard box, "this book I bought in 1937. It had just come out, it was a very important book, my wife and I we went without lunch for a week we should be able to afford it. And *this* book," he said, holding aloft a yellowed copy of *Ven Yash iz geforn (When Yash Set Forth),* Jacob Glatstein's powerful account of his travels in interwar Europe, "have you read this book?"

"Well, no, actually I haven't," I conceded.

"In that case, I want you should sit down right now and read this book."

It was a long afternoon. Every book he handed me had its story. This wasn't at all what I expected, and too spellbound and polite to interrupt, I fell hours behind schedule. But I did begin to understand what was taking place. Sitting together in that crowded apartment—he an eighty-seven-year-old man in a wool suit, I a bearded twenty-four-year-old in jeans and a T-shirt—we were enacting a ritual of cultural transmission. He was handing me not merely his books but his world, his *yerushe,* the inheritance his own children had rejected. I was a stranger, but he had no other choice: Book by book, he was placing all his hopes in me.

It was late afternoon before I was finally able to carry the books out to the van. I made a few quick calls from a pay phone in the lobby to apologize to the next people on the list. And then, as I opened the door to the van and was about to drive off, Mr. Temmelman came running over, grabbed hold of my arm, and spoke in Yiddish. *"Eyn minut, yungerman, vuhin loyfstu?* (One minute, young man, where are you running?)"

"Where am I running? I'm heading to Philadelphia and then on to New York. I have other stops to make, I'm hours behind schedule and—"

"*Oy yungerman, ir farshteyt nisht* (Oy, young man, you don't understand). When I got your telegram I told everyone in the building you were coming. They also have books for you!"

I peered up at the twelve-story building.

"*All* of them have books?"

"*Vu den?* Of course all of them!" he responded, proudly indicating the full height of the building with a sweep of his hand. We walked back inside, Mr. Temmelman leading the way, and proceeded floor by floor, knocking at every door.

"*Zayt mir moykhl,*" he'd say, "*ober der yungerman darf hobn bikher* (Excuse me, but this young man here needs books)."

People smiled. They clapped their hands. They came out with shopping bags, cardboard boxes, wicker baskets, suitcases . . . all filled with Yiddish books. To a greater or lesser degree, every person had to enact the same ritual of cultural transmission. They sat me down at their kitchen tables and poured *a glezele tey,* a glass of hot tea, which they served with homemade cookies, *lokshn kuglekh* (noodle puddings), or Entenmann's cakes. They all told stories. Some cried. One, a retired tailor, made me sit for twenty minutes while he stood and recited his latest Yiddish poetry. Everyone made sure I ate, at least half tried to fix me up with their granddaughters, and they all kissed me when I left. The sun was low in the sky when I finally said good-bye to Mr. Temmelman. By that time the van was so overloaded that the muffler scraped bottom at every bump, and I for my part was so full of tea and cake that I had to stop at every gas station between there and Philadelphia.

6. "Don't You Know That Yiddish Is Dead?"

My first inclination after leaving Montreal in the spring of 1979 was to make New York my home base, since, to paraphrase Willy Sutton, that's where the books were. But my teacher, Ruth Wisse, was dead set against it. The politics of the Jewish world there were too contentious, she explained, and the rancor of the Yiddish world was even worse. "If you're going to succeed," she insisted, "you have to start fresh. What you need is a Jewishly neutral location." So I returned to Amherst, the New England town where I had gone to college, moved in with friends, and, while finishing my master's thesis, began to lay the groundwork for what I was calling the National Yiddish Book Exchange. (Two years later we changed the name to National Yiddish Book Center, to reflect our expanding mission; for the sake of consistency, in this book I have used Center throughout.)

At the age of twenty-three, the first thing I needed was credibility, so I wrote letters to prominent Jewish writers and intellectuals. The response was heartening. Irving Howe and Alfred Kazin said it was "an idea whose time has come." Joshua Fishman, distinguished professor of linguistics at Columbia, called it "the only truly brilliant substantive/ administrative plan suggested in the entire Yiddish Studies field in the past decade." And Saul Bellow spoke from personal experience: "I was recently given a set of the complete works of Sholem Aleichem from a woman who didn't know what to do with them and would otherwise have thrown them out. So I understand the urgency and wish you good luck."

While universally supportive, almost every letter carried the same caveat: *Hurry*—it may already be too late! I consulted with scholars who, after some deliberation, estimated that there were seventy thousand Yiddish volumes extant and recoverable in North America. I figured it would take me two years to collect them all. But first I needed money: approximately $10,000, I thought, to cover the cost of a truck, gas, insurance, travel expenses, storage, and a modest living allowance for myself. So I sent off proposals to the major Jewish organizations, cut my hair, trimmed my beard, ironed my shirt, borrowed a suit and tie from a friend, and boarded the train for New York.

For the next two days I trudged from office to office, meeting with the leaders of the American Jewish community. My enthusiasm matched only by my naïveté, I assumed they'd review my proposal, listen to my irrefutable arguments (a chance to rescue an entire literature, after all!), ask a few probing questions (all easily parried), confirm my qualifications, applaud my initiative, and hand me a check. Instead, across one titanic desk after another, I met not with encouragement and support but condescension and dismissal:

"*Yiddish* books? You want us to help you save books in *Yiddish*? Why? Who cares? Don't you know that Yiddish is dead?"

Admittedly, some were kinder than others, but the sentiments remained:

"The Jewish future lies with Hebrew, not Yiddish."

"Only *bubbies* read Yiddish anymore."

"Your plan is a throwback, an anachronism."

"You're riding the wrong horse, barking up the wrong tree; why don't you just go back to school and forget the whole idea?"

"I don't think you understand," I protested. "If we don't save these books now they'll be lost *forever*! We as a people can't afford to lose our literature, our history, our culture. . . ."

S'hot geholfn vi a toytn bankes—it helped like cupping helps a corpse. At first I took it personally: Maybe my proposal wasn't clear enough, my borrowed suit didn't fit properly, I'd done a poor job ironing. But after listening to the same riff three, four, five times in a row, I began to see that it didn't matter how long my proposal or how short my hair. The priorities of the Jewish establishment had been set in stone years before: Israel, anti-Semitism, social services. In 1980 the national allocation for culture—literature, history, continuity, creativity—was less than one tenth of one percent of the total monies raised.

Of course, when you're talking about a $1.5 billion annual campaign, even one tenth of one percent begins to look like real money. So I made an appointment and the next day found myself in a skyscraper on East Forty-second Street, sitting across from Mr. Cohen, the head of the umbrella agency charged by the Jewish establishment with disbursing national funding for Jewish culture. I was optimistic. For one thing, there were books on the wall: real books, literature and scholarship, in Hebrew and English. For another, the meeting did not begin with a peremptory dismissal but with a sincere expression of interest.

I spoke at length, and when I was through, Mr. Cohen nodded in agreement. "You're absolutely right. The Jewish community should not allow Yiddish books to be destroyed," he said. "I'm with you all the way. There's only one problem. We have no money to give you."

"But I thought you're the national agency for Jewish culture."

"We are," he said, "but it's not so easy. After our own expenses, the money we get is divided among ten constituent cultural organizations. Some are big, some are small, and you can imagine what it took before we finally worked out a formula for who gets what. Now no one wants to risk their own percentage by reopening the discussion. We haven't made an allocation to a *new* organization since we began, and I can't see our board members starting now, no matter how good your cause."

"But that doesn't make sense!" I protested. "The solution isn't to cut the pie smaller. The solution is to bring in new organizations, encourage young people with fresh energy and ideas, and create such a buzz that the federations will give you more money. That way you'll end up with a bigger pie for everyone!"

Mr. Cohen sighed so deeply, it sounded like an outbound commuter train releasing its air brakes across the street at Grand Central Station. "You're right, of course," he said softly, "but it just can't be done. Not yet. Not now." A kind man, he did offer one small measure of hope. As I was getting up to leave, he assured me that the entire process was "in transition," and that major changes in the structure of Jewish cultural funding were imminent.

"What do you mean by 'imminent'?" I asked.

"Well, the committees are being formed, and we're about to begin a thorough reevaluation along some of the lines you're suggesting. I think we'll start to see some real changes within the next three to five years."

"Three to five *years*! But books are being destroyed right now! What am I supposed to do in the meantime?"

He shrugged. "I guess you're on your own till then. Maybe that's why no one has succeeded in establishing a new national Jewish cultural agency in America in almost twenty years. Who knows — you've got a good cause, maybe you'll be the first."

I left Mr. Cohen's office, walked across town to Penn Station, and boarded the Amtrak for New England. I was tired. I was disappointed. Above all I was angry. Yiddish books were being lost *right now*. There wasn't time for committees and studies. If the Jewish establishment wouldn't supply the modest funds I needed to save Yiddish books, I'd just have to find the money someplace else.

So I spent that summer picking blueberries with a crew of migrant workers in Maine, and the next fall I took a job teaching evening Yiddish classes at the University of Massachusetts. My earnings were modest, but they were enough to live on as I began to lay the foundation of a new organization.

My first step, after printing business cards and letterhead, was to convene a board. I turned to the people I knew best: local professors and college administrators. Some, like Haim Gunner, Rich Alpert, Ruth Stark, and, later, our successive early board chairs, Joe Marcus, Penina Midgal Glazer, and Gail Perlman, accepted my invitation immediately and remained mentors and stalwart allies for years. Only one person turned me down: He told me he could not possibly jeopardize his "unsullied reputation" by associating with an enterprise "which in all likelihood will not succeed."

With help from my father, who's a tax lawyer, we incorporated and won tax-exempt status from the IRS. Then, on a cold night in April 1980, the entire board gathered around a simmering woodstove in the home of Nancy and Jules Piccus, my first Yiddish teacher, for our initial meeting. The agenda was brief: They signed the articles of organization, appointed me executive director, toasted *l'khayim,* and then adjourned to a table of white wine and brie, leaving it to me to work out the details.

The first detail was to find a building—a task complicated by our having no money. Space was at a premium in our area, but in early May I came across a want ad that sounded promising:

6,000 square feet on second floor of older industrial building near Northampton. Ideal for small business. Loading dock, elevator, ample parking. Reasonable rent. Inquire now for immediate occupancy.

The space was in a nineteenth-century redbrick silk mill, located in Florence, just three miles north of Smith College. I prevailed upon my old college professors Leonard Glick and Jules Piccus to drive over with me. The building's owner, Steve Cahillane, greeted us in person.

"We run a trash-hauling business out of the first floor," he explained, "and on the third floor is a clinical psychologist with a table tennis club on the side. The whole second floor is available: six thousand square feet at a dollar fifty a foot, nine thousand a year. Some people I've showed it to have found the space a little, well, *unconventional,* but that's something you'll have to judge for yourselves."

He wasn't kidding. The previous tenant had been a nonprofit group called Women in Construction, and one of the construction skills they taught was wallpapering. They practiced with remnants, and as a result, in the entire space virtually no two strips of wallpaper were the same. There were pinks, greens, yellows, and blues, flowers, stripes, paisleys, and polka-dots; the crowing roosters of a kitchen pattern alternated with the seashells of a bathroom, the tumbling astronauts of a kid's bedroom, the ducks and hunting rifles of a man's study, and the gold fleur-de-lis of a formal dining room. But apart from the funky wallpaper, the space was remarkably well suited. About half the floor had been left open as a single warehouse space, the rest divided into offices. There was more than enough room for all the Yiddish books our experts thought existed. Without so much as a word to me or Len, Jules walked over to the landlord and said, "It's not perfect, but what the hell, we'll take it!"

Leonard and I looked at each other, aghast. We didn't have enough cash to cover the first week's rent, let alone a year-long lease. *"Gelt,"* Len addressed Jules in an urgent whisper, *"m'darf hobn gelt* (you need money first)."

Jules was unfazed. He may have been a college professor, but somehow he was also a surprisingly astute businessman. There he was, negotiating on our behalf, using terms like "liquidity," "balloon payments," "accrual," and "deferral." The upshot? The landlord agreed to let us move in on June 1, with the first payment not due until September. "That way we'll be able keep our cash flow liquid until our major grant comes through at the end of the summer," Jules explained.

"Major grant? What major grant?" I asked as soon as we were alone.

"Don't worry," Jules assured us, "September is three months away. We'll come up with something before then. In the meantime we've got a space. Let's start collecting books."

WE MOVED IN on June 1, 1980. My best friend, Noemi Schwarz, contributed half her household furniture. Paul Novak, a master scrounger, drove in from Omaha with a large van and, for $100, managed to buy us a desk, two file cabinets, a picnic table, and a second-hand IBM Selectric typewriter. The next day I sat down at the IBM and wrote my first press release, announcing the formation of the National Yiddish Book Center and encouraging anyone with unwanted volumes to send them to us.

I made copies at the local Xerox shop and mailed them to three hundred newspapers. Then I sat down in the empty factory loft and waited: one day, two days, three days . . . The only sound was the occasional *boing-boing* of a Ping-Pong ball dropping through holes from the floor above. With no money for a telephone, I had routed calls through my friend Rich Alpert at the dean's office at Hampshire College. Toward the end of the week Rich phoned me at home to tell me that Jean Caldwell, the western Massachusetts correspondent for the *Boston Globe,* had seen a copy of the press release and would be at the loft to interview me at ten the next morning.

I woke early, bicycled the thirteen miles from Amherst to Florence, and changed from my bicycle shorts into carefully ironed clothes (well, at least they *were* carefully ironed before I stuffed them into my rucksack for the ride over). Jean was right on time and her appearance was reassuring. An older woman with a warm smile, she carried a pencil and notebook and was dressed in comfortable clothes covered by an old London Fog coat. We sat down at the picnic table, surrounded by the dizzying display of wallpaper, and I began to explain my plans. I told her how important Yiddish was, how many young people were beginning to study the language, how urgently books were needed, and how, until now, unwanted Yiddish books had been regularly abandoned or destroyed. "Now all that will change," I assured her. "Soon this entire loft will be filled to the rafters with Yiddish books." And then, pointing to the only two boxes of books in the place—books I had picked up the day before by bicycle from a woman in Northampton—I boldly proclaimed, "You see, the deluge has already begun!"

Jean looked doubtful: two boxes weren't much of a deluge. But when I pulled out a jackknife and opened them, her whole attitude began to change. There were the usual books from Russia and Poland, printed before the war. "Imagine the miles those books must have traveled!" Jean marveled. There were novels, poetry collections, history, and essays—each with its own story. And as luck would have it, there was a copy of Harkavy's *Brifn-shteler,* a curious volume published in New York in 1902 offering a selection of form letters in Yiddish and improbably baroque English for use by newly arrived Jewish immigrants. Jean laughed aloud over choice selections, such as "From an Ardent Lover to a Lady," "Letter from a Young Lady to a Gentleman Declining the Offer of His Hand in Marriage," and "Telegrams of Ten Words or Less."

Objectively, there probably wasn't much of a story in an empty factory loft with two boxes of books. But Jean was charmed by the books she did see, and she was at least bemused by my vision of the deluge to come. Several days later her story appeared in the *Globe;* then the news went out on the AP wire, and before long the deluge did begin: so many books that our local post office balked at the prospect of delivering them all, and we had to ask our congressman to intervene.

Along with the books came letters. Elderly Jews, often writing in Yiddish, offered their own libraries "so that someone should read these books after I'm gone." Younger Jews—often typing their messages on the letterhead of law firms, medical practices, businesses, or universities—told how they had inherited Yiddish books from parents or grandparents and had held on to them all this time, waiting for someone to come along who wanted them. By the end of June I was spending ten and twelve hours a day in Florence, swiveling between the IBM and an old Yiddish manual, answering the letters one by one. I advised everyone the same: Get sturdy boxes from your local liquor store, pack the books carefully, take them to the post office, and mail them in.

Fortunately, along with the books some people sent contributions. Modest, yes, but enough to install a telephone and buy planks from a local sawmill, which my housemate, Scott, sawed and planed and nailed into shelves.

Some of the letters I received were enormously touching. Martin Moroff, an elderly immigrant who ran a cigar store in Reading, Pennsylvania, wrote in Yiddish that he had been collecting Yiddish books on his own for many years, storing them in his home. Among the boxes he was preparing to ship were several that he recovered at the last minute from the *meysim shtibl,* the room where corpses are prepared for burial at the local Jewish cemetery. He whisked them out of there as fast as he could, he assured me, because *"Di bikher zenen geven lebedike nefoshes* (The books were living souls)."

In a later letter Mr. Moroff had another story to tell, about a scholarly Jew from Poland who had settled in Reading shortly after the war. The scholar and his wife loved books, and they amassed a large Yiddish library. But gradually, as the man became more successful in business, he became more assimilated. He changed his name and spent less and less time reading. When his wife died he remarried, this time to an American-born woman who had little regard for literature. She promptly decided to renovate the house, and the first thing she did was get rid of her husband's books, piling them up on a neighbor's porch. As fate would have it, it began to rain that day, and by the time Mr. Moroff arrived at night—in response to an urgent phone call—the books were soaked through:

> *S'hot mir farklemt baym hartsn. Ikh hob oyfgehoybn a por bikher, es hot gekopet fun zey der regn. Neyn, s'hot getripet trern, di bikher hobn geveynt.* (My heart tightened with emotion. I picked up a few of the books and the rain dripped off of them. No, they were tears that fell, the books were crying).

Mr. Moroff was able to ship his books—and we were able to visit him in person some years later. But there were many people who, like Mr. Temmelman, could not manage to pack their books or carry them to the post office: They lived in walk-up apartments, or were too old or too infirm or simply had too many books to give away.

7. A Day in the Life

The visit to Mr. Temmelman was my first and last trip alone. After that, I tried whenever possible to travel in a team of three: two to do the shlepping and the third to be the Designated Eater. The latter was the really hard job: While the others carried boxes, you had to sit with the host at the kitchen table, listening to stories, sipping endless glasses of tea, and valiantly working your way through a week's worth of dishes cooked "special," just for you — gefilte fish and *khareyn* (horseradish), kasha varnishkes, blintzes and sour cream, potato latkes, and *lokshn kugl*. Given a choice, I preferred to shlep: better to strain muscles, I figured, than to sit at the table, watching your arteries harden before your eyes. And that's not to mention the care packages: So many people gave us a "little something for the road" that we had to unload the van with great care, lest a bag of onion bagels or a Tupperware container of chopped herring end up buried in our warehouse. Eventually we devised an "emergency kit" that we carried with us on every trip: an old Boy Scout knapsack packed with Ben Gay ointment and Ace bandages for the shleppers, and, for the Designated Eater, a roll of Tums, a jar of salted Japanese umeboshi plums (great after too much sugar), a canteen of water, and six packets of Alka-Seltzer.

As news of our efforts spread, the number of letters and calls increased exponentially. The staff of the local post office was learning more about the extent of Yiddish literature than most Jews in America would ever know. And we were learning more than many truck drivers knew about the intricacies of interstate highways and New York City streets.

I had four regular traveling companions now: my college friend Roger Mummert, whose Second Avenue apartment became our "crash pad" in New York; Fran Krasno, a writer and archivist from Northampton who would soon become the Center's assistant director; Pat Myerson, a freelance radio producer from Amherst with an interest in oral history; and Noah Glick, the son of my teacher, a strong, good-natured seventeen-year-old available only during school vacations.

It wasn't long before I was on the road more than I was at home. True, we were often exhausted, but we were also energized: Every day was a new adventure, a new opportunity to meet amazing people, discover great books, and—a privilege granted to few—to watch as a historical epoch passed before our eyes.

We made hundreds of trips over the next ten years. Here, taken from our truck logs and my memory, is a more-or-less typical day:

Fran Krasno and I came down by train the night before and slept in sleeping bags on the floor of Roger's apartment. We got up at six, roused Roger, and walked together to the Bowery to pick up a truck. Our regular rental company, Hittner, was the cheapest in town—and for good reason. The clerk sat in a grimy office behind a cloudy sheet of bulletproof glass, with a gun beneath his jacket and a German shepherd at his side. A sign behind him read In God We Trust—All Others Pay Cash. We paid $300 up front, with the balance to be returned when we returned the truck in good condition.

Of course, "good condition" was a relative term. There wasn't a truck in Hittner's fleet that wasn't dented or covered with graffiti. The one-ton Chevy van we rented that day was pretty much par for the course: The turn signals didn't work, both side mirrors were broken, and someone had repaired a gaping hole behind the passenger's seat by welding a stolen city street sign (Trucks Keep Right) to the floor. It could have been worse; two weeks earlier, reaching under the driver's seat of a Hittner truck to silence a rattle, I came up with four empty beer cans and a six-inch kitchen knife with a sharpened tip.

It was 7:15 before we were finally under way, leaving us just enough time for a quick breakfast at the B & H Dairy Restaurant on Second Avenue. An old *milkhig* haunt, the B & H had no waiters, just a short-order cook in an egg-stained apron who leaned across the counter and yelled, "Wha'dya want?" There were no menus either, just hand-painted signs Scotch-taped above the counter:

Gefilte Fish—*Mit dem Yiddishn Geschmack*—Try It with Some Delicious Horseradish!
Chopped Herring: Say No More—The *Best*!
Really and Truly Fresh Fruit Salad: Pure and Unadulterated!
Vegetable Roast: To Your Health!
Chopped Eggplant: Try It, You'll Like It!

We opted for the French Toast (3 Inch Thick Slices of Chalah Bread!) and Orange Juice (Of Course It's Fresh, We Squeeze It Ourselves!). While we waited we reviewed a clipboard on which Fran had posted a typed copy of the day's itinerary, and then we consulted a stack of street maps to plan our route.

Our first stop that morning was supposed to be the "Editorial Office" of *Zayn (To Be)*, a quarterly Yiddish literary journal. The office turned out to be a one-room residence in a down-at-the-heels SRO (single-room-occupancy) building occupied by Mr. Rosoff, the magazine's editor and publisher.

"*Kumt arayn, kumt arayn,* come in, come in, so many young people, it's so good to see you," Mr. Rosoff greeted us as he herded us into his tiny room. It was a tight fit, since, in addition to his furniture, the single room was filled from floor to ceiling with tottering piles of back issues of *Zayn*.

"A few of the issues didn't sell so well, so I stored them here in my apartment," Mr. Rosoff explained. "But I'll tell you the truth, they're not getting any younger and neither am I. It's not good they should sit here with me collecting dust. That's why I called you—maybe you can find young people who will want to read them?"

Most young people I knew weren't exactly waiting in line, but we promised to store the volumes carefully, list them in our catalog, and try to get them into libraries. A gentle man, Mr. Rosoff said he couldn't ask for more. Since he had no boxes, we had to load the dusty, paperbound issues loose onto handtrucks and roll them out to the truck. The more recent the dates, the higher the piles of unsold copies. We understood all too well: the higher the piles, the fewer the subscribers who remained.

We loaded the issues of *Zayn* as carefully as we could into the back of the van and headed back downtown to our next stop, the home of Mr. and Mrs. Arthur Rosenberg. According to the clipboard the Rosenbergs had two thousand books for us. But after double parking, offloading the handtrucks, and wrestling them through a revolving door (almost strangling a poor Chihuahua in the process), when we showed up at the Rosenbergs' apartment there were no books in sight.

"Excuse me," I asked, rechecking the clipboard, "but where are the two thousand books?"

"Why, in a warehouse, of course," answered Mrs. Rosenberg.

"So why did you give us this address?" asked Fran, who had scheduled the pickup herself.

"Why? So my husband and I could look you over before we trust you with such a treasure."

They led us into a tastefully furnished den, poured tea (in fine china), and proceeded to discuss with us Jewish history, Yiddish literature, and our plans for the Center. They were interesting, erudite people, and apparently we passed the test, because after a half hour they finally brought the conversation around to the books.

"You understand, of course, that the books we have are brand new. In fact, they're still packaged in the publisher's original cartons," Mr. Rosenberg told us.

"Brand new?" I asked. How often did one find two thousand brand new Yiddish books in 1980?

Mrs. Rosenberg explained that the books had been written by her father, Mendl Osherowitch, a well-known Yiddish scholar. Osherowitch's magnum opus was a two-volume work entitled *Yidn in Ukrayne (Jews in the Ukraine),* an anthology that included contributions by Max Weinreich, Eliyahu Cherikover, and other leading historians of the day. Because of the author's untimely death in 1965, just as the second volume was coming off the press, the books were never properly distributed. Instead they were stored in a friend's warehouse in the Fulton Fish Market, where they remained for the next fifteen years. Now the Rosenbergs were ready to turn them over to us, so we could distribute them, albeit belatedly, to libraries around the world.

Having grown up in New Bedford, the country's largest fishing port, I was familiar with the smell of fish. But nothing could have prepared me for the olfactory assault that greeted us twenty minutes later when we arrived at the Fulton Fish Market. Developers had not yet transformed the area into the tourist Mecca it is today, and frankly, it could have used a bit of gentrification. The address Mr. Rosenberg gave us was a dry-storage warehouse almost directly underneath the Brooklyn

Bridge. Roger, Fran, and I hopped onto the loading dock and were greeted by a warehouseman in his early sixties wearing a quilted blue jacket.

"What can I do you for?" he asked, leaning back on a wooden chair.

"Well, I hope this is the right place. Mr. Rosenberg sent us. We're here for the books, the Yiddish—"

The warehouseman was on his feet. "Hey, Smitty," he yelled into the building, "c'mere! You ain't gonna believe this, some kids have finally come for them Jewish books we got upstairs!"

Smitty, a big man carrying a metal hook with a well-worn hardwood handle, emerged from the darkness. "You bullshittin' me?"

His partner assured him that we were for real, and giving us strict instruction to "Wait right here!" the two of them disappeared into the darkness. Standing on the dock, we had time to look around at what could have passed as a stage set for *On the Waterfront*. Forklifts bounced along the cobblestones, pallet jacks clashed, roughnecks cursed, workers in rubber boots plied their hoses, and everywhere, trucks moved back and forth, leaking fish guts as they went. When the two men finally reappeared, they were using their hooks to pull ancient wooden dollies piled high with big, sturdy boxes lashed together with sisal twine. It was obvious that the boxes had never been opened; they still bore the stencils of the Yiddish printer.

We cut the twine and started loading them onto our truck. As we did so the warehousemen chuckled to themselves. "Hey, don't get me wrong," said the man in the quilted jacket. "I mean, I like Jewish people and all. But I'm gonna tell you something, them books have been a regular pain in the neck. 'Long as I been here—never mind how many years—we gotta step over 'em, move 'em around, pull 'em outa the way. I'm glad you kids can do something with 'em, 'cause just between you, me, and the wall, I'm glad to see 'em go."

Smitty agreed. "Good riddance!" he yelled, smiling and waving as we loaded the last box, secured the door, and pulled away from the dock. "Good riddance—and good luck!"

Next stop Brooklyn. We headed over the bridge, asked directions several times, and eventually made our way to the home of Mr. and Mrs. Kirshenbaum. Well into their eighties, the Kirshenbaums were moving to a Maryland suburb to live with their daughter. The daughter, a well-dressed woman in her fifties, was with them when we arrived. The apartment was upside down, furniture covered, closets emptied, the possessions of a lifetime packed into movers' boxes. Only the kitchen table was still uncluttered, an oasis amid the chaos, and Mrs. Kirschenbaum insisted we sit down first, apologizing because all she could offer was instant coffee.

"My parents don't want to leave," their daughter told us while her mother filled the kettle. "But they have no choice. My mom is going blind; she can't take care of the house anymore. My father is still active, but what kind of a neighborhood is this for him? Last month he went to a Yiddish poetry reading near the house, a mugger steps out from under the El and hits him over the head, he could have been killed. At least at my house they'll be safe, they'll have the grandchildren to talk to—"

"The grandchildren?" her father interrupted. "The grandchildren who are so busy *mit* the television and the sports and the making their parents drive them everywhere, the grandchildren are going to have time to talk to their old *bobe* and *zeyde*? Oh no. You want to know what we'll do there? We'll sit by ourselves in the den and *tsiter* (tremble) all day, we shouldn't be in the way. You call that a life?"

It was apparent that he and his daughter were reenacting, for our benefit, the final act in a long-standing argument. What made Mr. Kirschenbaum's point of view so poignant was that, as he explained, he and his wife had always been activists. They were leaders in the Bund, the Jewish labor movement in their native Poland. They survived the

Holocaust. After the war they fled to Argentina, where together they established a socialist Yiddish day school. Later they came to the United States, where he worked as a Yiddish teacher and they were both active in cultural and educational organizations. He was still the secretary of the local branch of the Workmen's Circle. "All right, it's true, our health isn't what it used to be, maybe the neighborhood isn't what it used to be either, but at least we have our friends here, we have our cultural life, our discussions, our meetings . . ."

His wife patted his hand. "All our lives we've fought. But now we're old. There comes a time you're too tired to fight anymore."

We spoke for another hour before they were ready to give us their books. Like so many of the people we met, they were home-grown intellectuals, and they had a large and impressive library, including rare Yiddish imprints from South America. Many of the writers had been personal friends. "*Ay, tayere bikher, tayere fraynt* (precious books, precious friends)," Mrs. Kirschenbaum sighed as we carried the boxes out the door. "It's a shame my eyes are going, I can't read them anymore."

"It's a shame we won't have room for them in Maryland," added her husband.

We wheeled hundreds of volumes out to the truck. But as he emptied the last bookcase, Mr. Kirshenbaum had a change of heart and decided to keep three well-worn sets for himself: the collected works of I. L. Peretz, Sholem Aleichem, and Avrom Reisen. "They're my favorite writers," he said, almost apologetically, his eyes beginning to well with tears. "True, I've read them a hundred times already, but at least this way I can read them out loud for my wife. She's right: They're old friends, these books. We'll take a few along; maybe when we get to Maryland we won't feel so lonely."

It was neither the first time nor the last in the course of our travels that I had to fight back tears of my own. I, too, loved Peretz and Sholem Aleichem, and not all that long before, I had even read Avrom Reisen—

once one of the most popular Yiddish writers in America, now largely forgotten. I recalled a particular story called *"Dem bruders koyl* (My Brother's Bullet)," which takes place during World War I. A Jew, living in the Austro-Hungarian Empire, takes a job in a defense plant making bullets, while his brother, living on the other side of the border, is pressed into service in the tsar's army. The factory worker, increasingly distraught, begins pocketing first one, then another and another bullet, certain that each time he is saving his brother's life. No wonder Mr. Kirschenbaum would want to hold on to books like that.

But there was little time for either tears or reflection as we piled back into the van, already several hours behind our carefully typed schedule. We stopped only long enough for Fran to phone our next appointments from a graffiti-covered pay phone, letting them know we'd be late, while Roger ducked into a nearby bodega in search of lunch. Returning with bread, cheese, and seltzer, he made sandwiches atop a box of books in the back of the van as we sped off to the Jewish Geriatric Center in Coney Island.

According to our clipboard, there were two boxes awaiting us at the Geriatric Center. When we arrived a tired-looking social worker led us down to the basement. There were two boxes all right, but they were the kind used to pack full-size refrigerators, and each was piled to the top with Yiddish books.

Roger went out to the truck and returned with two coils of manila rope. We lashed the first box to the hand truck and the three of us tried to heft it back. No luck—it must have weighed five hundred pounds, and there was no way we were going to budge it. So we were left with no alternative: We had to unload both boxes and spend the next hour carrying the books, loose, out to the truck. Fran said that next time she scheduled a pick-up she would ask people to define the word "box."

We made three more stops in Brooklyn and then headed over the Verrazano-Narrows Bridge for New Jersey. By now we were even further behind schedule, and Fran phoned several people to reschedule for the next day. (What a shame cell phones weren't widely available yet, what with our constant rearranging and apologizing.) We had developed a routine of sorts in the truck. Roger, a nondriver but the only resident New Yorker among us, insisted upon occupying the single passenger's seat so that he could "navigate." That left me at the wheel and Fran in the middle, balanced on boxes jammed as tightly as possible between the two seats. Traffic was heavy that late in the afternoon, and as we inched along we passed the time by singing the lyrics of every driving song we knew: "I've been doin' some hard travellin'," "Take me riding in a car car," "She's a little old lady from Pasadena," "Me and my Bobby McGee." When we ran out of songs we started making up our own, such as this impromptu version of "Lonesome Valley":

> You gotta shlep
> Them Yiddish books now,
> You gotta shlep
> Them by yourself,
> Ain't nobody here
> Gonna shlep 'em for you,
> You gotta shlepppppppp
> 'Em by yourself.

We tried Yiddish songs too, along with black spirituals, Frank Sinatra, folk songs, rock songs, campfire songs (Roger and I had both been Eagle Scouts), and protest songs gleaned from the *IWW Songbook*. Our singing was spirited but cacophonous, prompting Fran to suggest that next time we bring along an extra crew: "We can carry the books while they carry the tune."

> Oh, Mama, can this really be the end,
> To be stuck inside of Jersey
> With these Yiddish books again?

Like us, our repertoire was pretty much exhausted by the time we reached Passaic. After driving past rows of run-down factories we reached our destination: a synagogue where six boxes were supposed to be waiting for us at the back of a basement coatroom. The rabbi told us he didn't know where the books came from or how long they had been there, and he apologized because many were not Yiddish but Hebrew.

This wasn't great news: Several times in the past we had driven many miles, only to be weighed down with *siddurim* and *makhzeyrim,* old, worn-out Hebrew prayer books. But as soon as we pushed through the crowded coat room and opened the boxes, we realized that these books were something else entirely. Most were leather-bound tomes printed on rag paper, which likely dated them before 1850, when pulp paper was introduced. Along with volumes of Talmud were dozens of nineteenth-century rabbinic commentaries and an edition of *Yossipon,* a compilation of Hebrew writings by, among others, Josephus, a first-century Jewish historian. Distinguished by magnificent woodcuts, the book was one of the oldest we'd ever found, published in Durenfurth, Silesia, in 1759.

It was already dark and we were considerably more subdued by the time we returned to Manhattan. There were still two more stops to go. The first was at an elegant apartment building on Central Park West, where a group of cousins had gathered to divide the estate of their late great-aunt. By this point we must have looked pretty grungy, because the doorman, in his red coat with gold braid, curtly sent us around back, out past the garbage cans, to the freight elevator, where a sign read All Delivery Men, Repair Men, and Domestics *Must* Use This Elevator.

Up in the aunt's apartment, the half dozen cousins didn't treat us much better. They were our age or a little older, drinking white wine out of antique crystal while they argued over who got what from their great-aunt's estate.

"If you get the rug, then I want *both* lamps!"

Clearly no one thought their aunt's Yiddish books were worth very much, because they left us to empty her bookcase while they continued quarreling in the next room. The irony was that their aunt's library included some extraordinary volumes that one day could be worth more than all the furniture and *tshatshkes* combined. There were, for example, at least a dozen art books, including Avrom Sutzkever's *Sibir (Siberia),* a large-format volume of poetry based on the author's childhood in exile, powerfully illustrated by his friend Marc Chagall. No matter. The cousins studiously ignored us until we were ready to leave, and then, as we stood balancing our heavily laden handtrucks by the elevator, a new argument broke out as to who should get the receipt so they could claim the books as a write-off on their taxes.

The last stop of the day, at the home of an elderly widow and her daughter in Yonkers, was another emotional encounter over cookies and tea. We returned to Roger's apartment at midnight. Roger began preparing a late supper, but Fran and I fell asleep fully clothed on the living room floor before it was ready. It had been a good day: In eighteen hours we collected almost four thousand books. But there were many stops yet to go, and by seven the next morning we would be back on the road again.

8. A Brief History of Yiddish Literature

The only thing more exciting than collecting boxes of Yiddish books was opening them. What treasures lay within! The more we unpacked, the more we began to appreciate the remarkable scope of modern Yiddish literature.

What are Yiddish books? Who wrote them? When? Where? And for whom?

Despite their dust, their tattered bindings and yellowed pages, the books we recovered were not ancient. Most weren't even old. That's because Yiddish literature as we know it didn't really begin until the second half of the nineteenth century. Before that, when the traditional Jewish world was still intact, educated men spent their days studying in Hebrew and Aramaic. Although they spoke Yiddish, they considered it beneath them to read or write it.

What little literature did exist in Yiddish was intended for women—and perhaps uneducated men—who couldn't read Hebrew. Women used a folksy Yiddish prayer book called a *tkhine* and a loosely translated Yiddish bible called the *Tsene u'rene*. Beginning in the late fifteenth century, secular Yiddish works—fables, fairy tales, and fanciful stories drawn from European folklore—started to appear in Germany and

Northern Italy. One of the most popular was the *Bove bukh* (1541), a Jewish adaptation of medieval tales of chivalry and knights in shining armor. Although the book is now largely forgotten, it seems to have given rise to a familiar Yiddish expression: *"a bobe mayse"*—an improbable tale. Although most people assume that *bobe mayse* comes from the Yiddish word *bobe,* "grandmother," some scholars believe it to be a corruption of *bove,* referring to a story so outlandish that it sounds like something straight out of the *Bove bukh.*

It was not until the middle of the nineteenth century, when modern capitalism and Western Enlightenment finally made their way to eastern Europe, that the traditional Jewish world finally began to open up to other forms of literary expression.

At first the *maskilim* (Jewish proponents of Enlightenment) turned to Hebrew, a language so classical it was used for commencement addresses during the early years of Harvard University. There was only one problem: Like Latin, Hebrew hadn't actually been spoken for several thousand years, and nonscholars—presumably those who most needed enlightening—couldn't read Hebrew well enough to understand most of what the *maskilim* were trying to communicate. In 1857 the year's best-selling Hebrew novel sold 1,200 copies; the same year, a minor Yiddish novel by Isaac Meir Dik sold 120,000.

And so, slowly, with little enthusiasm, some of the braver Hebrew writers decided to try their hand at writing in Yiddish. The most important of these was an accomplished Hebrew stylist—he's often called the Father of Modern Hebrew Literature—named Sholem Abramovitsh, who made his Yiddish debut in 1864 under the pseudonym Mendele Moykher Seforim, Mendele the Book Peddler. Abramovitsh made no pretense: He regarded Yiddish as ugly and unwashed, and adopted it only as a "necessary evil," a utilitarian means of spreading enlightenment among the masses. But as I discovered in graduate school, he was enough of an artist to know a good thing when he saw it: The more he imitated the Yiddish vernacular—ostensibly to ridicule it—the more he came to appreciate its artistic possibilities. Although Mendele never ceased to poke fun at the foibles of the Jewish masses, it wasn't long before he was using his pen to defend them, as well. His works include a play about a tax revolt by the Jewish poor, an allegorical novel in which a talking horse demands bread before knowledge, a parody of Don Quixote, and Yiddish translations of the Hebrew psalms and classics of world literature. Fascinated by the literary possibilities of "a bird's-eye view," he translated Jules Verne's *Around the World in Eighty Days* from French to Yiddish. (Ironically, his own grandson became a test pilot and was killed in a plane crash in 1913.)

Mendele was followed by two other "classical" Yiddish writers: Sholem Aleichem and I. L. Peretz. They in turn were followed by hundreds more, and it wasn't long before the dynamism, wisdom, humor, and tragedy that had been cultivated in spoken Yiddish for a thousand years burst forth on the page. Between 1864, when Mendele published his first Yiddish story, and 1939, when the Nazis invaded Poland, nearly thirty thousand separate Yiddish titles appeared, constituting one of the most concentrated periods of literary creativity in all of Jewish history. Yiddish writers experimented with virtually every form of modern literary expression, from impressionism, romanticism, and naturalism to socialist realism, eroticism, and surrealism.

The new literature found astounding resonance. In Eastern Europe, and even more so in the countries where Jews took refuge, millions turned to Yiddish books for comfort and guidance in a confusing new world. They read widely and voraciously. They scrimped and saved to buy books. They devoured poetry, short stories, novels, drama, history, ethnography, sociology, folklore, linguistics, natural science, religion, and politics. They read about the world, about the Old Country, and about themselves.

In America, Yiddish books and newspapers played a central role in helping newly arrived Jewish immigrants adapt to life in a strange new land. Even religious Jews, who would never have seen a Yiddish book in Europe, bought them in America. *Grine,* greenhorns, studied etiquette books; schoolboys memorized ready-made bar mitzvah speeches; and aspiring Americans pored over Yiddish pamphlets—published by the D.A.R., no less—to prepare for citizenship exams. Another guidebook helped new parents choose a suitably American name for their child. *A Bintl Brief* (A Bundle of Letters), the *Jewish Daily Forward*'s advice column, was a cross between Dear Abby and Maimonides' *Guide for the Perplexed*—an invaluable introduction to American mores and manners.

Of course, Jewish housewives of the immigrant generation cooked the way their mothers did, with a *bisl* of this and a *smitshik* of that. Yiddish cookbooks tried to standardize recipes, adapting them to American ingredients, conventions, and tastes. When Jewish immigrants first arrived in America they assumed that coffee beans, like other beans, were not kosher for Passover—until an enterprising Maxwell House advertising agent came along. First he found a rabbi who publicly declared that coffee beans are really berries and therefore acceptable Passover fare. Then, to reinforce the point, he began distributing free Haggadahs (books used at the Passover seder) emblazoned with the Maxwell House logo. To this day, "Maxwell House Haggadahs" can be found on seder tables across the country.

Popular-science books in Yiddish taught everything from geology and astronomy to chemistry and physics. A Yiddish guidebook to human sexuality was censored under the federal government's puritanical Comstock laws; though hardly racy by modern standards, entire sections had to be blacked out before the book could be sent through the United States mail.

A surprising number of the books we collected were translations of world literature into Yiddish. We found Yiddish versions of "Bambi," *The Bhagavad Gita,* Chinese legends, and Finnish folktales. Favorite writers included Jack London *(The Call of the Wild—Di shtime fun blut),* Mark Twain *(The Prince and the Pauper—Der prints un der betler),* Knut Hamsun, Rabindranath Tagore, Robert Frost, Emily Dickinson, Emile Zola, Leo Tolstoy, Feodor Dostoyevsky, Harriet Beecher Stowe, Oscar Wilde, and last but not least, Guy de Maupassant, whose ubiquitous thirteen-volume *Collected Works* was distributed free as a subscription premium for a popular Yiddish newspaper. Thomas Mann's *The Magic Mountain (Der tsoyberbarg)* and Eric Maria Remarque's *All Quiet on the Western Front (Afn mayrev front keyn nayes)* were translated into Yiddish by the young Isaac Bashevis Singer, presaging the pessimism and disillusionment that later found expression in his own writing. Shakespeare was almost as popular in Yiddish as he was in English; a favorite title was *Kenig Lir (King Lear),* which dealt with a subject much on the minds of Jewish immigrants: *tsores mit kinder*—trouble with children. The Yiddish title page of one Shakespeare translation read *"Fartaytsht un farbesert*—Translated and Improved." Jews approached these works with great seriousness and respect; they were a window out of the tenement (or the shtetl), often giving Yiddish readers their first glimpse of the broader artistic and intellectual life beyond.

Meanwhile, by the early twentieth century, serious Yiddish literature was enjoying a golden age in the *goldene medine,* the golden land. Bohemian literary groups such as Di Yunge, The Young Ones, renounced social protest in favor of more personal artistic expression, largely through poetry. Their experimental language, exotic forms, and art-for-art's-sake philosophy made writers such as Mani Leib, Reuben Iceland, Moyshe Leib Halpern, Joseph Opatoshu, and David Ignatoff the "Beat Generation" of Yiddish letters. The *Inzikhistn,* or Introspectivist, movement brought Yiddish poetry into the jazz age through the work of Jacob Glatstein, Aaron Glanz-Leyeles, N. B. Minkoff, and others.

As we opened the boxes, we were intrigued to see how many works were written by women. Rachel Luria and Fradel Stock wrote vivid, gritty stories of daily life. Kadya Molodowsky was active in Yiddish literary circles in Kiev and Warsaw before coming to America in 1935. Here she continued her work as a poet, novelist, and editor, expressing her concern for the oppressed, exposing the depredations of war, and later responding to the tragedy of the Holocaust. After the founding of Israel her odes to the Jewish homeland were sung in the streets of the new state.

As oppression and violence escalated in Europe, other established Yiddish prose writers—including Sholem Aleichem, Sholem Asch, Lamed Shapiro, and I. J. Singer—fled to America, adding new momentum to an already teeming Yiddish literary life. They were joined after the war by Chaim Grade, Itzik Manger, Rokhl Korn, and dozens more.

For the most part, though, the accomplishments of American Yiddish literature lay more in poetry than in prose; when American Yiddish writers did write novels or stories, they usually set them in the Old Country. "The better Yiddish prose writers avoid writing about American Jewish life," observed Isaac Bashevis Singer, who arrived in the country in 1935. "Yiddish words that each day smell more and more of the past and of otherworldliness cannot convey a lifestyle which hurtles forth with such extraordinary speed that even the rich and ever resilient English language can scarcely keep pace."

Although Yiddish literature found its largest audience in America, until the outbreak of World War II its creative epicenter remained in Europe. In 1908 an international conference was convened in Czernowitz, Bukovina (now in western Ukraine), to discuss the role of

Yiddish in modern Jewish life. Among the seventy delegates were many of the greatest Yiddish writers and intellectuals of the day, including Nathan Birnbaum, Chaim Zhitlowsky, Jacob Gordin, David Pinski, Avrom Reisen, Sholem Asch, Hirsh Dovid Nomberg, and I. L. Peretz. Debate was spirited. "Yiddishists" wanted to recognize Yiddish as "*the* national language of the Jewish people," whereas Hebraists and Zionists argued that Yiddish should be discarded. In the end cooler heads prevailed, and Yiddish was declared "*a* national language." Although the Zionist leader Ahad Ha'am later characterized the conference as a "Purim *shpil*" (a farcical spectacle like those performed on the Jewish carnival day of Purim), others credited it with granting legitimacy to Yiddish, fostering new scholarship and literary creativity.

The peace treaty that ended the First World War granted special rights and protections to the ethnic minorities of Eastern Europe; for Yiddish-speaking Jews it seemed a godsend. Jewish political and intellectual life flourished, and hundreds of new Yiddish writers emerged. Even as anti-Semitism intensified, poverty deepened, and storm clouds gathered over Europe, a brilliant literary and cultural renaissance took place in the Jewish communities of Warsaw, Vilna, and other cities. Many of their titles featured imaginative design and typography, and when we opened boxes, we could usually count on finding at least some of these distinctive volumes inside.

It was the Holocaust, in the end, that sounded the death knell of Yiddish literature in Europe—and paradoxically gave rise to its most powerful expression. In the late 1930s, before the German invasion of Poland, the Yiddish poet Mordecai Gebirtig wrote with blood-chilling prescience:

> *Es brent, briderlekh, es brent!*
> *Oy, undzer orem shtetl, nebekh, brent!*

S'hobn shoyn di fayer-tsungen,
Dos gantse shtetl ayngeshlungen—
Un di beyze vintn hudzhen,
S'gantse shtetl brent.

On fire, brothers, it's on fire!
Oh, our poor little village is on fire!
Tongues of flame are wildly leaping,
Through our town the flames are sweeping—
And the cruel winds keep it burning,
The whole town's on fire.

Gebirtig went on to write powerful poems about the Holocaust until he, his wife, and two daughters were murdered by the Nazis in 1942. Of course, the consuming fire he foretold could not be extinguished, and as the horror unfolded, reportage and literary imagination, as much as armed struggle, became weapons of resistance.

In the Nazi-imposed ghettos of Lodz and Warsaw, the Jewish historian Emanuel Ringelblum handpicked a clandestine group of scholars, poets, playwrights, novelists, and journalists to chronicle daily life. Operating under the Hebrew code name *Oyneg Shabes* (The Joy of the Sabbath), they started out as social scientists, reporting in meticulous detail on everything from mail delivery to food and sanitation. But as conditions worsened, as starvation and disease ran rampant, as horrifying accounts came back from the death camps—and as it became clear that most of the ghetto's inhabitants would not survive—many of the *Oyneg Shabes* chroniclers turned to literature, in both Yiddish and Hebrew, to better convey the unspeakable human tragedy taking place before their eyes. Before the ghetto was liquidated, they buried three separate caches of documents. Part of the first cache, packed into ten tin boxes, was recovered shortly after the war; and the second, sealed inside two aluminum milk cans, was found by Polish construction workers in December 1950. The location of the third cache remains unknown.

In the Vilna ghetto young Jewish writers, including the Hebrew poet Abba Kovner and the Yiddish writer Avrom Sutzkever, played a central role in organizing a movement of armed resistance. Later they fled to the forests, where they fought on as partisans. In one poem, Sutzkever imagines the partisans melting the lead printing plates of the Talmud to forge their bullets. In another, one of my own favorites, he describes a young woman named Mira who continues to teach Yiddish literature to her students as the ghetto falls around them.

Immediately after the war, Jews in the displaced persons camps of Europe published firsthand Yiddish accounts. When they couldn't find Hebrew type, as was often the case, they settled for what was at hand, transliterating their Yiddish memoirs and setting them in German or Polish fonts. Although the survivors eventually rebuilt their shattered lives, Yiddish writers continued for years to wrestle with the political and existential implications of the Nazis' crimes. Among the most moving volumes we found were *yizkor bikher* (memorial books), massive compendia in which émigrés and survivors reconstructed their vanished hometowns through prose, photos, personal recollections, hand-drawn maps, and endless lists of names of those who died.

Of course, even without the depredations of the Holocaust it's not clear that Yiddish would have prevailed as the spoken language of the majority of Jews. In interwar Poland, Yiddish was already losing ground against Polish as younger Jews acculturated. In Palestine and later in the State of Israel, Zionist ideology predicated itself on "negation of the *galut*," rejection of the diaspora, leaving little room for Yiddish, a language redolent of Jewish marginality. In America, a land of unprecedented freedom and opportunity, Jews found tolerance for religious differences but not for differences of language or culture. Although a handful of writers continue even today to publish in Yiddish, for the most part they are very old, and their remaining readers are few and far between. With one or two exceptions, there has never been a significant Yiddish writer born in America. Like it or not, Yiddish literature is finite, bound to a specific time and place.

But precisely because Yiddish literature *is* finite, it is enormously important, a link between one epoch of Jewish history and the next. Its world's having been ferociously attacked and almost destroyed only serves to underscore its significance. The books we collect are the immediate intellectual antecedent of most contemporary Jews, able to tell us who we are and where we came from. Especially now, after the unspeakable horrors of the twentieth century, Yiddish literature endures as our last, best bridge across the abyss.

9. "People Are Dying Today Who Never Died Before"

There was a Sisyphean dynamic to our work: The more books we collected, the more the word spread, and the more the word spread, the more books there were to collect. By midwinter of that first year on the road it was clear that immigrant Jews had been more avid readers than anyone imagined. Yiddish books were scattered in virtually every city in North America, and there was no way that we, a handful of young people with extremely limited resources, could collect them all on our own. We needed help! So I decided to organize a network of zamlers, volunteer book collectors, who would gather books in their own communities and ship them to our Massachusetts headquarters.

The idea was not without precedent. In the late nineteenth century the great Jewish historian Simon Dubnow issued an appeal for zamlers to round up communal records and other historical documents in the remote *shtetlekh* of the Russian Pale. These documents served as primary sources for Dubnow's many books, including the *History of Jews in Russia and Poland* and *The World History of the Jewish People*. When the YIVO, the Yiddish Scientific Institute, was founded in Vilna in 1925, hundreds more zamlers answered the call, shipping bundles of documents to its archive. This ingathering continued until the Nazis invaded

Poland and seized the YIVO headquarters, hoping to use its extensive resources for their own racist research. Although many of YIVO's scholars were forced to work for the Nazis, they did so with quiet courage, often risking their lives to smuggle documents out of the archives, to be reclaimed after the war. Were it not for those early zamlers — and the heroism of librarians and scholars, many of whom were killed — the documentary record of almost a thousand years of Jewish life in Eastern Europe would have been lost.

It was this *yikhes,* this model, that I had in mind when I drew up plans for a "second wave" of zamlers — this time to save Yiddish books. I spent several days with a typewriter, a T square, and a bottle of rubber cement, putting together a prototype Zamler's Packet, a do-it-yourself kit containing posters, fill-in-the-blank press releases, shipping labels, and step-by-step instructions — in short, everything a volunteer would need to run a successful local Yiddish book drive. I borrowed money to have the packets printed, and then sent out letters and press releases in the hope of recruiting a small group of volunteers. The response was enthusiastic. People signed on all across North America. Some were elderly, others were young people who didn't speak a word of Yiddish; but they were all grateful for the chance to *act,* to do something practical to reclaim a culture that was disappearing before their eyes.

In New York City, so many volunteered that I decided to call a meeting to coordinate their efforts. Stuart Schear, a recent graduate of Oberlin College who had been fielding calls for us as an assistant in the education department at the Workmen's Circle, graciously agreed to serve as host. The Workmen's Circle — or Arbeter Ring, as it's known in Yiddish — is a fraternal organization deeply committed to Yiddish culture, and the use of their conference room lent a *hekhsher,* an imprimatur, a sense of historical connection, to the proceedings. The meeting took place at 7:30 on a Tuesday evening in early February of 1981.

The weather was windy and bitter cold, but that didn't stop a dozen people from showing up. Several were in their early twenties: Stuart; Roger Mummert; Danny Soyer, another Oberlin graduate, who was now doing research on the Jewish labor movement; and one or two others. The rest were in their seventies and eighties. There was no one in between.

We started out with coffee and cookies, and then I called the meeting to order. "Since many of you will be working together here in New York, I'd like to go around the room and ask each of you to introduce yourselves."

That was a mistake. Not for nothing are Jews called "a nation of priests." Everyone had something to say. I was looking for names, and instead ended up with life stories. The most memorable was Mr. Berger, a dapper octogenarian who, in defiance of the howling weather outside, sported a dazzling suntan (as though he had just spent the day playing pinochle on Miami Beach), carried a pearl-handled walking stick, and wore a cream-colored linen suit, a silk shirt open at the neck, a straw cap, and shiny white loafers. Alas, for a man who positively radiated good health, he was utterly preoccupied with death.

"I'm here tonight," he began when it was his turn to speak, "because my friends, the ones who really care about Yiddish, couldn't make it. Do you know where my friends are tonight? They're *toyt, geshtorbn, nayn eylen in drerd* (dead, deceased, nine cubits under the ground)! I'm here tonight to do the work they can no longer do themselves."

It was an hour and a half before all twelve people at the table had had their chance to *davenen baym omed,* to take the floor and speak. I then stood up, told a bit about the Yiddish Book Center, outlined my plans for a network of volunteers in New York, and passed around Zamler's Packets with freshly printed instructions, posters, and press releases.

"Now just one minute!" interrupted Mr. Berger. "I can see from these packets that you know all about marketing. If I ever need a good public relations man I'll be sure to call you. But let's face facts, PR isn't going to help us collect Yiddish books. The people with Yiddish books don't read PR. In fact, they don't read anything anymore! Do you know where the people with Yiddish books are now?"

"Florida?" ventured Roger.

"Dead!" shouted Mr. Berger, with a whap of his walking stick on the table. *"Toyt! Geshtorbn! Nayn eyln in——"*

"Excuse me, Mr. Berger," I broke in, "but if you'll just let me finish I think you'll see we've made adequate arrangements to pick up books after people have passed on."

"After they've passed on? Let me tell you something, yungerman, you may run an organization but by me you're still a *pisher,* wet behind the ears. You don't know the first thing about how the world works, you haven't seen what I've seen, you don't walk around with death breathing down your neck every day like I do. Take it from me: You don't go to people *after* they die, you go *before* they die!"

"And how do you propose doing that?" asked Stuart, who, working with older Jews every day at the Workmen's Circle, was having trouble hiding his annoyance.

"Simple!" shouted Mr. Berger, whapping his walking stick again against the Formica tabletop; "You go to the hospitals! You set up shop in the Intensive Care Unit."—*Whap!*— "When it looks like some old Jew is about to breathe his last"—*Whap!*—"you rush over to him and ask him for his Yiddish books!" *Whap! Whap! Whap!*

Stuart was aghast. "Mr. Berger, if you think I'm going to walk into a hospital and——"

"Why not? You'll be doing these old Jews a favor! You'll take a load off their chests! They can die easy, knowing someone will take care of their books after they're gone!"

The strategy was unsettling at best, and it was some time before I could restore order and bring the discussion around to my original if admittedly less sensational plan of canvassing apartment buildings and hanging posters in Laundromats, synagogues, and senior centers. After the meeting, Stuart, Roger, and I stayed behind to clean up. When we finally made our way to the elevator, Mr. Berger was waiting for us. He pushed the Lobby button with his walking stick.

"Do you want to know what the real problem is?" he asked as the elevator descended. *"The real problem is that people are dying today who never died before!"* With that he donned his straw hat, turned smartly on his white loafers, and tapping with his pearl-handled walking stick, proceeded calmly into the winter night.

Mr. Berger must have returned to Florida, because we never heard from him again. But notwithstanding his pessimism, the zamler network proved successful. More than two hundred people signed up, from Edgartown on Martha's Vineyard to Nome, Alaska. Where we could, we set up drop-off points: In El Paso, Texas, it was the Ave Maria Religious Store, where the proprietor, Jules Novick, advertised "Crucifixes, Wholesale and Retail" and set aside room in the back for Yiddish books.

For many of our zamlers, saving Yiddish books became their life. Sorell Skolnik, for example, was a resolute woman in her seventies who lived in the Mohegan Colony, a community of anarchists and other progressive Jews just north of Peekskill, New York. The first time we visited Sorell was in 1981. Pat Myerson, Fran Krasno, and I arrived cold and tired at the end of a particularly trying day. We had been drinking caffeinated tea and eating sugary cakes at the homes of older Jews since early morning, and we cringed at the idea of having to force our way through the frosting of one more Entenmann's. What a surprise, then, when we entered Sorell's house at the end of a beautiful country lane and inhaled the aroma of simmering chickpea soup! The meal she served us was an organic feast, with homemade bread, and herbs and vegetables picked fresh from her own garden.

Sorell and her husband, Nathan, had been living at Mohegan since the 1920s, shortly after they arrived in this country from their native Russia. Nathan was a garment worker who commuted each day to New York; Sorell was a dressmaker who worked at home. There, amid the pines, they and their neighbors had fashioned a rich Jewish cultural life with weekly study groups in Russian and Yiddish literature, a communal Passover seder, and an annual event to raise scholarship money for young people to study Yiddish each summer at Columbia. (I myself had been a recipient, the summer before I headed off for grad school.)

Sorell proved an amazingly energetic zamler. She had an old Dodge Dart, which she drove to pick up books all over Westchester County. She'd take them back to her house, and we'd come with a truck every three thousand volumes or so to transport them to Massachusetts. We became close friends in the course of these frequent visits. When we launched our annual summer program in Yiddish culture in 1984, we enlisted Sorell as one of our teachers, a position she held with distinction until she was in her late eighties. Her husband died shortly after our first meeting; she herself had a stroke several years back and is now confined to a wheelchair, living in her own apartment near her daughter on Long Island. But she retains every bit of her dignity and determination. As I write she is almost a hundred years old, and though her zamler days are behind her, she still keeps in touch with a loyal following of students, some of whom, themselves in their eighties, travel sixty miles each way for a weekly Yiddish reading circle in her home.

The prize for the most ambitious zamler has to go to Jacob Schaefer of Los Angeles. A survivor who lost his wife and three daughters at Auschwitz, after the war he made his way to New York, where he worked as a tailor, a trade he learned as an apprentice in his native Kovno, Lithuania. It was only after he retired and moved to L.A. that he became a zamler. "I'll tell you the truth," Jacob told us one day in his crowded Fairfax apartment. "I never wanted to be a tailor. All my life what I really wanted to do was work with books, but my father wouldn't let me, he wanted better I should earn a living. So I sewed. Now that I'm retired, I can do what I want. Every morning I get up early and go out with the car. I drive to Venice, Santa Monica, Beverly Hills, I talk with people and they give me their Yiddish books. This is the kind of work I've always wanted to do; for the first time in my life I'm really and truly happy."

With assistance from David and Sylvia Davidson and their fellow volunteers at the L.A. chapter of the Workmen's Circle, Jacob shipped us more than 45,000 volumes—an all-time record.

Meanwhile, back in New York, Mr. and Mrs. Field, elderly zamlers living on an upper floor of a Co-op City high-rise, used to summon us every six weeks. Each time we came they would have several hundred books waiting for us, all carefully tied with string in neat little bundles of three or four books each.

"You know, Mr. Field," I told him one day, "you don't have to tie the books in separate bundles. We're young, we have handtrucks, we can carry the books loose or pack them into boxes. . . ."

"Oh no," Mr. Field explained, "*ir farshteyt nisht* (you don't understand). *Mir hobn nisht keyn machine, darfn mir forn mitn bus kidey oyf-tsuzamlen di ale bikher* (We have no automobile; we have to travel by bus in order to collect all these books)."

A frail couple in their eighties, they regarded the rescue of Yiddish books as a matter of self-preservation: They had helped build this culture, and they were not about to see it abandoned. With halting steps but an unshakable sense of purpose, they set out every day on the city bus, traveling all over the Bronx, ringing doorbells and carrying donated books back to their apartment, two small bundles at a time.

10. "Pretty Soon We'll Have a Whole Forest in Israel and No More Members Here"

I t was a gray, wet morning, the streets clogged with slush, when Pat Myerson and I arrived in New York City with a twenty-two-foot diesel truck. On our clipboard that day were four special pickups, each of which promised to yield more books than could fit into a single van.

The first was Knight Printing, a venerable Yiddish firm that was going out of business. We double-parked the truck on Lafayette and entered the dim lobby of an old industrial building. Knight Printing was on the eighth floor. We rang for the elevator, waited what seemed like ten minutes, and finally started up on foot. The stairs were caked in dust, and in front of some doors several years' accumulation of phone books lay unclaimed. At the eighth floor we knocked on an unmarked steel door and were greeted by Mr. Kupferstein, a small, wiry man who, we soon learned, had owned Knight Printing for the past twenty-two years.

"What are you doing on the stairs?" he wanted to know. "Why didn't you take the elevator like a *mentsh?*"

We explained that we had pushed the elevator button in the lobby, but it was apparently out of order.

"Out of order? What out of order? Where out of order? The elevator operator has been sitting right here talking with me all morning. When you rang he finished his tea and went downstairs but no one was there—you must have started hiking already—so of course he came back up."

We stepped inside and sure enough, there was the elevator operator, sitting on a well-worn oak swivel chair inside his elevator, which opened directly onto Mr. Kupferstein's loft. He wore an English driving cap pulled low over his eyes, and his elevator was decorated with calendar pictures of mountains and beaches. An antique parabolic electric heater whirred at his feet.

"You know, Mr. Kupferstein," said the elevator man in a strong Yiddish accent, speaking directly to his compatriot and ignoring us altogether, "it just goes to show you, the young people these days, they're always in a rush, they push the button, they expect the doors to open right away, they forget maybe the elevator operator is a person, too, maybe he's busy for a minute somewhere else. No, Mr. Kupferstein, times are changing, nobody has time to wait anymore."

Mr. Kupferstein nodded sadly in agreement. After all, his company was going out of business for that very reason, its old letterpresses and hot-lead Linotypes as obsolete as the books they printed.

"What we had here at Knight Printing was *craftsmanship*," said Mr. Kupferstein as he showed us around the floor. "We were a union shop, our workers took pride in their work. Today no one wants craftsmanship, no one wants union. Now all they care about is quick, all they care about is cheap." Over the last decade, he explained, what little Yiddish publishing remained had shifted to nonunion shops run by Hasidim who used computers to set the type and inexpensive offset presses to print it. With his old presses and union crew, he didn't have a chance.

We followed Mr. Kupferstein to the corner of the large loft; there, next to packed crates of metal galley trays, chases, wooden "furniture," quoins, and other tools of hot-type printing, were wooden dollies loaded high with what appeared to be new Yiddish books. Knight had been a contract printer, manufacturing books for many of the largest Yiddish publishers. Piled on the dollies were several hundred samples: one copy of every Yiddish title they had printed over the past sixty years.

Mr. Kupferstein deftly secured the books to the dollies with binder's twine and then, like the warehousemen we'd met near the Fulton Fish Market, grabbed a heavy metal hook and towed them across the room, where the elevator operator, with practiced professionalism, brandished his own hook and pulled them onto the elevator. We and the books rode downstairs together, and then the two older men helped us carry them from inside the building out to the truck. Despite their age, they showed remarkable strength and agility as they ran back and forth through the rain and slush, covering the piles of loose books with their jackets.

When the job was done we stood together in the entryway to say good-bye. The cold rain pounded against the metal roof of the truck. The elevator operator shook my hand. "Maybe next time you'll wait for the elevator!" he grumbled. I promised I would do just that. But deep in our hearts all of us—Pat and I, Mr. Kupferstein and the elevator operator—knew that there would be no next time. After six decades and countless thousands of volumes, we had just carried out Knight Printing's very last load.

It rained harder as we hopped back in the truck and headed for the South Bronx. The week before, a Jewish Consolidated Edison worker had entered an apartment building to check the meters and stumbled over boxes and piles of what he recognized as Yiddish books. He phoned the Workmen's Circle, and they in turn phoned us.

In the early 1980s, the South Bronx was a war zone. Whole blocks were burned out. Buildings with broken windows and charred beams alternated with empty lots of brick and rubble. We could see little children staring out of empty window frames on this raw, bone-chilling February morning, whole families living in gutted buildings without water or heat.

It took us a long time to find the address the meter reader had supplied. Many street signs were missing and few buildings had legible numbers. After asking directions several times we finally came to a run-down apartment building, the only intact structure on a block of ruins. Acutely aware of the crime rate in the South Bronx, we were at first apprehensive about leaving the safety of the truck, but as we looked about us we realized that despite the devastation the daily lives of decent people still went on. A gray-haired woman, probably a grandmother, was wheeling a baby carriage, covering the child with an umbrella as she herself bent her head into the driving rain. At the corner grocery a delivery man in a Coca-Cola uniform was unloading crates of soda.

We went up to the apartment building and rang for the super. An elderly black man came to the door. Oh yes, he knew all about the books in the basement. "They belonged to an old Jewish lady, lived in the building since God knows when, died just last month. Far's I know, she hadn't kith nor kin, so there was no one to call to come claim her stuff. The landlord told me to clear out her apartment so he could rent it to someone else, so I just took everything and stashed it in the basement. You two can take whatever you want . . . assuming the junkies haven't beat you to it."

The super put on his raincoat and led us around back, past a mountain of garbage, into a dark, dank basement. The smell of urine and excrement was overpowering. Piled in a corner, already ransacked, were the Jewish woman's worldly goods: a bed and mattress, two stuffed chairs, a broken table, a threadbare carpet, kitchenware, bundles of old clothes, empty pill vials scattered in all directions, and beneath it all, two bookcases lying on their backs, still full of Yiddish books. Pat and I wondered aloud about their owner. As the ethnographer Jack Kugelmass later documented in *The Miracle of Intervale Avenue,* small numbers of immigrant Jews still lived in the South Bronx in the early 1980s, either unwilling or unable to leave the neighborhood they had called home for so long. We met such people ourselves in the course of our subsequent travels: some too feeble to move, living what was left of their lonely lives behind locked doors; others too stubborn to move; and still others too idealistic, determined to live in peace with their neighbors, whoever they may be.

We never learned the story—or even the name—of the woman whose books we hauled out of the basement that day. Many of her books were about the Holocaust, including a *yizkor bukh,* a memorial volume chronicling the destruction of the Jewish community of Kovno, so maybe she was a survivor who had run enough in her life and didn't want to run again. Whatever the case, Pat and I tied bandanas over our noses, pulled on leather work gloves, and set to work. We were so anxious to get out of there that we didn't even try to unload the bookcases: We just dragged them onto the handtruck and maneuvered them through the basement and out to the street. We took only the books and bookcases; all the rest of the dead woman's belongings—clothes, furniture, carpets, curtains, dishes, pots and pans—we left behind, one more pile of refuse amid the wretchedness all around.

It was already noon before we arrived in Elmhurst, Queens, to retrieve seven thousand books we had collected by van the previous month and temporarily stored in the basement of an apartment building belonging to our board member Sidney Berg. The rain had tapered to a drizzle, and we hauled the boxes in silence for two hours, until the job was done. We picked up cheese and crackers at a corner grocery, then settled into the truck for a long ride to the southern shore of Long Island, where we were to pick up our last load of the day. The truck was now laden with nearly four tons of books, and we could barely hear each other above the rattling of the cab and the roar of the engine. We were both cold and miserable: our muscles ached, our clothes were damp with sweat and rain, and our boots were soaked. Par for the course, the defroster on our rental truck was broken; every few minutes Pat had to reach across the big windshield with a towel so I could see where we were going.

It was 3:30 when we arrived at the Long Beach home of Mrs. Baram, a widow in her seventies. We must have looked awfully bedraggled as we climbed the stairs to her seaside bungalow, because she took one look at us and immediately sat us down in her well-heated kitchen, plied us with hot tea and kugel, and took what she could of our wet clothes and tossed them in the dryer.

As we slowly revived, she told us her story. As a young girl she had belonged to a socialist Zionist youth group in Poland. Eventually she made her way to Eretz Yisroel, the Land of Israel, where she lived as a *halutznik,* a pioneer farm worker helping to reclaim the soil. She spoke Yiddish and Hebrew fluently, as well as Russian, Polish, and English.

She asked us about ourselves, and before long Pat and I were pouring out our hearts about the morning's experiences in the South Bronx: the ill-clad children, the broken windows, the unheated buildings, the fetid basement in which a lifetime's books and belongings had been unceremoniously laid to rest.

Mrs. Baram let us talk. When we finished it was not we who were consoling her, as was so often the case on our collection trips, but she who was comforting us.

"*M'tor nisht miyaesh zayn* (You must never despair)," she said in a voice that bespoke decades of personal and political struggle, in Poland, Israel, and America. "It says in *Perek* (a two-thousand-year-old Hebrew text): '*Loy alekho hamelokhe ligmor* . . . It is not up to you to complete the task, but neither are you free to desist from it.'"

In the end it was her example, even more than her words, that lifted our flagging spirits. Here was a woman who had *lived* her Jewishness. All her life she had marched in demonstrations and raised money for the hungry. Like Sorell Skolnick at the Mohegan Colony, she ran a weekly *leyenkrayz,* a Yiddish reading circle. For twenty years members of the local Jewish community gathered under her leadership to read and discuss Yiddish literature. When they began there were 150 participants and they met in a rented hall; now they met in her living room. "Every time one of our members dies," she told us, "we remember them by planting a tree in Israel. Pretty soon we're going to have a whole forest in Israel and no more members here." She was a realist, but not a pessimist. Her very next words were to tell us, with great enthusiasm, about the Yiddish novel her small group would be discussing later that week.

And the books she had for us? There were many. For twenty years, whenever anyone in her circle died, she would drive over to save their Yiddish books. Almost three thousand volumes were waiting for us in the back room of her house.

"It's not enough to cry for the past," she told us after we loaded the last box onto the truck. "It's more important that we build for the future. You young people are our *hemshekh,* our continuity. We've done the best we could. Now it's up to you."

She hugged and kissed us each in turn, and then gave us a big bag of food for the long drive back to Massachusetts. The rain had stopped, and as we pulled away the setting sun suddenly broke through the scudding clouds in the western sky. Pat and I drove several blocks, pulled into an empty parking lot, and ran down to the beach to watch the sunset. A strong salt breeze was blowing off the ocean and the weather was turning cold, but we took our shoes off anyway and ran barefoot all the way to the water's edge. Since starting out early that morning, it was the first time we felt warm.

11. "Love and Peace"

As Jules Piccus foretold, a grant did somehow appear before the first rent payment on our factory loft came due: Rabbi Harold Kudan of Glencoe, Illinois, the father of a college friend, approached one of his congregants, and we received—in the nick of time—$2,000 from Col. Henry Crown, a prominent Chicago philanthropist. Other checks followed, from book donors and friends, though most of these were of the $18 variety (it is traditional for Jews to give in multiples of 18, the numerical equivalent of *chai,* life). By November, when the New England wind began whipping through the chinks of our old brick building, our tiny staff—Galina Rothstein, Fran Krasno, and I—were wearing heavy sweaters, wool hats, and *lange gatkes,* long underwear. We cut the fingers off of old gloves in order to type. Even so, cash was running low and the end seemed near when, one cold morning, an older woman with a bright silk scarf wrapped around her head walked into our workroom, stuck out her hand, and proudly announced, "Sonya Staff, Greenwich Village!"

Sonya was the daughter of the late Aaron Staff, a Russian-born lace manufacturer and a patron of many Yiddish writers and organizations.

In the 1930s Sonya and her husband, Otto, had founded the first multicultural, multiracial camp in western Massachusetts. Back in the area to visit a friend, she had heard reports of "young people in a loft trying to save Yiddish books" and rushed right over to see for herself. It was love at first sight. Within a week she had written a sizeable check and joined our board, and she remained a generous supporter—and a great personal friend—until her death seventeen years later.

Another break came when an article about us appeared in the *New York Times*. The paper had just hit the streets when I was awakened by an insistent phone call.

"Yungerman," said the good-natured voice at the other end of the line, "where have you been all my life?"

The caller introduced himself as Sidney Berg, a real estate developer from Great Neck who, like Sonya, had also grown up in a *yidishe svive,* a world of Yiddish culture. I went to see him the next day and liked him immediately, and he, too, became a major supporter, helping us out during the Dumpster episode in New York and participating in innumerable adventures in the years that followed. Our financial woes were far from over, but thanks to Sonya and Sidney we were at least able to pay the rent, crank the heat up to sixty, satisfy the most insistent of our creditors, and keep our truck on the road.

Then we met with a yet another bit of good luck. I was sitting at my desk one morning, opening the mail, when I came upon an unusual letter:

Dear Friends:

I read of your project and I am writing to inquire if you would be interested in a collection of books which came from my family.

My mother was a Yiddish poetess named Aliza Greenblatt. She was friends with many outstanding Yiddish writers, who presented her with their own books. I have a collection that includes many copies of my mother's two books. One is a story of her life, the other a collection of children's poems.

Please do let me know more about your project.

Love and peace!
Marjorie Guthrie

I had heard of Aliza Greenblatt. Many of her poems had been set to music, and some, such as *"Fort a fisher afn yam* (A Fisherman Sails Forth on the Sea)," I could sing by heart. A letter from Aliza Greenblatt's daughter would have been cause enough for excitement. But then I looked at the signature: "Marjorie Guthrie." At the upper left-hand corner of the letterhead was a picture of a little man with a guitar, and then there was that sign-off, *"Love and peace!"*

"Hey Fran!" I called into the next room. "Do you know the name of Woody Guthrie's widow?"

"You mean the one who sits by his bedside in 'Alice's Restaurant'? I'm not sure, I think maybe Marjorie."

Amazing. Could it be that the daughter of *"Fort a fisher"* was also the wife of "This Land Is Your Land"—and, come to think of it, the mother of "Alice's Restaurant"? Well, whoever she was, she had Yiddish books for us. We'd find out soon enough.

At the risk of namedropping, I have to point out that Yiddish has a certain cachet, and even at this early date in the Center's history we had met more than our share of famous people—or at least the *parents* of famous people. For example, we once picked up books in Philadelphia from a highly cultured man named William Uris. We enjoyed several pleasant hours of conversation with him and his wife, and then he handed us most (but not all) of his large Yiddish library, which he lovingly removed from a beautiful glass-fronted bookcase. "The rest of these books you'll come back for another time," he said, "*iz kenen mir farbrengen a bisl vayter* (so we can talk a little more)."

We were already standing in the hallway, waiting for the elevator, when he began complaining about his son, who had absolutely no interest in Yiddish books or culture. "*Efsher hostu gehert fun im?* (Maybe you've heard of him?)" he asked.

"I don't know," I answered, "who's your son?"

"*Er is epes a shrayber,*" he responded, "*er heyst Leon Yuris* (He's some sort of writer; his name is Leon Uris)."

Among other notables were Abbie Hoffman's mother: "Abbie would really love what you're doing here!" and Allen Ginsberg's stepmother: "Allen used to bring all his friends over to the house. Kerouac couldn't get enough of my *flunken* (stewed meat)!" And now here was Marjorie Guthrie: the daughter of an important Yiddish writer and, just maybe, the wife and the mother of two pivotal figures in American music. Fran phoned her and arranged to pick up her mother's books at the family's old house in Howard Beach, Queens. She would meet us outside her apartment building in Manhattan, next door to the Dakota, and ride out there with us.

The appointed day dawned brisk and clear, and Roger and I arrived right on schedule in a particularly large and ratty rented truck. We pulled up across the street, and almost immediately a beautiful, spry woman of about sixty came skipping across the street to meet us. Small and neatly dressed in a gray cardigan sweater, a knee-length gray wool skirt and gray wool knee socks, she moved with the grace of a dancer. Without a moment's hesitation she hopped up onto the running board and leaned in through Roger's open window.

"Are you the boys for the Yiddish books?" she asked, brightly.

We introduced ourselves, Roger stepped out of the truck to let her in, and in a flash Mrs. Guthrie was sitting poised and smiling on the seat between us.

"I hope you don't mind riding in the truck with us," I apologized.

"Why, don't be silly!" she shouted back over the roar of the engine, "I'm used to it! I ride in my son Arlo's truck all the time!"

That took care of that. I put the truck in gear and we chatted amiably the whole way out to Howard Beach. We plied her with questions about her mother and Woody. She in turn asked a thousand questions about us, our work, our prognosis for Yiddish culture. Her curiosity was genuine, her enthusiasm contagious, and it wasn't long before we learned she was not only a famous daughter, wife, and mother, but also an accomplished person in her own right. She had been a professional dancer, serving for eighteen years as Martha Graham's assistant before founding her own dance school in Sheepshead Bay. As Woody slowly succumbed to Huntington's disease, it was she who cared for him. Later, she founded and ran a nonprofit organization for the support of Huntington's patients and their families. She still traveled all over the world, lecturing, educating, encouraging research, and working with families. More recently she had begun speaking out in support of other health care issues, including "orphan drugs": medication for diseases that claim too few victims to make them profitable.

By the time we reached Howard Beach we were old friends. Marjorie directed us down a narrow, seaside street to the small, one-story house where she and Woody had lived and raised their family. Their daughter Nora lived there now: Not much older than we and the spitting image of Woody, she greeted us warmly and led us downstairs to a small finished basement. Only in America! Against one wall was a pile of cardboard boxes containing Woody's books and manuscripts, which Marjorie was preparing to ship to an archive in Oklahoma. Against the other wall, waiting for us, were boxes jammed full of Aliza Greenblatt's Yiddish books and papers.

A bit in awe, we loaded the boxes onto the truck. Many of the books had been written by Aliza's friends and were personally inscribed. At least several hundred were by women writers. Some boxes contained unsold copies of Aliza's own books, and others contained her personal letters and manuscripts, which, since we maintained no archive of our own, we agreed to pass on to the American Jewish Historical Society.

After the boxes were safely loaded we sat down with Nora and Marjorie at the kitchen table. Nora served up fresh coffee and home-made cookies, and Marjorie began to speak about her own childhood and her lifelong relation to Yiddishkeit. Although Woody was not Jew-ish, she said, he always struck her as having a *yidishe neshome,* a Jewish soul. For one thing, he was a voracious reader: "One time my father gave him a copy of a tractate of the Talmud in English translation, and he read it over and over, highlighting the passages he liked with dif-ferent colored inks." He was also unusually helpful around the house. "Our Jewish neighbor used to watch Woody as he wheeled the carriage or helped with the chores. She was so impressed with his domesticity that one morning, while he was carrying out the garbage, she came up to him and said, 'Woody, you're a regular Jew.' Woody said it was the nicest compliment he ever received."

Although Woody's relationship with his father-in-law, Izzy, had been stiff, he and his more literary mother-in-law had gotten along famously. They were, of course, very different writers: Woody was folksy, ver-nacular, and political, while Aliza tended to be lyrical and refined, writ-ing more about nature than about people. But they shared a love of words, and they both wrote a great deal for children. According to Marjorie, Woody enjoyed Aliza's work and actually learned the Yiddish words to *"Fort a fisher"* and other songs, which he performed in public. But he never stopped chiding her for not being more political. "'Enough flowers and butterflies!' he would say, 'What about the working masses?' My mother just laughed, but one day she surprised him. She presented him with a political poem she had written—in

English, no less! Woody loved it and praised her to the sky, although later they both had to admit it really wasn't very good."

Sitting there at the kitchen table, Nora as transfixed as Roger and I, Marjorie went on to explain how she had tried to give her children a good Jewish education.

"When the children got older I decided it was time for them to learn Hebrew. I didn't want anything halfway. I figured, better to expose the children to the real thing and let them decide for themselves. So I phoned the orthodox shul in Howard Beach and asked them to please send over a tutor. They sent a very intense young man with a beard and yarmulke. One afternoon a week the three children sat down right here at the kitchen table and that young man taught them Hebrew. I could see that he was very, how shall I say, *earnest* about his work. Frankly, I don't think the children paid too much attention. Whenever I looked I could see Arlo and Nora kicking each other under the table. But the tutor didn't seem to notice; he just went on with his lesson, pacing back and forth and reciting the Torah while the children squirmed and watched the clock.

"The weekly lessons went on for a year or two. Then one day I got a call from the rabbi at the shul. He told me that we had to fire the tutor.

" 'Fire the tutor?' I said, 'but *why?*'

" 'Because we've found out he's too fanatical,' said the rabbi.

" 'Oh, posh,' I told him. 'The Guthrie children are not afraid of ideas. They'll listen to whatever this young man has to say and then they'll make up their own minds.'

"So the teacher remained with us until he decided to move to Israel. That was the last I heard of him until one night fifteen years later, when I was watching the news on television. There was a big demonstration somewhere, and there on the screen was a young man with a beard and yarmulke giving a most impassioned speech. I looked closely and sure enough, it was the children's Hebrew teacher. Of course, he was older now, he was a rabbi, but he was just as earnest as when he stood here in our kitchen. I can still remember his name: Meir Kahane. How's that for a Hebrew teacher for the Guthrie children?"

We talked for another hour at the kitchen table, and continued talking the whole way back to Manhattan. Before she left the truck Marjorie asked us how our organization was supported. Not very well, we conceded. A week later we received a $1,000 check in the mail from the Woody Guthrie Foundation. When we told Sidney Berg about this godsend, he decided to go see Marjorie in person. They didn't exactly travel in the same circles, but they found enough to talk about for two hours, and by the time he left she had agreed to become a member of our board. By spring she and I were traveling together, speaking at synagogues, cultural centers, and fund-raising events. We developed a regular routine. Marjorie would kick it off, telling stories about Aliza and Woody—"who," she was always quick to remind her audience, "was not 'Yiddish.'" I followed with a "good news, bad news" talk: "The good news is that more young people are studying Yiddish than ever before; the bad news is that Yiddish books are being destroyed, and unless we act now a whole literature will be lost forever." Then Marjorie concluded with an eloquent appeal for membership. Five hundred people, including Nora and Arlo, turned up to hear us at the Center's first-anniversary celebration in the fall of 1981. The event was held in a softball field beneath a green and white tent, and after we finished the Klezmer Conservatory Band played a Yiddish version of "This Land Is Your Land." We raised some money—and, perhaps more important, a week later Arlo's secretary called: He had decided to learn Yiddish and was looking for a good primer.

Still, for all her enthusiasm and hard work, I always felt that Marjorie retained a certain ambivalence about her Jewishness. After all, she had

rebelled against Jewish provincialism when she set out to become a
dancer, and again when she married Woody. Meir Kahane notwithstanding, she had little formal Jewish affiliation. So I was surprised
when Sidney Berg phoned me one day to tell me that he and Marjorie
had just returned from a Yiddish banquet held in memory of Aliza
Greenblatt at an old Labor Zionist Center in Brighton Beach. "It was
beautiful!" Sidney enthused. "There were a hundred people and the
whole program was in Yiddish. As soon as Marjorie walked into the
room she was surrounded. Many of her mother's friends hadn't seen
her since she was a child! They came up to her, hugged her, kissed
her . . . I'm telling you, it was a sight to behold. Then we sat down at
round tables and the program began. They made speeches, read Aliza
Greenblatt's poems, sang her songs, and served refreshments. Marjorie
was so touched she cried."

A few days later Marjorie called and offered her version of the same
event. "Oh, it was very lovely," she said, "there were so many people I
hadn't seen for years, they still remembered my mother and sang her
songs. And of course Sidney was a dear to take me. But I'll tell you the
truth, the longer I stayed the more upset I became. Suddenly my whole
childhood came back to me. I remembered how I used to go to these
events with my mother, and how I always found everything so, well, so
aesthetically displeasing. One thing I remembered about those banquets
was that they always sat at tables covered with dirty oilcloths. Why
couldn't they use a nice piece of linen? No, always the same dirty oil-
cloth. Well, there I was with Sidney, forty years later, and when it came
time for refreshments they brought us to the tables and they were *still*
covered with the same dirty oilcloths. I took one look and I couldn't
help myself, I just broke down and cried."

12. "Ostroff! Sea Gate!"

Excuse me, Mrs. Ostroff, but is this whipped cream you're serving with the strawberries?"

"Whipped cream? God forbid—whipped cream is too *fettening*. That's *sour* cream!"

We were in the home of Sam and Leah Ostroff, sitting down to yet another twelve-course breakfast. In the six months since Marjorie Guthrie had introduced us to her late mother's best friends, they had joined the ranks of our most active zamlers—and our favorite hosts. For us, they represented everything that was good about the old Yiddish world: humor, generosity, intelligence, kindness, social consciousness, and an almost preternatural sense of Yiddishkeit.

Actually, the Ostroffs found us even before Marjorie did. On June 13, 1980, less than two weeks after I mailed the first press release, Sam wrote to me in Yiddish:

Tayere fraynt,
Mir, dos heyst mayn froy un ikh, hobn gehat shoyn a por mol shverikaytn
tsu bazorgn a heym far undzer tayerer yerushe.

Dear Friends,
We, that is to say my wife and myself, have already encountered many difficulties in securing a home for our precious
inheritance.

I assumed that their precious inheritance meant their books, but
when I wrote back suggesting they mail them to us, as I usually did in
those early days, he responded immediately, saying he and his wife had
no intention of giving up their own books *biz a hundert un tsvantsig,* until they were both 120 years old (the number of years Moses lived and
the traditional Jewish wish for longevity). Instead, what they wanted
was for us to visit them, so we could get to know one another better
and discuss what they could do to help.

They weren't the only people who wanted just "to talk," and given
the urgency of collecting actual books I put the letter aside, in a
Shmooze Pile, for a less hectic time. It might have remained there in-
definitely had it not been for Marjorie. When she returned from the
Yiddish banquet she told me that, despite the oilcloths, there was one
couple whom she had been thrilled to see. "Sam and Leah Ostroff were
my mother's next-door neighbors and her closest friends. They are the
most wonderful, generous people I have ever known, and I didn't even
realize they were still alive until I saw them at the banquet. They were
so happy to hear about my involvement with the Book Center. They
said they already wrote to you and are waiting for you to come. Really,
it's an experience not to be missed. I hope you don't mind, but I took
the liberty of telling them to expect you soon."

Pat Myerson was working on an oral history project at the time, and
she agreed to go as the Book Center's emissary. She set off one morning with a professional tape recorder and five hours of blank tape.
When she returned the next day she told us that she had not only used
up all her tape, but had remained talking and eating at the Ostroffs'

table for another four hours after that. Like Marjorie, Pat assured us that a visit to the Ostroffs was an experience not to be missed.

So a month later, while collecting books on Coney Island, Fran, Roger, and I decided to pay the Ostroffs a visit. They lived in Sea Gate, a fenced-off community at the very tip of Coney Island. Founded in the late nineteenth century, it was originally a summer colony for the Yankee yachting set, but during the 1930s, when money was tight and housing in short supply, large numbers of Jews began moving in, buying up summer cottages and converting them into year-round homes. By 1980, 80 percent of Sea Gate's seven thousand inhabitants were Jewish. The community maintained it own police force, its own community center, its own beach, even its own lighthouse—the last civilian-manned lighthouse in the country.

The Ostroffs lived in a small apartment on the first floor of a converted hotel. We rang the doorbell and were greeted by an effusive couple in their eighties, neither of whom was much over five feet tall. Mrs. Ostroff had white hair and a beatific face with high cheekbones. She was dressed in an old-fashioned but still elegant wool skirt with a white shirtwaist and a matching wool jacket. Mr. Ostroff, a bald, stocky man with powerful shoulders and mischievous eyes, wore a red plaid flannel work shirt buttoned to the collar, with a sweater and tie.

"*Nu, sholem aleykhem, kumt arayn, kumt arayn, s'iz genug vos tsu esn!* (Hello, come in, come in, there's plenty to eat!)"

Each Ostroff kissed each of us at least twice, they inquired about "Petty" (whom I took to be Pat), and then sat us down in the living room at a folding metal card table piled so high with food it was literally sagging under the weight. I looked around. Every square inch of their two-bedroom apartment was crammed full: tottering piles of books and papers on the floor, sculptures portraying Jewish themes atop overflowing bookcases and cabinets. The wallpaper was barely visible between all the paintings, collages, photographs, awards, testimonials, and framed certificates announcing the planting of trees in Israel.

"You like *mayn krefts?*" asked Mr. Ostroff.

"Your what?"

"*Mayn* krefts*!*"

He meant his crafts. As Mrs. Ostroff served up the first course, homemade gefilte fish, Mr. Ostroff explained that he had been a plumber until he suffered a heart attack twenty years ago and was forced to retire. He'd had five heart attacks since, as attested by the four-foot-tall green metal oxygen tank visible in his bedroom. But he wasn't about to let his health slow him down. To the contrary, once it became clear that he couldn't go back to work, he went to the Coney Island Community Center and decided to become an artist instead. His first medium was oil on canvas, and his subject—visible on the walls around us—was the Old Country: his mother at the family seder, a bearded rabbi, a train billowing smoke and steam across a snowy plain. In more recent years he had ventured into other media: sculptures carved from *markh* (marrow) bones, jewelry fashioned from old silver spoons, miniatures painted on the lenses of old eyeglasses. On one wall was a replica of the famous wooden synagogue in his home town of Zabludow, Poland, rendered in *lokshn,* sticks of spaghetti, with rice for grass and cantaloupe seeds for shingles. On another wall was a Hasidic rabbi composed entirely of beans: navy beans for his face, pintos for his eyes, turtles for his yarmulke, and limas for his long white beard. Mr. Ostroff jokingly referred to him as the "Beanzer Rebbe." His workshop, a small room at the back of the apartment, was crammed full of tools, paintbrushes, scraps of cloth, paper, leather, lengths of pipe, wood, sheet metal, soup bones, egg cartons, coat hangers—whatever his *krefts* required.

"You see, it's like this," he explained, speaking in an inimitable mixture of English and Yiddish, both leavened with a heavy Litvak accent.

"When I came home from the hospital for the first time, the doctor told me I had had enough excitement already in *mayn* life, now I should just sit home and do nothing. But I think to myself, What, I'm going to sit here in the apartment and wait for the *Malekhamoves,* the Angel of Death, to come take me away? The *Malekhamoves* will come when he's ready; in the meantime, I don't have to sit still and wait for him. Instead, I make things for myself, and I go to the senior-citizen center, I teach other old people, they should make, too, instead of sitting around waiting for You-Know-Who to come calling."

During all this monologue neither Sam nor Leah—we were already on a first-name basis—ever stopped moving. They walked back and forth to the tiny kitchen, returning each time with another heaping platter of Jewish food: matzo brie, herring in cream sauce, *lokshn kugl,* latkes, blintzes. When we protested, Mrs. Ostroff assured us it was no trouble: "*Mir zenen shoyn tsugevoynt*. We're used to it already." She explained that Sea Gate was once the summer home of many of New York's greatest Yiddish writers: I. J. Singer, Peretz Hirschbein, Avrom Reisen, Moyshe Nadir, Itzik Manger. Even the young Isaac Bashevis Singer lived there when he first came to America. (He later wrote, "Sea Gate was a quiet little village of retired people, Jews, intelligentsia. And Coney Island was Coney Island. When I went out from Sea Gate to Coney Island I went from paradise into hell. I couldn't believe that such a quiet place and such a loud place could exist next to each other.")

The Ostroffs' next-door neighbor was Marjorie Guthrie's mother, Aliza Greenblatt, who wrote a book called *Si Geyt afn yam (Sea Gate by the Sea)*. Two doors down lived Israel Zetser, a scholar of Jewish mysticism. "Zetser, he was a little strange," Mrs. Ostroff confided. "Most people didn't know, but he was a polar bear. Every morning he went down to the beach to swim in the ocean, even on the coldest days. We used to see him when he walked home in the wintertime, the icicles were hanging off his trunks."

Another neighbor and close friend was the Yiddish actress Bella Ballerina. As Roger, Fran, and I progressed from the matzo brie to the *kugl,* Mrs. Ostroff told us that Bella Ballerina had once been in a play on Second Avenue where she portrayed a Jewish woman who abandoned her children to run off with another man. "For years after that she couldn't walk down the street without people yelling at her and spitting. *'Feh!'* they would say, 'leaving three little children like that. How could you do such a thing?'"

Of course, none of these Yiddish writers, actors, and intellectuals made much of a living. Where did they congregate when they came to Sea Gate? "In our home!" Sam said proudly. Since Sam and Leah actually *worked* for a living, he as a plumber and she as a pattern maker and seamstress, and since they only had one child, they could afford to keep a huge apartment, occupying the whole second floor of a big house across the street from the main hotel where they lived now. At night they would cook great feasts, and all the writers and intellectuals would come over to eat and talk.

"Oy, what talking!" Mrs. Ostroff remembered, clapping her hands to her cheeks. "We had a big balcony where we set up chairs. The writers would come and they'd talk about literature, politics, Jewish culture. And what arguments! My non-Jewish neighbors, they used to wonder, 'What do you do over there? People come over, you don't play cards, you don't listen to the radio, all you do is talk. Talk, talk, talk, night after night. What is there so much to talk about?'"

"Often we would stay up till two or three in the morning," Sam added. "At three-thirty I would go to bed, at five-thirty I had to be up to go to work. But I didn't mind, because culture, *Yiddish* culture, for us that was the most important thing in the world."

Remembering the Ostroffs after all these years, I'm amazed by how much ground we covered—and how much food we ate—in just that first visit. Among the many writers the Ostroffs recalled, perhaps the most memorable was Itzik Manger, author of the *Khumesh lider (Bible Poems)*, a cycle in which the familiar characters of the Bible are transformed into Yiddish-speaking Jews. Abraham, for example, wears a long Hasidic coat and eats gefilte fish, Isaac studies Talmud with his children, and Leah cries her eyes out over silly French novels. The anachronisms are funny, but they also serve to underscore Jews' seamless sense of history and the evolving nature of Jewish identity—how the *rakhmones,* the empathy and sensibility gleaned from a few thousand years of exile, can be read back into our own history. Take, for example, one of the more unsettling stories in the Bible, in which, at Sarah's insistence, Abraham exiles his lover Hagar and their son Ishmael to the desert, knowing they will almost certainly die. As Abraham haggles with a local peasant for their passage, Hagar pours out her heart—in Yiddish—to her son:

> *Veyn nisht, Yishmeylikl tate,*
> *Azoy iz undz shoyn bashert,*
> *Ot azoy firn zikh di oves*
> *Mit di lange frume berd.*

> This is our portion, Ishmael;
> Darling, dry your tears.
> This is the way of the Fathers
> With their long and reverend beards.

Manger was brilliant, but he was also rootless, hard-drinking, and self-destructive. Born in rural Romania, he was a literary sensation in Warsaw as a young man, dodged the Holocaust by working on a British ship, lived with a non-Jewish woman in England, moved to France, and in 1951 took passage to America, where, in his own words, "financially, physically and spiritually bankrupt," he eventually washed up at the Ostroffs' door.

"For so many years we had read Manger's work," Leah Ostroff re-counted. "Now here he is, no money, no friends. So Sam and I took care on him." The Ostroffs organized an evening in his honor and raised $300. Manger called the Ostroffs *folksyidn,* "my kind of Jews," and became a regular guest in their home. In later years, when he hit rock bottom, he moved in with them altogether and lived there for two years.

"Of course we loved to have him," Mrs. Ostroff explained. "But I'll tell you the truth, sometimes it got a little difficult. Our son Nokhum was still young yet, and when he'd be sitting watching television Manger would come in and change the channel. Nokhum would come running to me, 'Mama, Mama, Manger changed the channel.' I'd wipe his tears, but I'd have to explain to him that Manger is a very great writer, if he wants to watch a certain show we have to let him watch. It wasn't so easy, but what else could we do?"

Another frequent guest at the Ostroffs' home was Arlo Guthrie. After Woody got sick, Marjorie would take Arlo to spend the day with his grandmother, Aliza Greenblatt, who took him next door to the Ostroffs'. "Arlo used to call me *Der Professor,*" Mr. Ostroff told us. "'Oy,' he would scream, '*der Professor kitselt,* the Professor is tickling me.'"

Now, of course, Arlo was grown up, Aliza Greenblatt was dead, and the Yiddish writers, actors, and intellectuals who frequented the Ostroffs' home had all passed on. Which may explain why the Ostroffs welcomed us with such open arms. After Fran, Roger, and I had eaten our last spoonful of compote, Mr. Ostroff poured us each a glass of *shnaps,* wished us *L'khayim,* and then said, "Okay, now let's get down to business. In whatever time Leah and I have left, we're ready to work. We have no more writers to take care on, so we've talked it over and now we want to become your biggest zamlers." All we had to do, they said, was leave it to them, and they would assume sole responsibility for collecting Yiddish books in Sea Gate, Coney Island, and Brighton Beach.

We gladly agreed. During the coming weeks Sam posted hand-painted signs on telephone poles throughout the area: *Az ir hot alte yidishe bikher, iz klingt on Ostroff* (If You Have Old Yiddish Books, Then Phone Ostroff). Business was good, especially in Brighton Beach, where newly arrived Soviet immigrants were displacing an older Jewish population and everyone, it seemed, had Yiddish books to donate before they moved.

For all his energy, after five heart attacks Mr. Ostroff could not actually carry the books himself. Instead he and Leah acted as the advance team: They'd go to see people in their big, old Pontiac, confirm what was there, and schedule a time for "the young people to come with the truck." Every two weeks, like clockwork, we'd arrive at the Ostroffs' door. After feeding us ("You can't lift boxes on an empty stomach!") they'd climb into the truck with us and off we'd go. Somehow Mr. Ostroff got the idea that my friend Roger was my valet: He called him "Rogers!" and expected him to do all the shlepping himself. Every time I'd prop a heavy box onto my shoulder he would berate me, "Lahnsky, *s'past nisht*, you shouldn't be shlepping yourself, you haven't got the build for it. Let Rogers take it."

Mr. Ostroff felt it was not enough that people just give books: They should also become zamlers. Once, he spent fifteen minutes trying to convince a ninety-eight-year-old man to hang posters outside his building. The man kept smiling and nodding his head and Mr. Ostroff kept speaking louder and louder until the man's wife finally came out of the kitchen and politely informed us that her husband was deaf.

Sometimes Mrs. Ostroff stayed home ("I want to have a meal ready; you'll be hungry when you get back"). Then all the widows would flirt with Sam. They loved it when we asked them to stand beside him to pose for pictures. "And why not? I'll take any excuse to hug such a nice man."

MOST OF OUR encounters with older Jews consisted of a single, oft-times emotional meeting: They'd feed us, tell us their stories, hand us their books, and before we had time to dry our tears or wipe the lipstick off our cheeks, we were already back in the truck, rushing to the next stop to start the process all over again. With the Ostroffs it was different. We spoke regularly by phone, exchanged letters, and spent a full day with them every other week. Sometimes, after collecting books elsewhere in New York, we'd drop by just for a social call. Not only did they feed us, but no matter how blue or discouraged we might be, they were always able to lift our spirits and remind us—just by being themselves—why we were collecting Yiddish books in the first place. Sometimes, after a meal, they would bring out boxes of old photographs and tell us stories. What was most striking was how respectful they were of one another. They held hands, they exchanged smiles, they took turns *kvell*ing, beaming with pride, while the other spoke—except, of course, when they both happened to be speaking at once. "*Ir zent undzere kinder.* You are our children," Mrs. Ostroff once said, and month after month she and Sam did their best to bequeath their *yerushe,* the stories of their lives. For me they represented a civilization—they were as close as I was likely to get to the lost, living world of Yiddish literature. So I often placed a tape recorder on the table, propped between matching bowls of horseradish and sauerkraut, to capture what they had to say. Sam called it *der geylem,* the golem, the monster. Sometimes, when they came to the juiciest part of a story, they'd say "Now this the *geylem* can't hear," and they'd make me shut it off. But most of the time they forgot it was there. Here, gleaned from those tapes, in their own words, are the broad outlines of their lives, a portrait of what I. J. Singer called "*a velt vos iz nishto mer* (a world which is no more)."

LEAH BEGINS:

"Me, I come from Vilna. I was born in 1907. Vilna in those days was known as *Yerushalayim d'Lite,* the Jerusalem of Lithuania. It was a city of scholars, of learning. Believe me, it was some *yikhes,* it was really some-thing to be born in such a city.

"What went on during the [First World] War don't ask. I was sepa-rated from my mother and my sisters, I lived with a neighbor, we didn't have what to eat. Before the war I went to Russian school. After the war, when my mother came back, she sent me to Yiddish school. We had to speak only Yiddish; they charged us a penalty if we spoke a word of Russian. We wanted to go to America, but it wasn't so easy. My fa-ther died, and then we couldn't get a visa. So finally my mother decided we would *ganvenen dem grenets,* cross the border illegally. My uncle in America wired the money. On the way over, in Antwerp, there was a quarantine, we had to go through an inspection. They took us into a bathhouse, we had showers, then the doctors came and examined us. They looked everywhere, in the hair, even in the underwear, to make sure that you're clean. So I thought, they go to all this trouble, when I get to America it's going to be cleaner than what we had in Poland, it's going to be immaculate.

"But then we got to Ellis Island, we had to wait two days for my uncle to come for us. I never saw a cockroach in my life before I got to Ellis Island—but the cockroaches there! So already I'm a little disap-pointed. Then my uncle came and we left Ellis Island and we came to the Lower East Side and I saw the big tenement apartments with the lines of clothes, the bloomers, the brassieres, the girdles. And then the streets—*azoy shmutsik,* so dirty like I never saw in Poland. So my uncle looks at me and he can see that I'm sitting like this and he says, 'What's the matter?'

"I didn't know what to say. I asked him, 'Is this New York already?'

"He said, 'Yes, this is New York.'

"I was so disappointed. But I didn't say anything. I figured look, the man tried so hard, he spent a lot of money to bring over a family of seven, so I didn't say a thing."

Eventually Leah and her family found an apartment of their own. She went to school, became active in Yiddish cultural organizations, learned English, and studied dressmaking.

"As hard it was," she concluded, "my life was easy compared with Sam."

SAM'S STORY:

Sam was born in Zabludow, a shtetl in White Russia, in 1900. In many ways his story is the story of Jews in the twentieth century, for, perhaps more than most, his life was shaped by the larger historical events that shook the world.

At the age of six he entered kheyder, *Jewish religious school, where he learned Hebrew and traditional Jewish texts. Later, at a modern school, he studied Russian and basic German. In 1915, when the Germans invaded White Russia, he was pressed into service on a German road crew.*

"I was just fifteen. I said good-bye to my mother, I didn't know if I'd ever see her again. The Germans paid us ninety pfennigs for a twelve-hour day. A loaf of bread cost a mark. So I did a little business with benzoil [gasoline] on the black market. Two people got arrested, an official shot himself, but me they never caught.

"After we finished building the road near Bialystok they sent us to build roads in the Ukraine. That's where the front was. One day the medical corps, German doctors, came through to vaccinate us against typhus and cholera. They needed help giving shots to so many people, so they asked, 'Who can read German?'

"I raised my little finger. The doctor says, 'I see that little finger there. Come on.'

"They taught me to call out the names, to wash the arms with alcohol, then to cross the names off the list. The doctor liked me and asked me if I wanted to become his assistant. He called me Mr. Shmuel. He said, 'Mr. Shmuel, it's going to be dangerous.'

"I told him, 'Professor, it's less dangerous than being here. Here you suffer from hunger, you get swollen up, and then you die. From a bullet you just die one-two-three.' So for four years I was the doctor's assistant, on the front, in the hospitals. I saw bombings, shrapnel, bullets, terrible things. There was one attack in particular, a medic I worked with was killed, I was hit with shrapnel but I survived.

"After the war I was still with the Germans. The doctor took me to Berlin, he got me into medical school, I should become a doctor. I studied for several months. Then in 1919 the German Revolution broke out. I was walking down a big parkway, under the linden trees, on my way to class, when suddenly a man walks in front of me, pulls out his revolver and shoots another man.

"I thought, that's nothing new for me. I've seen so much killing in my life: on the Russian front, the French front. I lived through the Russian Revolution. Now I have to live through the German Revolution. So I said, 'Enough. If I'm going to die it's better I should die among Jews.' So I left medical school, I left everything, I went back home to Zabludow."

When Sam returned home he found Zabludow in ruins. The streets were full of orphaned children, and crime and violence were rampant. After four years with the German army Sam had forgotten Yiddish, and he had to work hard to relearn it in order to communicate with his family. He worked part-time at a Yiddish school and helped to open a local Yiddish library, but most of his energy was devoted to reopening the family business, a restaurant. He renovated the building, added hotel rooms, and kept the dining room open twenty-four hours a day. Within two years the business was thriving and he and his mother were making good money for the first time in their lives.

"We worked so hard, but the Poles wouldn't leave us alone. One day they came, they told us we had to keep the door closed because we were too close to a church. So I had to go to Grodno, the capital, to get papers to keep the door open.

"I took the train. I carried with me a revolver, I was a businessman,

I had a permit. There comes into my car an old Jew, a *khosid* with a long beard and *peyes*, and he sits down near me. Then a little while later some Polish soldiers come into the car and they say, 'Where are the Jews?'

"I was sleeping. They woke me up and they said, 'Are you a Jew?'

"I told them 'Yes' and I took out my revolver. Once they saw the gun they got scared and they moved away. It was dark—there were no lights in the car because of the war with the Bolsheviks. Next morning the old Jew creeps out from behind my seat. He tells me, 'If you didn't have that revolver they would've killed us.'

"When I got back to Zabludow I told my mother, 'Mama, I don't care what you'll do. I will not stay here. I'm going to leave Poland.'

"She said, 'Look what you're doing. You're throwing away gold, you're going to go look for crumbs.'

"I said, 'Mama, I'll beg in America, but I don't want to be in Poland.'

Sam had a brother in the United States who was able to arrange a visa. He and his mother sold the restaurant and arrived in New York on May 1, 1921.

"I was free, and I was very proud of it. I went to evening school, I should learn English. And I started to learn a trade.

"Then one day I read in the *Forverts,* the Jewish paper, that there's going to be a strike in the needle trades. [Many immigrant Jews were employed in the garment industry, usually under deplorable conditions.] I never saw a picket line before and I was interested to go see. So I took a ride to New York [Manhattan], to Broadway. I look—there's the picket line. And then the police come. What I saw the police do to those girls, with the sticks over the head, the ears, it was terrible. I got so disappointed that time. That night I went to evening school, it was just before graduation and the principal gives us a lecture. He talks about the freedom of the United States, what a beautiful thing we have here.

"So I got up. I said, 'And what I saw today, for a policeman to take a stick and knock a girl over the head and drop her to the floor and step on her, is that freedom, too?'

"He says to me, 'You're a Bolshevik, I'm going to have you deported, I'm going to send you back to Europe.'

"My friends pushed me out the door, they were afraid for me. I had to quit school, and I never got my diploma. So instead I became a plumber. In Germany I was going to be a doctor, here I became a plumber, but I'll tell you the truth, it's pretty much the same thing."

Sam and Leah met at a dance sponsored by their landsmanshaft, *an organization of immigrants from the same region in Europe. Leah remembers:*

"At first I looked down on Sam on account of I was from Vilna and he was from a shtetl. But then I said to myself, 'Look, you're in America now, you can't be too fussy.'"

They were married four years later.

Sam mastered his new trade and entered the Plumbers and Pipefitters Union, working primarily on new construction. As we traveled together through Brooklyn he would point proudly to various buildings he helped build: the Wabash Houses, Luna Park, the Coney Island Aquarium. During World War II he was the only Jewish member of a construction crew sent to work on government projects in New Mexico.

Sam and Leah shared a passionate commitment to culture and to learning l'shma, *for its own sake, for the simple joy and ennoblement of knowledge. Their after-work hours were devoted to literature, theater, music, and ideas. In this sense they represented a tradition common among Jewish immigrants from Eastern Europe:* halb-inteligentn, *homegrown intellectuals for whom learning was not the exclusive province of the academy but the fountainhead of the home, the activity that gave dignity and purpose to everyday life. After their son was born, they became active in the Sholem Aleichem Folks-Institute, a network of nonpartisan Yiddish afternoon schools for children. Sam still recalls his role with pride:*

"I was the volunteer plumber for all the Yiddish schools in New

York. I was always on call. Maybe it's eight o'clock in the evening, we're all dressed up ready to go to a show. It doesn't matter. If they called that a toilet is broken at the Sholem Aleichem School in the Bronx, I got on the subway and went to fix the toilet. By me education always came first."

13. The Great Newark Book Heist

S ome wonderful people joined the Center's staff in those early years. Nansi Glick, the wife of my college teacher, offered to help us run a small printing press scavenged from an old Yiddish school in New York, and she stayed on, as a printer, editor, writer, and administrator, for the next eighteen years.

And then there was Sharon Kleinbaum: a smart, feisty, and acutely political young woman whom I happened to pick up hitchhiking one day outside of Amherst.

"Excuse me," she said as she hopped into the van and noticed the open boxes of books in the back, "but aren't these *Yiddish* books?"

"You read Yiddish?" I replied, raising an eyebrow in the rearview mirror.

"*A bisl.* A little. I studied at Columbia for two years while I was a student at Barnard."

I took her to the Center and we continued talking the whole afternoon. Her father was the head of the Jewish federation in Bergen County, New Jersey, where she had attended a modern orthodox high school. She had just left a job at the War Resisters League and was looking for a new position—"a new cause" is the way she phrased it—

where she could direct her considerable energy. I offered her a job and she immediately accepted, with one proviso:

"I'd love to start working tomorrow, but there's a problem."

"Really, what's that?"

"Well, I won't be available for another six months. First I have to serve."

"Serve?" I thought maybe she had taken a summer job as a waitress on the Cape.

"No, no," she corrected me, "I mean *serve,* as in federal prison."

Two days later she reported to Alderson Federal Reformatory for Women, in West Virginia, where she spent the next six months repaying her debt to society for having tried, together with several thousand other women, to wrap the Pentagon in yarn. When she got out she joined the staff of the Yiddish Book Center, well rested and ready to fight.

Which was a good thing, because by that point there was plenty of fighting to do. Not two weeks after Sharon's arrival, I received a call from a young staff member at the Newark Public Library, in New Jersey. The library had been in disarray since 1969, when, in the aftermath of the Newark riots, a newly elected administration targeted it as an elitist white institution and tried to shut it down. Philip Roth, who had spent much of his childhood in the Newark Library, wrote a powerful defense in the *New York Times:*

When I was growing up in Newark we assumed that the books in the public library belonged to the public. . . . In the forties, when the city was still largely white, it was simply an unassailable fact of life that the books were "ours" and that the public library had much to teach us about the rules of civilized life, as well as civilized pleasures to offer. It is strange (to put it politely) that now, when Newark is mostly black, the City Council (for fiscal reasons, we are told) has reached a decision that suggests that the books don't really belong to the public after all, and that what a library provides for the young is no longer essential to an education. In a city seething with social grievances there is, in fact, probably little that could be *more* essential to the development and sanity of the thoughtful and ambitious young than access to those books. For the moment the Newark City Council may have solved its fiscal problem; it is too bad, however, that the councilmen are unable to calculate the frustration, cynicism, and rage that this insult must inevitably generate, and to imagine what shutting down its libraries may cost the community in the end.

In the face of scathing criticism from both blacks and whites, the city council relented. But only barely. By the early 1980s chronic underfunding, long-standing hostility from local officials, and the Reagan budget cuts all conspired to bring the orderly operation of the library—such as it was—to an end. Experienced librarians were laid off, professionals who resigned or retired were not replaced, and the institution was reduced to a skeletal staff, with front-line tasks handled largely by sullen teenagers who were given little adult supervision. According to our informant, these young people often discarded returned books rather than reshelve them, and when shelf space was needed, they just cleared off whole collections and wheeled them to the Dumpster. The library's excellent foreign-language collections had been especially hard hit. He believed its three thousand Yiddish books, many of them extremely rare, were in immediate danger, and he urged us to get to Newark as soon as we could.

Sharon and I arrived two days later. The rest of the city looked like a third world country, but the Newark Public Library and its neighbor, the Newark Museum, stood like Greek temples commanding a broad boulevard. The person who summoned us was well prepared. He directed us to a service entrance around back, where we were greeted by one of the library's senior administrators and the chief custodian, an elderly black man. The administrator, a white-haired woman, confirmed everything we'd been told. All public libraries periodically cull their collections, she explained, but in this case unsupervised workers were indiscriminately discarding as many as two thousand books a day. The most valuable books—the oldest and rarest—were often the first to go. Nearly one third of the Yiddish collection had been lost already, and those books that remained would soon be discarded unless we could remove them first. "There are few Jews left in Newark," she explained, "and the Yiddish books are rarely read. That's why we phoned you. We have to work quickly and quietly. We have a very big job ahead of us."

We followed the administrator up a maze of cast-iron stairways, along heavy glass floors, until we reached a mezzanine section where the foreign-language books were stored. The Yiddish collection was the largest, occupying an entire wall. We had been given Yiddish books by public libraries before, mostly in small New England factory towns such as Lowell and Fall River, but they were usually limited to literature popular among Jewish immigrants at the turn of the century: proletarian poetry, inexpensive pirate editions, and Yiddish translations of world literature, including Shakespeare, Tolstoy, and Dickens. Such books were represented here as well, many in sturdy library bindings with romanized titles on their spines. But there were also more recent and more sophisticated titles I wouldn't have expected in a public library: fiction from interwar Warsaw and Vilna, and more recent titles by Chaim Grade, Avrom Sutzkever, Isaac Bashevis Singer, and others. What really caught my eye, though, were several hundred prewar imprints from the Soviet Union, scholarly studies in history, folklore, linguistics, and literary criticism published by research academies in Moscow, Minsk, Kiev, Kharkov, and Odessa, which were among the rarest books in all of modern Yiddish literature. Most of them, the staff member explained, had come from a single donor, a prominent Newark intellectual who had made several trips to the Soviet Union in the 1920s and 1930s and brought these rare books and brochures back with him specifically for the Newark Library. It was heartbreaking to note that at least two shelves of these Soviet treasures were empty, their contents already trundled off to the Dumpster.

Alongside the Yiddish books was an equally dismaying sight: an extraordinary collection of books in Esperanto, the "universal language" invented in Warsaw in 1887 by a Yiddish-speaking Jew named L. L. Zamenhof. It is said that at the international Esperanto conferences held each year in Warsaw before the Second World War, papers were delivered in Esperanto but conversation in the halls took place in Yiddish—the only truly international language the delegates shared in common. From these shelves, too, books were missing, as though to mock the enlightened dream that had created them.

The administrator assured us that she was making arrangements for someone else to save the Esperanto collection; our job was to clear the shelves of books in Yiddish. We set to work, and as we did, a half dozen library workers, including several teenagers, came over to help. We finally left with almost twenty-five hundred volumes. Sharon and I were pleased that our guerilla operation had gone off so smoothly. But we were also indignant and sad: sad for the residents of Newark, whose crown jewel, this wonderful library, was being so diminished; and sad, too, for all those great books, in English, Esperanto, and a dozen other languages, that we left behind to an uncertain fate.

PART THREE

"Him I Don't Talk To!"

14. "You're a Liar!"

Early in 1985 I was invited to speak at the Yablon Center, a formerly communist (they now called themselves *linke,* leftist) Jewish culture club that met in a modest storefront directly across the street from the gleaming-white colossus of NBC's "Television City" in Los Angeles. Seventy-five people were waiting for me, seated on folding metal chairs. There was only one other young person in the room: a reporter for the *Los Angeles Times,* who was writing a story about the Yiddish Book Center and the "Yiddish revival."

I began my talk with a quick overview in which I mentioned, more or less in passing, that Yiddish had not died a natural death, that one out of every two Yiddish-speaking Jews was murdered in the Holocaust, and that increasing persecution in the Soviet Union had culminated on August 12, 1952, when Stalin ordered all of his country's leading Yiddish writers shot on a single night. No sooner was this last statement out of my mouth than an old man in the back of the room jumped to his feet, waved his fist in the air, and shouted at me in a heavy Yiddish accent, "You're a liar!"

"Excuse me?" I said.

"I said you're a *liar!*" repeated the old man, more vehemently than before.

I glanced at the reporter. "Um, I'll be happy to take questions after the lecture."

"It's not a question, it's a *fect!*" thundered the old man. "It never happened what you said, Stalin never killed those writers."

The audience was growing restless.

"*Sha!*"

"Sit down, better!"

"We came to listen to the yungerman, not to you!"

The old man faced off against the crowd. "*Ikh vel nisht zayn keyn Bontsha Shvayg!* (I won't be a Bontsha the Silent!)*" he screamed, invoking the name of the long-suffering title character of a story by I. L. Peretz. "The yungerman is a liar. It never heppened, it's all propaganda, Stalin never did it."

A woman in the front row turned around to face him. "Okay," she demanded, "if it never happened, then where are all the Soviet Yiddish writers today?"

"Where are they? They're all *hiding,* to embarrass Stalin!"

Pandemonium ensued. Only the reporter was still in his seat; the others were on their feet—some were actually standing on their chairs— and everyone was yelling at once. Arguments, accusations, and epithets flew through the air. The old man gave as good as he got, holding his ground for ten minutes or more until, his face red and his body trembling with rage, he invoked several unprintable Yiddish curses on his erstwhile comrades and stormed out of the building, slamming the door behind him.

I tried my best to restore order and resume my lecture. I was concerned, naturally, lest the incident color the *Times*'s coverage, but I needn't have worried: Much of the uproar had been in Yiddish, a language the young reporter didn't understand. And even if he had understood, he wasn't the least bit interested: He was there, he told me afterward, to write an "upbeat" article about the *joys* of Yiddish, and bitter political debate was simply not part of the story.

Except, of course, that it *was* part of the story, and a central part at that. After the assassination of Tsar Alexander II of Russia in 1881, reactionary decrees forced large numbers of Jews out of the countryside and into the cities, where they found work in factories: sewing clothes, tanning leather, or rolling cigarettes. They were not exactly the sort of proletariat Marx had dreamed of. A typical Jewish factory might consist of two workers and an owner, all three working side by side, bent over their machines sixteen hours a day. Class conflict in the Pale, according to one observer, meant the struggle of *kaptsn kegn dalfn,* the pauper versus the destitute. Still, in a country as overwhelmingly agrarian as Russia, Jews comprised a significant percentage of the urban population in the Pale and were pretty much the only urban proletariat there was. By the early 1890s young Marxist revolutionaries seeking to organize the workers (as opposed to the peasantry) had no choice but to turn to these poor Jews as the vanguard of the revolution.

At first their organizing efforts were comical. The early revolutionaries were mostly intellectuals from wealthy, highly assimilated Jewish families, and their idea of agitation was to teach the workers *gramota,* Russian grammar. The few workers who, after a long day at work, managed to stay awake quickly put their newfound knowledge to good use, leaving the factories altogether. Eventually the revolutionaries realized—just as Hebrew writers had realized a few decades before— that the only way to reach the Jewish masses was to speak to them in Yiddish, the only language they understood.

Since many of the revolutionaries didn't speak Yiddish themselves, they mobilized a homegrown cadre of what they called *halb-inteligentn,* "half-intellectuals," who in turn organized *Zhargon Komitetn,* Jargon Committees, making use of the nascent Yiddish literature to spread revolutionary consciousness among their fellow workers. The Jewish poor, schooled in the tradition of social justice espoused by the Hebrew prophets, oppressed both as workers and as Jews, rallied to the cry. The Jewish Workers' Bund of Russia and Poland, founded in 1897, quickly became one of the most powerful forces in East European Jew-ish life. It played a key role in launching the Russian Social Democratic Workers' Party in 1898, in precipitating the split between Mensheviks and Bolsheviks in 1903, and in fighting the Revolution of 1905. After that revolution failed, the tsarist authorities sought to redirect popular dis-content by unleashing a wave of anti-Jewish violence. The Bund responded with armed resistance, and then, as reaction and disillusionment took hold, by turning inward, transforming what until then had been a util-itarian expedient — the use of Yiddish to reach the Jewish masses — into a far-reaching cultural program rooted in Yiddish language and literature.

And the Bund was not alone. Ber Borochov, a professional Yiddish linguist, synthesized Marxism and Zionism, giving rise to an influential Labor Zionist movement. Territorialists championed Yiddish-speaking Jewish settlements outside of Palestine. Jewish Communists threw in their lot with the new Soviet Union, while other Jews allied themselves with Polish socialist movements. Together, these groups challenged the political status quo, reshaped Jewish culture — and expended consid-erable energy fighting among themselves.

When all was said and done, however, the most powerful social movement of all was emigration. Between 1881 and 1924, when the United States effectively closed its doors, some 2 million East Euro-pean Jews packed up their meager possessions and made the long jour-ney across the sea to *di goldene medine,* the Golden Land, seeking economic opportunity and an escape from violence and oppression. Like Mrs. Ostroff, many of those immigrants were, at least at first, bitterly dis-appointed. Population density on the Lower East Side of New York ex-ceeded that of the worst slums of Bombay. Living conditions in the dark, airless tenements almost defied description, and working con-ditions in the sweatshops were even worse. In 1911 fire broke out at the Triangle Shirtwaist Company, at the edge of Washington Square.

"In the eighteen minutes it took to bring the fire under control, one hundred and forty-six workers, most of them Jewish and Italian girls, were burned to death," Irving Howe recounts in *World of Our Fathers.* The factory owners had locked the doors to keep out union organizers, and the only way the girls could escape the flames was to jump nine floors to the street below. The Lower East Side was plunged into mourning—a mood captured in a Yiddish poem by Morris Rosenfeld that appeared on the front page of the *Forward:*

> Over whom shall we weep first?
> Over the burned ones?
> Over those beyond recognition?
> Over those who have been crippled?
> Or driven senseless?
> Or smashed?
> I weep for them all.
>
> Now let us light the holy candles
> And mark the sorrow
> Of Jewish masses in darkness and poverty.
> This is our funeral,
> These our graves,
> Our children, . . .

For many Jews, there was nothing left to do but organize. They joined unions, such as the Amalgamated Clothing Workers and the International Ladies Garment Workers Union. They struck for better wages and shorter hours, they walked the picket lines and stood up to the thugs, they suffered setbacks, went hungry, and through victories large and small, they changed the face of the American labor movement forever. In 1914 the Lower East Side elected Meyer

London, a Yiddish-speaking socialist and trade union lawyer, to the United States Congress.

If in Europe many Jews still clung to tradition, in America the flood of change was unstoppable. When my sixteen-year-old grandmother arrived in America, she took a job sewing muffs in a sweatshop. "We worked fourteen hours a day, Saturday included," she remembered. "The first time I had to work on Shabbos I cried so hard I soaked every muff I sewed."

Torn from their traditional moorings, Jews turned to new, secular Jewish institutions. *Landsmanshaftn* were mutual aid societies for immigrants from the same city or town. The Workmen's Circle provided everything from health insurance to burial plots. The old political movements staked out new ground on American soil—socialists, communists, anarchists, Zionists—each with its own Yiddish newspapers, radio stations, publishing houses, libraries, lecture halls, musical groups, schools, and summer camps. They skirmished constantly with one another, and held only two things in common: Yiddish and the dream of *a besere un shenere velt*—a better and more beautiful world for their children.

It is impossible, today, to understand how important these old Yiddish organizations once were. They attracted hundreds of thousands of members, shaped American Jewish culture, and exercised enormous political influence. Yet they were not to last. For all their proletarian solidarity, Jewish workers couldn't wait to escape the sweatshops and move their families away from the stifling streets of the Lower East Side. They scrimped, they saved, they took in boarders, they did whatever they had to until they had enough money to move uptown, to Harlem or the Bronx. Many went into business. If they did remain factory workers, it was almost certain that their children would not. And why should they? After all, *they* were Americans, they spoke English without an accent, they were educated, they became professionals, they moved to the suburbs. What need did they have for unions or radical Yiddish organizations?

There was one other factor. In Eastern Europe many Jews were swept up in the spirit of nationalism, seeking to create a new, modern Jewish culture rooted in Yiddish (or modern Hebrew) instead of religion. In America it was different: Rather than Minority Treaties we had a melting pot. Religious differences were okay; cultural and linguistic differences were not. Upwardly mobile Jews were quick to redefine their identity: not as nationalism, not as culture, but as religion—exactly as assimilating Jews had done in Germany several generations before. It didn't take long before membership in America's Reform and Conservative synagogues outnumbered the membership of all Yiddish cultural and political organizations combined. Even those who remained in the Yiddish organizations tacitly acknowledged that America was different. They created many Yiddish afternoon schools in this country but, unlike in Eastern Europe, unlike in Canada, Mexico, and Argentina, not a single Yiddish day school. No matter how rich and varied the Yiddish cultural life they built for themselves, deep in their hearts they must surely have known that their own children wouldn't or couldn't follow. To quote Michael Chabon, Yiddish in America became "a tin can with no tin can at the other end of the string."

Arriving as I did very late in the game, I felt for these once proud Yiddish organizations. For five decades or more they had watched as their members died and were not replaced. They saw the spotlight of history grow dim, they saw themselves marginalized and then forgotten, until, inevitably, their idealism gave way to disappointment, their disappointment to resentment, their resentment to bitterness. They were mad at their children, mad at America, and—because no one else was listening—they were mad at one another. By the time I came along, anarchists wouldn't speak to socialists, socialists to communists, communists to Zionists. I marveled that Yiddish still existed at all, since it seemed everyone I met who spoke the language refused to speak with everyone else.

For my generation the personal was political; for many of the older Yiddishists, the political was intensely, even frighteningly, personal. I once received a call from the widow of a distinguished Yiddish writer. Many years before, her husband had had a political falling out with Sholem Asch, the most widely translated Yiddish writer of his day. Asch had now been dead forty years, her husband nearly ten years, and still the widow couldn't give it up. "Mr. Lahnsky," she said on the phone, "I have the most wonderful news. I just read a memoir which I obtained from the Yiddish Book Center, and I want you to hear what the writer had to say. I quote: 'I used to get up early in the morning to have more hours in the day to hate Sholem Asch.' I ask you, have you ever heard a more beautiful passage?"

Wherever I went in the Yiddish world, otherwise rational people continued to fight old battles with a tenacity that left me speechless. One night Roger, Fran, Noah, and I arrived at a high-rise building in Chelsea to pick up books from Diana Sandler, the widow of Philip Sandler, a prominent Yiddish journalist. While Roger and Noah removed hundreds of her late husband's books from the living room shelves, Fran and I sat with Mrs. Sandler at her kitchen table and talked. She was leaving New York to be near her daughter in Michigan. Given her age she felt too lonely and isolated to remain.

"Don't you have any friends in this building?" Fran asked.

"No," she said sadly. "Once, many Jewish people lived here, educated people, Yiddish writers and scholars. My husband and I had many good friends. But over the years they either died or moved away." She sighed and stared into her coffee for a long time. When she looked up again, she shook her head and added softly, "Actually, there *is* one other person in the building that I know — very well, in fact — but *him,* him I don't talk to."

The other person was Paul Novik, then more than ninety years old and still the editor-in-chief of the *Morning Freiheit,* the communist Yiddish newspaper. For many years, Diana Sandler explained, her husband had worked under Novik as the *Freiheit*'s city editor. Their families were close friends, so close that they took apartments in the same building. Then came 1956, when Khrushchev made his speech to the Party Congress confirming the magnitude of Stalin's crimes. Deeply shaken, Sandler quit his job and moved to the noncommunist *Tog;* Novik remained at the *Freiheit,* and although they continued to live in the same building, the two men and their wives never spoke to one another again.

Except once, Mrs. Sandler explained. Five years earlier, in the middle of an unexpected blizzard, she went downstairs to get her mail and saw Novik pacing back and forth in the lobby. Usually, she said, Novik was a vigorous man, but that night he looked small and frail, and she knew something was wrong.

"There were already big drifts outside. I looked at the snow, I looked at Novik—I could see he was worried. I felt terrible, I knew I shouldn't speak to him, but what could I do, I'm also a mother. 'Mr. Novik,' I said, 'is something the matter?' It was the first time I had spoken to him in maybe twenty years. 'Yes,' he said in a daze, 'my wife, she went out shopping, she should have been back an hour ago—' I didn't let him finish. I said, 'Mr. Novik, it's all right, it's snowing, the buses are running late, she'll come home soon.' And then I took him by the hand and we sat down together on a bench in the lobby. We talked quietly for a long time until the door finally opened and his wife, poor thing, came in half frozen, covered with snow. I waited to make sure she was all right. Then Mr. Novik, he turned to me and he said, 'Thank you.' Just that, 'Thank you.' Me, I didn't answer him, I went into the elevator and back up to my apartment. That was five years ago. We still see each other from time to time, in the elevator, in the lobby, but we haven't spoken a word to each other since."

The battles still aren't over. As recently as December of 2002 I received a phone call from a Yiddish editor in New York, asking if the Yiddish Book Center could help underwrite the cost of *Der yidisher kemfer (The Jewish Fighter),* the hundred-year-old magazine of the Labor Zionist movement. To be honest, I didn't even know the magazine was still alive. But I wasn't completely surprised by the call. Three months earlier, I was approached by the ninety-seven-year-old editor of another Yiddish journal, who needed help to keep his faltering publication alive, and I knew of at least two other New York Yiddish journals that were on equally shaky ground. "You all seem to be in the same boat," I pointed out to the *Kemfer* editor when he called. "There are four separate Yiddish magazines, all without enough writers or readers or money to survive. Why don't you just join forces and create one single, viable Yiddish periodical?"

The editor laughed. *"Ummeglekh!* (Impossible!)" he said, explaining why the ideologies and personalities of the various publications couldn't mix. His vivid characterization of the respective editors—all insisting on autonomy, all at odds with one another—was entertaining, but it was also tragic. Even at this very late date, they'd rather die alone than work together. I was reminded of a Yiddish expression: *Yeder makht shabes far zikh,* Everyone is making Shabbos for himself. Itche Goldberg, the erudite head of the erstwhile communist Yiddish cultural world and himself no stranger to bitter internecine Yiddish polemics, once characterized the present state of Yiddish culture as a conflagration: "The entire edifice of Yiddish culture is on fire," he told me, "it's burning out of control. Every once in a while a lone individual or organization comes along with a little bucket of water to throw on the flames. But before he can get close, he has to pass by a committee of representatives of all the other organizations, who check to make sure that his *tsitses* (the fringes of his ritual garment) are kosher. Never mind that the members of the committee do nothing to extinguish the flames themselves, they still want to make sure that no one with the wrong political credentials should have a chance."

I so wanted it to be different. I wanted these old radicals to be feisty and funny, like the geriatric rabble-rousers in John Sayles's "At the Anarchists' Convention." But there was a danger in romanticizing them. My coworker, Sharon Kleinbaum, who was enamored of anarchist theory, once made a pilgrimage to the elderly editor of a Yiddish anarchist newspaper. She went expecting to talk about Kropotkin, Bakunin, and Emma Goldman; instead, the editor pinched her on the *tukhes* and chased her around the living room.

At least he still had the oomph to chase her; many of the people we met were just plain bitter—characters not from John Sayles but from Cynthia Ozick's masterful 1969 story "Envy; or, Yiddish in America." Envious they were—of each other, and even more so of us. They envied us our youth, our optimism, our success. Why should the newspapers publish pictures of us instead of them, who spoke Yiddish so much better and had been championing Yiddish culture since before we were born? Once, when an article about the Center appeared in the *New York Times,* the board of a major Yiddish organization filed into its public reading room (a friend of mine was sitting at an adjoining table) and convened an emergency meeting, the subject of which was "What to do about Lahnsky."

It wasn't only envy. When all was said and done, they regarded our work in rescuing Yiddish books not as a triumph but as a sign of their own defeat: If they had been doing their jobs, if they had succeeded in conveying Yiddish culture to their children, then Yiddish books wouldn't need to be rescued. Of course, the historical depredations and upheavals that unseated Yiddish were hardly their fault. But they couldn't see that, and their myopia only compounded the tragedy. I'd be lying if I said that their barbs didn't sting. But in the end we, unlike them, could grasp a deeper irony: No matter how harshly they maligned us or how stubbornly they refused to speak with one another, sooner or later they would have to call us to pick up their books, and when they did, we would make no distinctions: Their books and those of their antagonists would end up in the same truck and on the same shelves—side by side, together at last.

BECAUSE IT'S MY nature, and because I had studied enough history to impart a certain *rakhmones* for those who suffered the slings and arrows of Yiddish fortune, I tried my best to make peace with the old Yiddish organizations while they were still here. I didn't take sides (though I was often sorely tempted), and I made a point of speaking to everyone—though I learned soon enough whom not to mention to whom. I visited different organizations and appeared before their *eksekutives,* their executive committees. I attended and spoke at their *banketn,* the interminable banquets where their members got together in the gilded ballroom of one or another of New York's faded grand hotels to congratulate one another, celebrate the past, and mourn the future. The more radical the organization, it seemed, the more bourgeois its events. Whatever the ideology, though, the speeches were always the same: *"Vu iz undzer yugnt?* (Where are our young people?)" their orators would demand as they pounded the hotel podium. And I'd sit there at the head table, looking at my uneaten chicken swimming in grease (I was a vegetarian), looking at my parve ice cream (it never melted, no matter how long the program lasted), and I'd think, With food and entertainment like this, was it any wonder that their *yugnt* stayed home?

Fortunately, not everyone was bitter. Sometimes I connected personally with members of that older generation—and occasionally I even managed to turn them around. Take S. L. Shneiderman, for example. Barely a year after we began collecting books, he wrote a blistering article in the *Forward,* attacking the Yiddish Book Center for being out of touch with the *real* (meaning older) institutions of Yiddish culture. Why, he wrote, hadn't we contacted the *Forverts,* why had we ignored the Old Yiddish World, and most of all, why had we never taken the trouble to phone him, Mr. Shneiderman, and let him know what we were up to? The best he could conclude from such gross derelictions was that we were not really interested in saving Yiddish culture, but rather in hoarding books so as "*tsu mumifirn di yidishe shprakh,* to 'mummify' the Yiddish language."

Since I had never met Mr. Shneiderman, since he had never visited the Center or interviewed me or any other member of our staff before writing his article, I didn't think his attack was quite fair, and I phoned him at home to tell him so.

"*Shneiderman!*" he bellowed by way of greeting, in what I took to be a preemptive strike.

I introduced myself and explained where I thought his article had gone astray. To my amazement, he listened, and after an hour and a half—marked by frequent interruptions and pontifications—he was genuinely repentant. "I'll tell you the truth," he said, "I had no idea. When you started collecting books without getting in touch with *me,* I naturally assumed you weren't really interested in *der yidisher kultur* (the Yiddish culture). *Meyle* (no matter), it's never too late. When can I get a train to Am Hoyrst to see for myself?"

A week later Mr. and Mrs. Shneiderman arrived at the local Amtrak station. He looked like a Jewish Winston Churchill: short but powerful, with broad shoulders and a deep, resonant voice. His wife was considerably quieter and more refined, with a face that revealed both humor and intelligence. In keeping with what I had come to recognize as Yiddish custom, she referred to her husband by his last name alone, as in "Shneiderman was so looking forward to coming here today," or, "Shneiderman, *zay shtil!* Keep quiet!"

I loaded the Shneidermans into the back of a borrowed car and took them to the Center. They were impressed. In fact, the relentlessly voluble Mr. Shneiderman was actually nonplussed for a good twenty seconds. Then he wiped a tear from his eye and boomed out his verdict: "*A nes min hashomayim!* (A miracle from Heaven!) Such young people, to do so much! What's happening here is the *future* of Yiddish culture! *Ershtns* (first of all), I'm going to donate to you all my own books after I'm gone. And *tsveytns* (second), I'm going to write a three-part series for the *Forverts*. The whole world should know what goes on here and not listen to the *yentes* back in New York who only know to criticize and complain."

He was as good as his word. The *Forward* ran three successive, full-page articles by S. L. Shneiderman, one of which bore the headline AMHOYRST—NAYER PUNKT AF DER MAPE FUN YIDISH (Amherst, the Newest Point on the Yiddish Map). My grandmother couldn't stop *kvelling*: It's one thing, after all, to see your grandson in the *Times* and quite another in the *Forverts*! Before long I was receiving handwritten Yiddish letters from scores of older Yiddish organizations, some with checks and others offering to help us collect books in their communities. I responded in kind, accepting invitations to speak at their meetings, attend their banquets, accept their awards, and sometimes even write for their papers. In fact, I'm still waiting for the $25 honorarium I was promised for an article I wrote for the *Forverts* in 1983.

I met many people whom I genuinely liked—decent people, activists, visionaries, idealists—and I spent long hours sipping tea at their kitchen tables while they regaled me with recollections of great writers or eyewitness accounts of movements and events I had only read about in books. But even after hundreds of hours together, I think we both knew that on some level we would remain strangers to one another. Born in the shtetl, versed in Talmud, steeped in Marxism, tested on the streets (and sometimes in jail), well read in Hebrew, Yiddish, and the major languages of Europe, they possessed a depth of

learning, experience, and Jewish erudition that I could barely appre-
hend, let alone aspire to. And I, for them, was also a cipher: relatively
ignorant of Jewish knowledge, true, but an American through and
through, unbent by the past and heir to a new world—sexually, politically, intellectually—that could never be theirs no matter how long
they lived in America, no matter how much they read or how earnestly
they tried to understand. We were time travelers, inhabitants of different epochs stopping long enough to compare notes before returning whence we came. No matter how respectful I was, no matter how
intently I listened, it was never enough. They always wanted me to stay
longer, return sooner, understand better or appreciate them more.
And why shouldn't they? They'd been famous long ago, they'd lived
front and center on the stage of history, they wrote books, they led,
they learned, they taught, they organized, and now, in their old age, all
they lacked was a *yarshn*—someone to whom they could bequeath not
only their libraries but the sum total of their lives. God only knows they
deserved it. And God only knows I tried. But in the end, what history
had stolen from them, no one—not I, not anyone—could restore.

15. "They're Tearing Apart the Library"

I'd been working twelve hours a day, six days a week for many months when I decided to take a rare Sunday off to accompany my friend Andrea Kurtzman to her cousin's wedding in Nyack, New York. The meal was over and I, woozy from champagne, had just retreated to my hotel room for a much needed nap when I noticed the message light flashing on my phone.

"Hmmmph?" I muttered into the receiver.

"Hello, Mr. Lansky?" said the operator. "I have a message for you from a Mrs. Langert in the Bronx. She says it's urgent. She says, 'They're tearing apart the library.' She wants you to call her right away. She says she's sitting by the phone. She says she won't move until she hears from you. Do you want me to give you the number?"

Under the circumstances, my head spinning already, Celia Langert was the last person I wanted to talk to. A forceful woman in her late seventies, she was our zamler in the Coops, a complex of Gothic red-brick apartment houses at the corner of Bronx Park East and Allerton Avenue. The buildings were built by a cooperative of Yiddish-speaking communists in 1927, and two of my former professors had grown up there: Andy Rabinbach, who taught German intellectual history at

Hampshire, and Eugene Orenstein, who taught Yiddish literature and the history of the Jewish labor movement at McGill. The Coops had fallen on hard times in recent years. The cooperative itself went bankrupt, leaving the buildings to a succession of private landlords. What was once a Jewish housing project was now mostly black and Puerto Rican. Almost all the Jews who remained were elderly, and by the early 1980s they were either dying or moving out at an alarming rate—which kept our resident zamler extremely busy. Over the years, Mrs. Langert had summoned us on half a dozen occasions to pick up books from one or another soon-to-be-vacant apartment, and among the thousands of volumes we retrieved were a large number of monographs and periodicals published in the Soviet Union in the 1920s and 1930s—generally considered to be among the most valuable imprints in all of modern Yiddish literature.

But I also knew from experience that as much as Mrs. Langert cared about Yiddish books, she cared even more about the old Yiddish left and was not above a certain well-intentioned duplicity to further her political agenda. Sitting on the hotel bed in Nyack, my head between my hands, I thought about the last "urgent" phone call I had received from Celia Langert, barely a year before. At that time she had called me at home—after 11 P.M., naturally—to tell me she had books that needed to be picked up. As it happened we were planning to be in New York with a truck later that week, and I suggested we stop by on Thursday afternoon.

"Oh no, not Thursday," Mrs. Langert replied. "Thursday is too soon."

Unsuspecting, I offered to come on Friday instead.

"No, no, Friday is also no good. Tell me, maybe you young people could come on Sunday?"

We hadn't planned to be in the City that Sunday, but Mrs. Langert was insistent. "Please, these books are so important, you simply must come on Sunday. Monday could be too late already. Sunday is the only time, Sunday or never."

I reluctantly agreed. "Okay, Mrs. Langert, you win, Sunday it is. We'll be there at two in the afternoon."

"Oh no, two is too late. You must come earlier—more like eleven in the morning. I'll be waiting for you in the lobby at eleven sharp. Don't be late."

Fran Krasno and I hastily rescheduled the rest of our trip. Early Sunday morning we drove from Massachusetts to the Bronx in my big secondhand station wagon, intending to rent a truck once we got to Manhattan. When we pulled up to the Coops a little before eleven, Mrs. Langert was waiting for us in the lobby. We should have known something was up right then and there, because instead of her usual nononsense book-shlepping clothes she was wearing a satin dress, nylons, high-heeled shoes, a long coat, and a hat that had probably been the height of fashion in 1955.

"*Sholem aleykhem!*" I greeted her. "*Avu zenen di bikher?* (Where are the books?)" I expected her to lead us to some recently abandoned, book-filled apartment, as she had done so many times in the past. Instead she pointed to three plastic shopping bags sitting forlornly on the lobby floor. They couldn't have contained more than twenty volumes between them, mostly commonplace imprints from the *linke* Yiddish publishing house in New York.

"*Dos iz gor?*" I asked, astonished that she, who knew better, had made such a fuss over such slim pickings. "That's all?"

"Well, that's all in terms of *books,*" Mrs. Langert replied. "But as long as you're here, there *is* one other thing you could do for me. Maybe, if it's not too much trouble, you wouldn't mind giving an old lady a ride to Manhattan?"

Aha, *azoy kokht men lokshn* (so that's the way you cook the noodles), I thought as we carried the three bags to the station wagon, with Mrs.

Langert following close behind. She slid into the front, between me and Fran, and it didn't take long before the full truth was out. Our zamler's destination was the Roosevelt Hotel, where, "it just so happens," they were holding the *yerlekher banket,* the annual banquet of *Jewish Currents,* the English-language magazine of the Yiddish left. Mrs. Langert, a loyal subscriber, had never missed a *Jewish Currents* banquet before, she said, and she was not about to miss this one, either. "The person who usually drives me, he died last year. So I thought, the young people from Massachusetts, they have to come to see me anyway to pick up books. What would be so terrible if they came by on Sunday and gave me a ride?"

The ends justify the means. Fran and I, her unwitting fellow travelers, knew we had been duped, but Mrs. Langert was in such high, festive spirits, regaling us with stories of strikes and demonstrations and political triumphs, that it was hard to hold a grudge. *"A bisele gikher, zay azoy gut!* (A little faster, please!)" she cajoled. "Pass that car. No, don't turn here, the next exit is better!"

Nature, however, has its own designs. Not a mile from Manhattan the skies opened up. I reached down, turned on the windshield wipers—and nothing happened. I tried again. Still nothing. With the rain coming in torrents and visibility nil, I barely managed to bring the car to a stop in the breakdown lane. And there we sat: crowded in the front seat of an old station wagon with an iron-willed Yiddish-speaking communist, forty feet above one of the worst neighborhoods in New York, the rain pounding on the roof, the windows steaming up, traffic whizzing by, the roadway shaking under the weight of passing tractor-trailers, and Mrs. Langert oblivious to everything but "the *banket*—we must get to the *banket!*"

As Mrs. Langert continued her exhortations, I scrunched down on the floor, reached under the dashboard, pulled the fuse from the cigarette lighter, and exchanged it with the wipers.' No luck. As I later

learned, the wipers' transmission (I didn't even know they *had* a transmission) had given way, and it was impossible to fix without a skilled
mechanic and $80 worth of new parts—neither of which was available
up there on the Major Degan Expressway. But we did have a coil of
manila rope (which we carried to secure loads in the rental trucks). I
found a jackknife, cut off a twenty-foot length, opened my window,
getting splashed by passing cars in the process, and tied one end with
a Boy Scout's bowline to the metal arm of the left wiper blade. I then
passed the other end of the rope over Mrs. Langert and handed it to
Fran, who in turn opened her window and tied it to the right wiper.
Mrs. Langert marveled at what she called the *makherayke,* the contrap-
tion, and it worked: I pulled one way, Fran the other, and sure enough,
the wipers moved back and forth and visibility was restored. The only
problem, I realized, was that I couldn't pull and drive at the same time.

"Excuse me, Mrs. Langert," I said, "do you think you might be able
to hold one end of the rope and pull together with Fran?"

"*Pull together?* I've been pulling together all my life! Now *gey shoyn* (go
already), onward to the *banket!*"

And so we proceeded down the highway, Fran and Mrs. Langert
pulling back and forth on the rope like lumberjacks on a cross-cut saw.
We made fairly good progress through the downpour until, halfway
across a bridge, the rope, which had been chafing against the window
frame, suddenly snapped in two. Again I couldn't see a thing, and in order to avoid the cars in the next lane I allowed myself to drift ever so
slightly to starboard. But with zero visibility the distance was difficult
to judge, and I ended up brushing the right fender against a concrete
abutment, sending what was undoubtedly a superfluous piece of chrome
molding plummeting into the abyss. It didn't matter to Mrs. Langert:
By the time I managed to grope my way to a stop at the far end of the
bridge she was already cutting a fresh length of rope. We affixed this
in turn and resumed our journey, arriving at the Roosevelt just in time

for the banquet to begin. The hotel doorman in his caped raincoat barely raised an eyebrow as he glanced at the rope snaking through the window, opened the front door, and watched as Fran stumbled out cradling a sore, soaking-wet right arm, followed by a damp but unflappable Mrs. Langert. She straightened her coat, brushed the water off her hat, and fell in with her comrades, having made it to the *banket* at last.

In light of that experience—and the fog of champagne that still suffused my Nyack hotel room—I was understandably reluctant to return Mrs. Langert's call. But if I had learned anything from collecting books, it was that *you never know*. So I splashed cold water on my face and dialed her number.

She answered on the first ring, and even through the champagne I could tell from the sound of her voice that this time the emergency was real. The Coops, she explained, used to have a large cooperative library. Although it hadn't been used much in recent years, it was there all the same—or at least it had been there until two weeks ago, when a new owner bought the buildings. He came in, saw the library, realized no one was paying rent for the space, and without a word to anyone decided to clear it out and lease it as office space. For an entire week, unbeknown to the residents, workers had been unceremoniously dismantling the Coops library, pulling shelves off the walls and dumping thousands of Yiddish books into a big pile on the floor. Mrs. Langert had just discovered the demolition—and what's worse, she'd found out that a dump truck was scheduled to arrive the very next day to haul all the books to the dump. That's why she had tracked me down at the wedding in Nyack: to make sure we got there first.

Suddenly sober, I found my friend Andrea (as a young girl she had studied Yiddish at the Peretz School in Montreal) and then phoned Noah Glick, who together with his friend John Stevenson agreed to take a late-night train and meet us in New York. We also enlisted Josh

Stillman, a friend of Andrea's, and Sidney Berg, our ever-ready board member from Great Neck. Andrea and I rented a large Ryder truck. At 7:30 the next morning, a hot, humid, summer day, we all rendezvoused on the sidewalk in front of the Coops library, where Mrs. Langert and several neighbors were waiting for us. In one of the library's dusty windows, facing the street, a big printed sign read Office for Rent.

Not surprisingly, Mrs. Langert took charge, leading us around the side of the building to the library entrance. A faded, hand-lettered Yiddish sign locked in a glass case announced *"Aktivitetn fun klub* (Activities of the [Yiddish] Club),"followed by a long list of weekly events, including "Tuesday, 3 P.M.: *Leyenkrayz* (Reading Circle)," "Wednesday, 2 P.M.: Discussion Group," and "Thursday, 7:30 P.M.: Film," and at the bottom of the sign, in Yiddish and English: "Library Open Every Day, 8 A.M.—5 P.M." It was clear that it had been a long time since the Yiddish Club had last met, and longer still since the library had kept anything resembling regular hours. As we pushed open the door we saw the short flight of stairs leading down into the library, cluttered with debris: a snow shovel, a shattered light fixture, children's toys, and a broken mirror. But that was nothing compared to what awaited us in the library itself. A large, L-shape room, it once held reading tables and chairs surrounded by floor-to-ceiling wooden bookcases; now everything lay in ruins. In the center of the room almost ten thousand volumes were buried beneath the rubble of smashed shelves and huge chunks of plaster and laths pulled from the ceiling and walls. We had to keep a sharp lookout to avoid stepping on rusty nails.

Apparently the wrecking crew hadn't yet finished, because at the far end of the library, in the short leg of the ell, several thousand additional volumes were still on the walls. We recognized many of the titles: multiple copies of the collected works of Peretz, Sholem Aleichem, Sholem Asch, and Avrom Reisen; ten copies of Abraham Cahan's two-volume *History of the United States* (in Yiddish, of course); immigrant novels by Chaver Paver; Mark Schweid's *Treyst mayn folk (Take Comfort, My People)*, a biography of Peretz; and Yiddish translations of Zola and Balzac. There was also an unlikely mix of books in Russian, German, and English: *Co-op*, by Upton Sinclair; *Das Kapital,* by Marx; *The Correspondence of Carlyle and Emerson;* a paperback edition of *Peyton Place;* and right next to it *The Six-Year Plan for the Reconstruction of Warsaw*. On the floor were remnants of fifty years of cultural activity: a dented coffee urn, three big aluminum tea kettles, a broken podium, a coat rack with four wire hangers, a box full of brand new, unsold copies of Yiddish humor books by Sam Liptzin, cans of food, a ripped movie screen, a jimmied strong box (apparently used for ticket sales); framed pictures of Peretz, Sholem Aleichem, Sholem Asch, Moyshe Olgin (the founding editor of the *Freiheit*), and Abraham Lincoln; a faded reproduction of Picasso's *Guernica;* and strewn everywhere, playing pieces from chess, checkers, backgammon, and Chinese checkers.

We were still reconnoitering when the landlord appeared, demanding to know who we were and what we were up to. I explained that we were from a nonprofit organization and that we had come to retrieve Yiddish books that were the rightful property of Mrs. Langert and other members of the cooperative. The landlord was Jewish. He was also *prost un farbisn,* coarse and snappish, and he made it clear that he had no sympathy for a Yiddish library, let alone a left-wing Yiddish library that occupied good space and paid no rent. "Anyway, you're too late," he said. "I've got trucks coming in less than an hour to haul all this junk away. This isn't a pinko co-op anymore, this is private property and I'm the owner. As far as I'm concerned you and your hippie friends are trespassing and I want you out of here *now!*"

Thank God for Sidney Berg. A landlord himself, he stepped forward, introduced himself, and offered a deal: If the man let us have the books, we in turn would give him a receipt that he could use to claim a whopping write-off on his taxes. "All right," the landlord agreed, "I'll give you till four this afternoon. Whatever you can carry out of here between now and then is yours. Whatever's left goes to the dump."

We sprang into action—but our progress was painfully slow. It took forever to remove the wood and plaster under which the books were buried. The landlord had just had the whole space fumigated, and as the temperature climbed into the nineties we had to tie bandanas around our faces to keep from gagging on the acrid stench. By noontime we had removed fewer than a thousand books, and it was clear that with just the five of us shlepping, we didn't have a prayer of finishing by four.

That's when we realized that a bunch of neighborhood kids had gathered to watch us. When we removed our gloves and masks and stepped outside for a quick lunch in the shade of the truck, an eleven-year-old Puerto Rican boy named Victor came over and asked what we were doing. We explained that the apartment complex had once been a cooperative and that we were saving Jewish books from its former library. Although Victor had come directly from San Juan to the Coops less than two years before, his English was excellent and he responded to this news with greater interest than I would have expected. "Imagine," he said, "a whole library right here where we live!" When I told him that we were racing to meet a four-o'clock deadline, he looked genuinely surprised. "Do you guys need help here or something?" he asked.

Did we need help! In a flash Victor was off. Ten minutes later he returned with a dozen more black and Puerto Rican kids his age, whom he proceeded to organize into a brigade snaking from the library to the truck. I think every kid in the neighborhood ended up shlepping books that day—with the exception of Victor himself, who in light of his linguistic and managerial talents appointed himself foreman and stood at the top of the stairs supervising everyone else. Sidney went off twice to buy cold Coca-Cola to fuel the troops; other than that, they worked without stopping. By the time four o'clock rolled around, the job was done. Almost fourteen thousand books lay safely stacked in the back of the truck. For Victor, new to the neighborhood, it was a personal triumph: He had proved himself a leader. For Mrs. Langert it was also a triumph, although of a somewhat more political nature: Despite her sadness at the loss of the library, she was proud to have played such a crucial role in its rescue. Even more, she was proud of the way the library had been saved—all those local boys, black and Puerto Rican, passing Jewish books from hand to hand was, in her eyes, a shining example of working-class solidarity prevailing over racial and ethnic divides. In its final hour, its library in ruins and its books about to be driven off to points unknown, the Coops' progressive vision had been realized at last.

16. A Ghost in the Attic

When we got back to Amherst, our truck groaning under the weight of the Coops' library, we were greeted by a half-dozen staff members and volunteers and, as fate would have it, by Dr. Elias Shulman, a frequent visitor to the Center, an accomplished historian of Yiddish literature, and editor of *Di tsukunft (The Future)*, the oldest of the Yiddish literary magazines. Dr. Shulman was a *farbrenter* (passionate) anticommunist, and when he learned where the fourteen thousand books on the truck had come from, he couldn't help but gloat.

"So this is what the *linke* (the leftists, the Jewish communists) have come to," he tsked. "It just goes to show you. They don't care about Yiddish and they never did. For them Yiddish was just window dressing. If they really valued their books, they wouldn't have let them end up this way!"

As it turned out, the final disposition of the Coops library was not as dire as Dr. Shulman might have imagined. Once we sorted them out, we sent several hundred of the most valuable volumes to the Bodleian Library, at Oxford University, and most of the remaining books to a handful of other major university and research libraries. But how did

Mel Brooks put it? "We mock the thing we are to be." Deep in his heart Dr. Shulman must have known that the downfall of the Coops library was a result of its demographics, not its ideology, and he must have feared a similar fate for his movement as well.

Which was sad, because I liked Dr. Shulman. This tall man in a silk ascot possessed an encyclopedic knowledge of Yiddish literature, which he shared unstintingly with me and other members of our staff. He was European born but American educated (apart from two years as an *aspirant,* a research fellow at the Vilna YIVO), he was married to an American-born woman (an accomplished watercolor artist), and he spoke English with only the slightest trace of a Yiddish accent. For all that, it was no easier for him than for most people in the Yiddish world to communicate with an American-born generation.

I once invited Dr. Shulman to deliver a public lecture at the Center. I forgot to say that by that time we had moved from our original factory loft into an old redbrick schoolhouse in Amherst, which we rented from the town for a token sum. The only problem was that we couldn't afford to heat the building, so our few staff members usually worked huddled around a kerosene heater in the middle of a first-floor office. When Dr. Shulman arrived, we decided to fire up the big steam boiler in his honor. That was a mistake, because as the building heated up, several dozen dormant flies felt the warmth and came back to life, dive-bombing the overhead fluorescent lights of our public reading room just as the lecture began. That wasn't all. Dr. Shulman was of the old school who insisted on reading their lectures verbatim, and he needed a podium, which we didn't have. Sharon improvised by stacking four boxes of books and covering them with a *shmate,* a rag, in this case a shabby, red cotton horse blanket. Fifty people crowded into the room, most of them young and all of them enthusiastic. Dr. Shulman was in fine spirits, buoyed by the audience. But the minute he stepped to the makeshift podium he turned stiff and formal and began reading his lecture from a prodigious stack of yellowed three-by-five cards. He mumbled. The radiators hissed. The flies whapped against the lights. At one point he began reading from a book he was discussing, Chaim Grade's *Musernikes (Mussar Students),* a thin paperbound volume published in Vilna in 1939. When he turned the brittle pages they literally crumbled in his hands, and as he continued reading, the fragments fell in a steady rain until the red blanket was festooned with crumbs of brown paper. My old teacher Leonard Glick leaned across Sharon to whisper in my ear, "This isn't a lecture, it's a metaphor!" The radiators went on hissing and the speaker went on droning, until, on my right, to my horror, I could feel a volcano stirring: Sharon was giggling!

There's a Yiddish expression for uncontrollable laughter: *"Der nar shtupt mikh* (the fool is pushing me)." It was contagious: crowded *pulke* to *pulke,* thigh to thigh, I could feel Sharon's shaking, and before long the *nar* was shtupping me as well. I clapped my red bandana over my mouth, but I too started shaking, tears rolling down my face, which only got Sharon going more. *Hiss! Whap! Drone!* Sharon had her bandana out too: two paroxysmal cowboys at the front of the room for all to see. We were seconds from disaster when suddenly, deus ex machina, Dr. Shulman dropped his cards. Talk about fifty-two-card pickup— three hundred yellowed index cards went cascading down the horse blanket and onto the floor! Dr. Shulman was on his hands and knees, members of the audience jumped up to help—and in the confusion Sharon and I made a mad dash for the door, *pppffft,* hands over our mouths, just one step ahead of the explosion.

I don't remember exactly what happened next. We took refuge in the bathroom, splashed cold water on our faces, and somehow managed to compose ourselves. After five more minutes of chaos Dr. Shulman reshuffled the cards as best he could and continued reading as before, although his lecture had now turned kaleidoscopic, the paragraphs hopelessly out of order. By that point it didn't really matter, most people having lost track of the lecture long since. Even when language was no barrier, communication between the old Yiddish world and the new wasn't easy.

Although we booked no further lectures for Dr. Shulman, he and I remained good friends. I went often to his apartment in Greenwich Village to discuss Yiddish literature. He suggested books to read, and we discussed them the next time I came. For me our private tutorials were a gift of knowledge to be found nowhere else; and for him, I think, they offered a glimmer of continuity—the hope that at least an echo of his vast learning would live on after he was gone. But even he could not refrain entirely from the dark humor of the Yiddish world. When, in the face of dwindling readership, the *Forward* switched from daily to weekly publication, he told me that Yiddish writers were now trying to figure out a way to die on a Thursday "so they can make the weekly deadline and someone will show up for their funeral." And though he ridiculed the communist Coops for losing their library, I think he was not all that surprised when, a year later, his magazine and a host of other like-minded, anticommunist, socialist Yiddish organizations were forced to give up the building where they had been housed for decades and leave many of their own treasured Yiddish books behind.

Here's how it happened. For many years, the Atran House, a large, comfortable building at East Seventy-eighth Street, had been home to many socialist Yiddish groups, including the Congress for Jewish Culture, the Jewish Labor Committee, the Bund Archives, CYCO (the Central Yiddish Cultural Organization), and *Di Zukunft (The Future)*, Dr. Shulman's magazine. There was only one problem: The building was owned by the Atran Foundation, whose bitterly divided board was now dominated by third-generation family members who did not share their late grandfathers' interest in Yiddish culture. When real estate prices went through the roof and they were offered a substantial sum for the Atran property, they decided to sell. Their plan was to relocate the Yiddish groups to smaller, cheaper space elsewhere in New York, and then use the difference in cost to help fund Jewish nursing homes in Florida.

Rumors of the imminent demise of the Atran House had been circulating for several years, but whenever we checked with the tenant organizations they steadfastly denied it. Proud, defensive, suspicious of everyone, they insisted that their ailing organizations were as healthy as ever, their space was as secure as ever, and there was therefore absolutely no need for them to jettison their Yiddish books. We tried to be as deferential as possible—we respected their past accomplishments and didn't think it our place to shatter the illusions of their declining years—and so we kept our distance, reminding them only that we were there if and when they needed us. Unfortunately, by the time they were finally willing to admit what was happening to call for help (it turned out that they had known the sale date for almost a year and had been packing for months), it was the Monday before Thanksgiving, and the building had to be completely vacated by Wednesday afternoon. That left us exactly two days to remove almost fifteen thousand Yiddish books that, for lack of space in their new quarters, they could not take with them.

Sharon was off speaking in Cleveland the day the call came in. I tracked her down by phone, and she was able to rebook her return flight so as to rendezvous with us the next morning in New York. Noah, who had just returned home from college for his Thanksgiving vacation, agreed to drive down with me that night. I phoned the Ryder office in Manhattan and arranged for the one-way rental of a large truck. That evening, at about seven o'clock, Noah and I loaded handtrucks and dollies into the back of my big Ford station wagon, stopped to pick up juice and sandwiches, and then set out for New York.

Noah was at the wheel and I was in the passenger seat eating an avocado and cheese sandwich when, cresting a bridge over the Connecticut River at thirty-five miles an hour, we watched in sudden horror as the headlights of an oncoming car turned directly into our path. What happened next seemed to unfold in slow motion: the moment of impact, breaking glass, crumpled metal, the seat belt forcing the air from my chest, and then, ever so slowly, the realization that I was still alive. Noah was slumped over the twisted wheel. "I never saw him coming," he sobbed. I assured him it wasn't his fault, and then, because his right hand was hurt and because his own door was crushed, I helped him out through the passenger-side window. Together we ran over to the other driver, who was still sitting at the wheel of what little remained of his late-model sports car. His nose was bleeding and he seemed to have lost several front teeth. "It's my father-in-law's car," he moaned, his mouth foaming with blood. "I got no insurance, man. I got no insurance."

The police and ambulances arrived almost immediately. A friend happened to be driving by, and I vaguely remember asking her to help me remove the Book Center's handtrucks from the back of the station wagon. Both cars were a total loss. At the hospital the other driver was treated for a broken nose, two missing teeth, and a mild concussion. Noah had a badly sprained right hand, and I had five bruised ribs. Other than that, we had been very lucky. The doctor bandaged my ribs, gave me a prescription for painkillers, and told me to lie in bed for the next three days. Under the circumstances, that was hardly an option. A board member, Rich Alpert, came to the hospital and drove me to a friend's house. I managed to catch Sharon in Cleveland (she had just finished her lecture) and we agreed to postpone the pickup until Wednesday. I phoned Ryder to change the reservation, then took a good shot of *shnaps,* climbed upstairs, and fell into bed.

I slept fitfully, waking again and again with the thought that somehow it was all a bad dream. When I awoke a little before noon my ribs ached mercilessly, but my head was clear and the events of the night before did not seem quite so cataclysmic. I tucked a bottle of aspirin into my rucksack, took a bus to Springfield, and boarded the train for New York.

When I awoke on Wednesday morning in Roger's apartment I was, to my dismay, even more stiff and sore than the day before. The slightest movement sent streaks of pain shooting through my sides, and I was pretty doubtful as to whether I could handle a truck. Fortunately Sharon had greater foresight than I: She had arranged for several friends to help with the shlepping and enlisted her brother Aaron to drive. (An ardent feminist, Sharon was furious with herself for having to resort to male assistance, let alone her older brother, and she vowed on the spot to learn to drive big trucks herself. Within three months, after a series of nerve-racking lessons, she was a full-fledged *balegole* (teamster), piloting heavy truckloads of Yiddish books all by herself.)

The scene at the Atran House was predictably chaotic. It was the building's last day, and professional movers—big, strapping, tattooed men in sleeveless T-shirts and broad leather weightlifter's belts—were rushing to remove the last of the furniture. Books, papers, and junk were scattered everywhere. "All the books that are left are yours," we were told. So we began in the subbasement and systematically made our way up through the building, one floor at a time. In addition to thousands of abandoned Yiddish books we found boxes of periodicals, props and costumes from old Yiddish plays, vintage metal signs with old-fashioned painted hands pointing to things like *Kafeterye* (Cafeteria) and *Vashtsimer* (Wash Room), and a half-dozen sheet Royal and Underwood manual Yiddish typewriters. As sometimes happens when there's work to be done, my pain somehow, miraculously, eased for the day, and I was able to hold my own with the heavy lifting—although I paid the price for weeks to come.

Our truck was almost full and the sun beginning to set when we finally reached the top floor. I was alone, deeply absorbed in my work, collecting what books and papers I could find, when suddenly I came upon a large rolltop desk that had not yet been removed and, seated behind it, a very old man reading a newspaper. He looked up and we stared at each other for a long time. Here was I, a young man with a beard, long hair, jeans, and a dirty sweatshirt carrying an armful of Yiddish books, and there was he, a small man at a big desk in an otherwise empty building, silhouetted against a small, arched window, looking as though he had stepped straight from the pages of a novel by Isaac Bashevis Singer.

It was he who broke the silence.

"Ver zayt ir? (Who are you?)" he gruffly demanded.

I told him.

"And who are you?" I asked in return.

"Yud Shin Hertz."

Yud Shin Hertz? If this really were a Bashevis novel I would have sworn I was talking to a ghost. Yud Shin Hertz was a preeminent historian of the Jewish labor movement in Europe. His four-volume *Di geshikhte fun Bund (The History of the Jewish Labor Bund)* had been standard reading in graduate school, and I had read other books and articles by him as well, including his moving memoir of Jewish life in Poland, *Geshikhte fun a yugnt (The Story of a Young Generation)*. For me Yud Shin Hertz was a legend from another world. I'd assumed he had died many years before.

Suspicious at first, Mr. Hertz was astonished and then clearly pleased when I told him his books were still being read. He was ninety-two years old, he told me, and at his age it was too late for change: Although he knew the building was being emptied, he had decided to remain at his desk until the movers or whoever was in charge actually looked him in the eye and ordered him out.

I left him there, alone at his desk, leaving it to someone with a less acute sense of history to persuade him to leave. Although I was often exasperated by what I perceived as the stubbornness and intransigence of the old Yiddish world, I found myself rooting for Mr. Hertz in his lonely vigil in that darkling room. His determination struck me not so much as obstinacy as nobility: the Don Quixote of the Atran House attic resolute against the inexorability of change, the last defender of a world that was literally being pulled out from under him. But even before I passed the burly movers on their way up the stairs, I knew that Mr. Hertz's cause was lost: for as he sat at his rolltop desk, digging in his heels and waiting to do battle with history, the newspaper he was reading was not the Yiddish-language *Forverts;* it was the English *New York Times*.

17. "If Not Higher"

In Isaac Bashevis Singer's novel *Enemies: A Love Story,* the owner of a Yiddish bookshop is asked whether he is afraid of thieves.

"No," replies the bookseller. "My only fear is that some Yiddish author might break in at night and put in some more books."

Our own collection was growing by leaps and bounds. On average, we collected four hundred volumes a day, two thousand a week, a hundred thousand a year. Just finding space to store them all had become a major problem. Our new home in an Amherst schoolhouse proved a godsend, but we weren't there a year before the piles of incoming books grew so high that we had to park a borrowed tractor-trailer out back for the overflow. When that, too, was full we went looking for warehouse space, first in a defunct roller-skating rink, then in the attic of a spice merchant, where the air was so redolent it made us dizzy and the ancient wooden floor literally sagged beneath the weight of our overladen carts. It was only when those spaces, too, were full that our no-nonsense board chair, Joe Marcus, decided enough was enough. The dean of engineering at the University of Massachusetts, Joe prevailed on a former student to lease us two floors in a renovated nineteenth-century mill building in nearby Holyoke, at the rock-bottom price of one dollar per square foot per year, utilities included, with no increase for the next twenty-five years. Each floor was the size of a football field. We managed to *shnor* $125,000 worth of surplus steel library shelving—but not before the mountain of unopened boxes had grown high enough to crack a three-foot beam on the floor below.

Of course, our warehouse was never intended as *genizah,* a mausoleum for superannuated volumes, but rather as a clearinghouse through which we could place old books in the hands of new readers. We issued regular catalogs offering duplicate copies at reasonable cost, and it wasn't long before orders arrived. To the bewilderment of those who insisted that Yiddish was dead, our customer list eventually included four thousand individuals and more than five hundred national and university libraries in twenty-six countries!

How can we account for such a groundswell? Why, at the precise moment when older Yiddish organizations were waning, were younger Jews flocking to Yiddish like never before? Part of the reason, as I've already suggested, was academic: for a thousand years, Jews in central and eastern Europe spoke Yiddish, and Yiddish sources had therefore become essential for serious research in the emerging fields of Jewish social history and cultural studies. But when all was said and done, the number of scholars remained small, while interest in Yiddish continued to grow. Surely there were other factors to explain the mounting pull of this fading language on a new generation.

One answer, I believe, at least in the 1970s and 1980s, was political: not because of the role of Yiddish in proletarian struggle, as championed by many of the older Yiddish organizations, but because of its potential for *cultural* struggle, as championed by my generation since the Vietnam War. Consider, for example, *Soon to Be a Major Motion Picture,* the 1980 memoir by Abbie Hoffman, perhaps the best known of the self-described "cultural revolutionaries." It is, on the whole, a surprisingly Jewish book, but nowhere more so than in Abbie's account of the trial of the Chicago Seven, who were charged in federal court with conspiracy to incite riot at the 1968 Democratic National Convention. Half the defendants, both defense lawyers, and the judge were Jewish, and, according to Abbie, it didn't take long for the trial to develop into a confrontation between two competing American Jewish possibilities: specifically, himself, Abbie, the unabashedly Jewish, Yiddish-quipping, curly-haired activist from Worcester, Massachusetts, and the judge, Julius Hoffman, a highly assimilated German Jew. "We fashioned our own little battle," Abbie recalls, "the war of the two Hoffmans."

The contest came to a head in the final days of the trial, when the judge sent one of the defendants, David Dellinger, a pacifist, behind bars on contempt charges.

> I really exploded. "You're a disgrace to the Jews. You would have served Hitler better," I screamed [at the judge], "you *shtunk!*" And then, in the sharpest thrust of all, I called him *"a shande fur de goyim,"* which roughly translated is a Yiddish expression meaning "a front man for the gentiles."

I don't want to overstate the case. Abbie was no Yiddish scholar. His translation of *"a shande far di goyim"*—literally, "an embarrassment in the eyes of non-Jews"—was inaccurate, although whether he was mistranslating or intentionally reinterpreting is not clear. What is clear is that he saw Yiddish as a *counterculture,* and he didn't hesitate to use it to challenge the mainstream culture from which, in his eyes, the war derived.

Of course, what Abbie didn't know—what few Jews his age or younger could have known—was that Yiddish had been pressed into service to challenge mainstream values since at least 1878, when Mendele Moykher Seforim published a short novel entitled *The Travels* and *Adventures of Benjamin the Third.* Loosely modeled on *Don Quixote,* the book tells the story of two small-town Jews, Benjamin and his side-kick Senderl, who leave their wives and set off in search of the lost ten tribes of Israel. The book is openly satiric of its heroes' narrow horizons and *kleynshtetldik* (small-town) ways. When, just a few days' walk from home, they come to Teterevke, a provincial town with sidewalks and two-story buildings, they mistake it for Constantinople and stand philosophizing in the middle of a busy street until they're almost run over by a passing wagon. Some pages later Benjamin and Senderl are kidnapped from a *shvitz,* a communal steam bath, and sold into service in the tsar's army. For the first time in Yiddish literature, Jews come face-to-face with the non-Jewish world—with predictable results:

They were utterly bewildered. . . . Everything around them was strange and grotesque: the barracks, the other soldiers, the language and the rudiments of military drill. Their uniforms draped them with all the gracefulness of [beggars'] sacks, their caps were tilted at a ludicrous angle. To the casual beholder the whole thing appeared farcical: the pair looked like scarecrows got up to parody soldiers and to burlesque military bravado. *Az okh un vey tsu der biks, nebekh, vos iz arayngefaln tsu undzere parshoynen*—pitiful was the fate of any rifle that fell into the hands of either of the two recruits. . . . Their drilling was one endless comedy, and needless to say they came in for their share of resounding blows.

Benjamin and Senderl decide to escape. Late one night they sneak out of their barracks and head to the perimeter fence, where they are caught by a sentry and brought before a court-martial of resplendent Russian officers. The charge is desertion, the penalty is death. But Benjamin is undaunted. Instead of pleading for his life, he defends himself by challenging the military itself—from a decidedly Jewish point of view:

"Your honor," Benjamin vociferated. "Trapping people in broad daylight and selling them like chickens in the marketplace—that's permissible? But when these same people try to escape, you call it a crime? If that's the case, the world must be coming to an end and I fail to understand what you call 'permissible' and 'not permissible.' . . . Speak up Senderl—don't stand there like a *golem*! Come out with God's own truth . . . and say together with me: 'We want to tell you that we don't know a thing about waging war, that we never did know, and never want to know. We are, praised be the Lord, married men; our thoughts are devoted to other things; we haven't the least interest in anything having to do with war. Now then, what do you want with us? You yourselves ought to be glad to get rid of us, I should think!'"

We lose something in the translation. What Benjamin actually says about the "arts of war" is this: *"Zey geyen undz afile gor in kop nisht—* They don't even go into our heads." In other words, militarism lies outside their cognition: beyond their interest, their ability, or their comprehension. Their position, as Abbie Hoffman would have appreciated, is radical to the core, for it challenges not only the legitimacy but the very *premise* of military culture. And the incredible thing is that they get away with it. Roaring with laughter, the assembled officers set our Jewish heroes free on grounds of insanity.

To quote the title of another of Mendele's works, *"Aderabe, ver iz meshuge?"* (On the Contrary, Who Is Really Crazy?) If Mendele began writing in Yiddish to spread Western Enlightenment among the Jewish masses, it didn't take him long to recognize that Yiddish-speaking Jews—despite, or rather because of, their marginality—had something to teach the Western world. In short, the Yiddish medium had become the message—a point underscored exactly one hundred years later, when Isaac Bashevis Singer stood in Stockholm as the first Yiddish writer to accept the Nobel Prize in Literature:

The high honor bestowed upon me by the Swedish Academy is also a recognition of the Yiddish language, a language of exile, without a land, without frontiers, not supported by any government, a language which possesses no words for weapons, ammunition, military exercises, war tactics; a language that was despised by both gentiles and emancipated Jews.

It's true: Yiddish was despised, disparaged, and dismissed as insane because it was *different;* because the people who spoke it lived on the outside for a thousand years; because when Christian soldiers were marching as to war, they stayed home; because they didn't want to talk about weapons and tactics; because they valued peace, decency, and social justice not as abstract values but as the strategy for their own survival. All this was part and parcel of the Yiddish language, and the longer Jews wrote in it, the more implicitly radical and challenging their literature became. No wonder it was despised by gentiles and emancipated Jews; and no wonder so many young people of my generation, having grown up in a world gone amok, were suddenly so ready to embrace it anew.

BUT TIMES CHANGE. Today's college students are too young to remember Vietnam or Abbie Hoffman or countercultural struggle. And yet for them, the pull of Yiddish seems to grow stronger with each passing year. So if not politics alone, then what other forces are at work? The answer, I believe, lies deeper still in the nature of the Yiddish language—and in the pages of Yiddish books.

According to Max Weinreich, Yiddish—like much of Jewish culture—was the product of two powerful dialectical forces. On the one hand, Jews' core culture, rooted in Hebrew and Aramaic texts, was so strong that they could interact with their non-Jewish neighbors and, instead of being subsumed, could transmute foreign elements into their own frame of reference. Such familiar Jewish foods as challah, kugel, herring, and gefilte fish, for example, were first adapted from the kitchens of non-Jewish neighbors. The fur hats and black coats worn by Hasidim were an imitation of the finery of the Polish nobility in the eighteenth century.

The same magic played out linguistically, as Jews borrowed words and grammar from a host of languages and made of them something distinctly Jewish. The name Yenta, for example, which now suggests a meddling busybody, comes from the French *gentille,* genteel. *Yarmulke,* the head covering of observant Jews, shares its Turkic origin with the helmets worn by Ukrainian Cossacks. In every case, Jews strengthened their culture not by hiding from the world but by making the world their own.

An even more powerful dialectic existed *within* Jewish life, where a well-established system of ritual separation—between men and women, Shabbos and week, meat and milk, wool and flax, the holy and the everyday—found linguistic expression in the relationship between Hebrew, *loshn koydesh,* the holy tongue, the ancient language of scholarship and prayer, and Yiddish, *mame loshn,* mother's tongue, the language of women, the marketplace, and everyday life. The creative interaction between the two can be plainly seen in traditional Jewish proverbs, many of which begin in Hebrew and end in Yiddish (represented here by small capital and lowercase letters, respectively):

Ato bikhartonu mikol ho-omim—*to vos hostu gevolt fun dayn folk Yisroel?* Thou hast chosen us from amongst the nations—so why did you have to pick on us Jews?

Omru l'eylohim—*ober shray tsu der vant!* Speakest thou unto the lord—but go scream at the wall.

In short, Hebrew conveys abstract teachings, while Yiddish brings them down to earth. Like the dialectic between Jewish and non-Jewish spheres, which found expression in *Benjamin III,* the internal dialectic between high and low culture, Hebrew and Yiddish, is also radical and full of literary potential, as became clear in the writings of I. L. Peretz, another pioneer of modern Yiddish literature.

Consider, for example, Peretz's 1900 story about a rationalist Lithuanian Jew who visits the southern, Hasidic town of Nemirov, at the time of *slikhes,* the penitential prayers. When he asks where the rebbe is, the local Hasidim inform him that every year at this time the rebbe ascends to heaven to intercede on their behalf. Impossible, thinks the skeptical Litvak, and he vows to get to the bottom of things. That night he hides under the rebbe's bed. Before dawn the rebbe rises, puts on the clothing of a Russian peasant, takes an axe, and goes into the forest. While the Litvak watches in amazement, the rebbe cuts a load of firewood and carries it on his back to the home of a desperately poor, half-frozen Jewish widow. He lights her stove for her, and only then, as the flames grow brighter, does he quietly recite the *slikhes* prayers. The Litvak, having seen all this, returns to town and becomes a Nemirover Hasid. Thereafter, every year at *slikhes* time, when the rebbe disappears, the Hasidim insist as always that he has ascended to heaven. All but the Litvak. He listens, nods, and adds quietly, *"Oyb nisht nokh hekher* (if not higher)." Even higher than heaven are good deeds here on earth.

Here's another of Peretz's stories, although in this case the meaning may be less obvious: Bontsha, a *treger,* a public porter, makes his living carrying heavy loads in the marketplace. He suffers every manner of calamity—all without complaint. When he dies and goes to heaven the angels give him a hero's welcome. Like every soul, he must still stand trial for his actions on earth, but in his case, we're told, this will be a mere formality: "The prosecutor won't dare open his mouth. Why, the whole thing won't take five minutes. . . . Don't you know whom you're dealing with? You're dealing with Bontsha, Bontsha the Silent!"

As the trial begins, the defense attorney, an angel, reviews the sad story of Bontsha's life, a series of disasters, deprivations, and miseries through which he never uttered a word of complaint. At the end, the court is still and when the judge finally speaks, his voice is soft and tender. "Bontsha *mayn kind,* my child, Bontsha . . . For you there is not only one little portion of Paradise, one little share. No, for you there is everything! Whatever you want! Everything is yours!"

For the first time Bontsha lifts his eyes.

"Really?" he asks, doubtful and a little embarrassed.

"Really!" the judge answers. "Really! I tell you, everything is yours! . . . Choose! Take! Whatever you want! You will only take what is yours!"

"Really?" Bontsha asks again, and now his voice is stronger, more assured.

And the judge and all the heavenly host answer, "Really! Really! Really!"

"Well then"—and Bontsha smiles for the first time—"well then, what I would like, Your Excellency, is to have every morning for breakfast *a frishe bulke mit puter,* a hot roll with fresh butter."

A silence falls upon the great hall, and it is more terrible than Bontsha's has ever been, and slowly the judge and the angels bend their heads in shame at this unending meekness they have created on earth.

Then the silence is shattered. The prosecutor bursts out laughing.

What does the story mean? Ruth Wisse tells me that most of her students at Harvard think Bontsha is a hero, a paragon of humility. Professor Tzvi Howard Adelman points out that his students in Israel "want to see in the story a paean to piety rather than a critique of Jewish passivity."

A little more than a century ago, when Peretz wrote the story, few

Jewish readers would have missed the point. It may be true, as Shylock said, that "sufferance is the badge of all my tribe," but Jews rarely made a virtue of it. For Peretz, who had spent time in prison for socialist agitation, what mattered was protest in the here and now, and "Bontsha the Silent" was therefore a blistering critique of those who would remain silent, who would abstain from political engagement and wait for pie in the sky instead. It's not only in the last line, where the prosecutor gets the last laugh, that Peretz makes his meaning clear; condemnation of Bontsha is implicit throughout the story. After all, any eight-day-old baby who fails to cry during his own circumcision is demonstrating not moral conviction but neurological deficit. A person who fails to tell the police the identity of a hit-and-run driver is not being noble, he's abrogating a basic civic responsibility and thereby putting future pedestrians at risk. If Bontsha burns with moral fire, then why does the narrator tell us that his eyes were *"oysgeloshn* (extinguished)"? If his silence can be regarded as a moral stance in the face of evil, then why does the narrator tell us that *"er hot geshvign far shrek* (he was silent out of fear)"? Now that Bontsha is in heaven, now that his race is run, why does he need a third-person narrator? Why can't he tell his own story and extol the virtues of meekness for himself? And finally, why, when he's offered his just reward, does he opt for a *bulke* and butter, instead of, say, something a bit more ambitious, like world peace, Messianic redemption, or a Mercedes-Benz?

"Bontsha" was not intended as a terribly subtle or ambiguous story. The fact that so many students today conclude otherwise is, I think, a measure of assimilation: the degree to which we've been influenced, whether consciously or not, by the Christian ethos that surrounds us.

It wasn't always that way. In her trenchant introduction to *The I. L. Peretz Reader,* Ruth Wisse writes, "Isaac Leib Peretz was arguably the most important figure in the development of modern Jewish culture — and until 1939 one would not have had to argue the claim at all." Outside the door of Peretz's Warsaw apartment was a brass plaque in He-brew that gave the hours when he would receive aspiring writers from the provinces. Around him grew a literary circle whose luminaries in-cluded I. J. Singer (the elder brother of Isaac Bashevis Singer), Alter Kacyzne, Hirsh Dovid Nomberg, Sholem Asch, I. M. Weissenberg, and many others. In cities around the globe there were (and in some places still are) Peretz schools, Peretz libraries, Peretz Streets, even a Peretz Publishing House. Years ago, when the Book Center first began, I met an elderly man in New York who proudly informed me, *"Ikh bin a khosid fun Peretsn* (I am a disciple of Peretz)."

Nowadays it's hard to imagine any writer eliciting such devotion. If anything, young people who encounter Peretz for the first time seem to find him unsettling to the point of misinterpretation. But that, I think, is only a first reaction, because he's so different from the complacent Jewishness they've come to expect. If you read enough of Peretz and the countless Yiddish writers who followed, a deeper vision begins to emerge: of a Jewishness infinitely more interesting, more challenging, and more relevant, rooted in tradition, shaped by marginality, fueled by a relentless dialectic, and unafraid of the inextricability of art and action. If anything, Yiddish books are more of a counterculture to-day—more of a challenge to mainstream values—than they were when they were written. That, I think, even more than their scholarly significance, is what accounts for their growing popularity. And that's why I remain confident, even as once-powerful Yiddish organizations fade and the last native Yiddish-speaking Jews pass on, that, sooner or later, the old books we've saved will find the new readers they deserve.

18. "Hitler's Fault"

Ten years after we recovered books from the old Atran House, we were invited to the new Atran House. An improbably narrow building on East Twenty-first Street, it had almost no windows, as though the old organizations—most were still there—had turned their backs on the outside world for good.

We had come to meet with officials of the Congress for Jewish Culture, which was one of the world's younger Yiddish organizations, having been founded in the immediate aftermath of the Second World War. Subsidized by German reparations money, the CJC had published many extremely important Yiddish titles, including the eight-volume *Lexicon of the New Yiddish Literature,* Simon Dubnow's ten-volume *World-History of the Jewish People,* and Yehoash's masterful, two-volume Yiddish translation of the *Tanakh,* the complete Hebrew bible. Unfortunately the organization's refugee leaders had proved themselves more adept at editing and printing than at marketing and distribution. Their titles were beautifully printed and bound, yet a huge number of brand-new copies remained unsold.

Which is why we were there. Despite the truckload of books we had carted away from their old location almost a decade before, the Atran

House was still teeming with books, most of which belonged to the Culture Congress, which had overflowed its allotted space, taken over the offices of its neighbors, and spread throughout the building. There were books everywhere—on shelves and desktops, inside file cabinets, in corridors, closets, and bathrooms. Stacked boxes were used as partitions, and tottering piles leaned against every wall.

The CJC leadership had recently changed, and two of the new heads of the organization—Yonia Fain, a respected Yiddish writer and artist, and Manny Goldsmith, a personable American-born rabbi and scholar whom I had known for years—were eager to do something about these stockpiles. So they sat down with me and my colleague Jeffrey Aronofsky (who was even younger than I) and made us an offer: For the nominal cost of $2 a volume, they would give us every book in the place.

Under ordinary circumstances I would have rejected their proposal out of hand. We *never* paid for books. Even if we were willing to pay, where would we get the $80,000 needed to pay for the CJC's estimated forty thousand volumes?

But these were not ordinary circumstances. Not only had the books taken over every office in the building, they—together with most of the irreplaceable archive of the Jewish Labor Bund—had spilled over into the basement as well. Manny and Yonia gave us a tour. From floor to ceiling, the cellar was a solid mass of boxes extending to within four inches of what can only be described as a Byzantine web of pipes: cast-iron sewer lines, hot and cold water pipes, sprinkler mains, and steam pipes covered with ripped asbestos that was raining down on the boxes below. My stomach lurched. Twelve years before, when the Yiddish Book Center began, we had temporarily stored several hundred recently collected books in a similar space, a subbasement storeroom beneath the press room of the *Forward* on East Thirty-third Street. We had assumed the books were safe until we received a call one day telling us that a pipe had broken, the water had been running undetected for more than a week, and (although the pipe was now fixed) all of our books were soaked. By the time we got there the next day, it was too late by far. Immersed for so long and then left packed together in a warm, windowless room, the swollen books had sprouted a furry rainbow of mold. In three of the most dispiriting hours of my life, we donned masks, packed the soggy books into heavy trash bags, and hauled them up through the press room and out to the trash.

That was a few hundred books. By my estimate, fully half of the congress's forty thousand books were stored in its basement. When I expressed my concern I noticed Yonia and Manny exchanging glances with the congress's young, American-born executive director, who had joined us for the tour.

"What's the matter?" I asked.

"Well," the administrator said sheepishly, "a pipe did break about two years ago. We lost two thousand volumes. That's one of the reasons we're offering the books to you now."

As I saw it, there wasn't a moment to lose. I returned to Amherst and presented the proposal to our board. Several board members strongly opposed paying for books; they didn't want to establish a precedent we would live to regret. But there was no denying that the twenty thousand books in that basement were in imminent danger, and that further delay could have disastrous consequences. The board authorized the expense—provided I could find the cash.

It wasn't easy. The Center has always run on a bare-bones budget. At the time, in 1992, we had zero cash reserves and could barely meet payroll each week. The sum was, quite simply, beyond our imagination.

So Jeffrey and I went back and negotiated a reduced fee, to be paid in equal installments over the next five years, which took the pressure off our cash flow. Eventually we'd find the money; now was the time to act. Jeffrey hired a tractor-trailer and driver, reserved the Center's own truck (an Isuzu diesel purchased in 1987), and inveigled four of our staff members and former interns to join us. At 7:30 on a chilly October morning, we gathered in front of the Atran House, ready to begin.

Shlepping forty thousand books is no small job—especially when they're in movers' boxes weighing close to a hundred pounds each. My coworkers were not particularly brawny, but they were young (at thirty-seven, I was the eldest of the crew), and the day would have gone smoothly enough were it not for an unforeseen problem. The tractor-trailer, which was supposed to meet us in front of the Atran House at 8:00 A.M. (Jeffrey had arrived at six to stake out a row of parking spaces), didn't actually pull up until nightfall, a full nine hours late! By that point, the oversize boxes we had been assiduously hauling out of the building since early morning had grown into a solid wall, three boxes wide and four high, from the entrance to the far end of the block.

While the rest of us shlepped, Jeffrey had seen to it that at least one person remained on the street, keeping guard over the boxes. But as the day wore on, the sight of that growing ridgeline proved increasingly unsettling to the Culture Congress staff and just about everyone else inside the Atran House who ventured outside to have a look. For the first few hours they were still joking and kibbitzing with us. A few even kissed us, grateful that someone had finally come to clear the decks, freeing up badly needed floor space in their offices. *"Gotenyu!"* one secretary gasped as we removed floor-to-ceiling boxes from behind her desk, "who knew there was a wall there? Tomorrow I'm going to bring a framed picture. It will look so nice."

By midmorning, though, others were getting testy. The sheer size of that Berlin Wall on the sidewalk was becoming a *shtokh,* a goad, a vivid display of exactly how much they were giving up. Inside the building it was even worse. If you've ever moved, you know how shabby a room can look once it's stripped of its familiar furnishings. The effect on the Atran House was no different: As we descended on each office in turn, we left shmutz on the floor and unfaded rectangles on the walls where the boxes had blocked them. The inhabitants' growing uneasiness was not just aesthetic; it was existential. Now that the books were gone, who were they, exactly, what was their mission, and where was the culture they sought to maintain?

My young colleagues and I were not insensitive to what was happening. We took time to talk to people in every office, explaining where we were taking the books and what we would do to get them into the hands of new readers. We also let them know that the considerable money we were paying for the books would enable the congress to publish new titles and begin new programs. Some people were mollified by these explanations, but others only became more agitated. The executive director, not much older than I, started pulling individual volumes from boxes as our staff members carried them past. Then he started shouting orders: "Put that box down! Don't take *those* books— we spent two years putting them in alphabetical order, you'll get them all mixed up! No, not the ones in the bookcase—a bookcase is supposed to have books in it. How will it look without books?"

I didn't mind leaving some books behind: If the Culture Congress could use them, *gezunterheyt*. There were enough to go around. What the executive director seemed to forget, though, was that the books were ours, we had paid for them, we had a big job to do, the boxes weighed a hundred pounds apiece, and his kvetching was not making our work any easier. Fortunately, at about 10:30 Yonia Fain showed up. When I explained the situation he agreed immediately: We had bought the books fair and square, and he promised to do his best to keep the director out of our hair.

We kept on working, mostly upstairs. In the offices of the congress proper, boxes were stacked almost twelve feet high. Our bibliographer, Neil Zagorin, retrieved an extension ladder from the Center's truck, set it against the wall, and precariously positioned himself at the top. I balanced myself on a rung halfway down, from which I was able to re-lay the heavy boxes to our people on the floor below, who loaded them onto hand trucks and rolled them out to the street. We were nothing if not efficient—within twenty minutes the whole pile was gone.

Yonia took one look at the empty wall and now it was his turn to protest. We were moving very fast: American kids, boys and girls, long hair, blue jeans, shouting back and forth in fluent English, exuberant, laughing and joking as people engaged in hard physical work are wont to do, and all the while Yonia's books, his past, his very being, were dis-appearing before his eyes. Was it any wonder he started to yell?

"Why are you taking so many books?" he demanded. "You have to leave some for us! Why are you trying to liquidate us? What are *we* supposed to do when the books are gone?"

I reminded him of our mission: We were going to take the books to Massachusetts, store them safely, match them with new readers—and pay the congress enough money to continue its good work. But Yonia wasn't listening. "What will we be without the books? Go ahead," he shouted, "take them, take them all, finish us off! Everyone else wants to destroy us—why don't you just make an end of it?"

I admired Yonia, and I understood his passion. Born in Dneprope-trovsk, Ukraine, he hadn't learned Yiddish until the age of ten, when he and his parents fled to Vilna. He immediately fell in love with Yiddish literature. He spent the war as an art student in Moscow, then settled in Mexico as a protégé of Diego Rivera. Later he came to the States, where he became an art professor at Hofstra University. His paintings hang in the Whitney and other major museums. At the same time, he also became an important Yiddish writer. When, after

Dr. Shulman's death, the Yiddish literary magazine *Zukunft* needed an editor, he took the job, "writing half of each issue myself." He regretted he no longer had enough time to paint, "but someone has to do it." Presumably he felt the same way about his responsibilities at the Culture Congress.

I wasn't about to get into a shouting match with Yonia or argue with him in public, so I asked our staff members to take a break. Meanwhile Yonia stormed off into his private office. When I tried to follow he slammed the door. "I don't talk to people like you," he yelled. "I want nothing to do with you!" I pushed into the office anyway and shut the door behind me, trying to ignore the fact that the partition did not go all the way to the ceiling and people outside could overhear. At first Yonia was accusatory: We were *khazerish,* we were greedy, we wanted to build an empire, we couldn't stand the thought that someone else should have books, too.

That wasn't fair. "Who do you think we are?" I asked him. "Why do you think we're collecting these books? You think we're here to make money? To build an empire out of dirty boxes covered in rat shit, of books that no one's read for forty years?"

Yonia began to weep. "Look at these books," he said, lifting a volume of the *Lexicon* from his desk. "What are we doing, selling a book like this for two dollars? For one dollar? What about all the work that went into writing it, into printing it?" He held his head in his hands. "It's okay, Ahrn, I'm not mad at you. Do you know who's really to blame?"

I couldn't imagine. The truck driver? The dispatcher?

"Hitler!" he screamed. "If it hadn't been for Hitler you wouldn't be here now. We'd be selling these books ourselves for forty dollars apiece. Don't you see? Hitler killed our readers, Hitler destroyed our world.

"Here in America, the Jewish establishment, they won't listen, they think Yiddish is over and done with, they think we're all dinosaurs, they want to bury us, they want us to fade away, they want us to close up and disappear. But we *won't* disappear!

"It's okay, Ahrn, I know you're not our enemy. It's just that everywhere I turn, people want to destroy us, and I just can't take it anymore. I see these Jews today in America, I go to *simkhes* (Jewish celebrations) and see these fancy Jews, these rich lawyers and businessmen and bankers, they think they're so special, they spend fifty thousand dollars on a bar mitzvah, but they don't have a penny for us, for all of Yiddish culture. Let me tell you, Ahrn, those bankers, with all their money, not one of them has the *yidishkayt* of the lowest tailor in Vilna!

"I respect you," Yonia continued. "I respect so much what you've done, and I'm so ashamed that I spoke to you like that. I didn't mean it, you are close to my heart, I'm so hurt and frustrated and heartsick from all that's happened to Yiddish in this country that I just lashed out at the wrong person. I'm so ashamed."

I offered my hand, but it wasn't enough, so we stood up and hugged each other, and we both felt hot tears, undone by the irredeemable sadness of it all.

We had lost an hour's work, but I, for one, was glad for the catharsis. I opened the door of Yonia's office with a new sense of calm and determination . . . only to find the executive director up in arms. "Stop!" he cried. "You have to stop right now! I forbid you to take one more book. It's all illegal. Our board never voted to sell you the books, Yonia didn't have the authority to sign, let's just stop right now."

"You know, if you had called me last week, if you had called me yesterday, I would have understood," I replied. "But right now there are thousands of books sitting on the sidewalk, a forty-five-foot tractor-trailer is on its way, and I've got five staff members here in New York. We can't afford to come down again. If you want to sell us the books, then we need to take them now."

It was true: This was costing us a fortune, and I had no desire to come back. What's more, we weren't going to leave books on the street, and we certainly weren't going to shlep them back down to the basement. Fortunately one of the congress's board members, an elderly man, was present, and he spoke to the director. "Lahnsky is right," he said gently, "there's a contract, you can't cancel now. It costs a lot of money for a truck." The director was unappeased, but this sounded like the right tack, and so, in desperation, I uttered the only misleading statement I made that day: "Do you have any *idea*," I asked indignantly, "how much it costs for a *union truck driver?*"

To tell the truth, I had no idea, either: The driver who canceled on us was an owner-operator, and I didn't have a clue whether the replacement company, for whom we were still waiting, was union or not—though I rather guessed it wasn't. No matter. We were in union territory, the home turf of the Bund Archive and the Jewish Labor Committee, and my question garnered instant audience support. "He's right!" someone said in a heavy Yiddish accent, "a union driver isn't cheap!" "A union man is on his way, you can't just ask him to come back some other time."

God forgive me my trespasses, but the ruse worked: We went back to hauling boxes from the basement, and we continued hauling till late that night. When the truck driver finally did arrive (the delay, he assured us, was the dispatcher's fault, not his), he graciously agreed to help. So, too, did a rail-thin homeless man whom we recruited off the street. At 8:00 P.M. we all sat down on the boxes on the sidewalk for supper from a nearby deli: seltzer, sandwiches, pickles, and cookies. We continued working until the tractor-trailer and our own truck were overloaded, and even at that we had to send a truck and crew back the following week to retrieve the books that remained.

By that point most people in the Atran House were starting to appreciate their newfound space, and if any of them still had qualms, they were too exhausted to say. In the years that followed we made good on our promises: The Culture Congress was paid in full, the books we retrieved were sorted and cataloged, and many have been sent to students, scholars, and libraries around the world. Yonia and the Center remain on good terms: *Pakn Treger,* our magazine, recently published a translation of a wonderful short story of his, which he illustrated himself. The Congress for Jewish Culture is still here: I read recently on the Web that they've started a Yiddish coffeehouse for young people—presumably in space once occupied by boxes of books—and they're pursuing several interesting publishing projects. Meanwhile, announcements of the demise of other, older Yiddish organizations have also proved premature: Some may be little more than shadows of what they once were, but they still exist.

Some have even flourished. The Forward Association, publisher of the newspaper, had a *groyse gevins,* a great stroke of good luck, when they sold WEVD, their one-time Yiddish radio station (the call letters are a tribute to socialist leader Eugene Victor Debs), for an astronomical sum and used the money to shore up the Yiddish *Forward,* introduce a Russian-language edition, and in conjunction with private investors, to launch a new *Forward:* a first-rate, national English-language Jewish newspaper. YIVO, the Yiddish research institute, met with similar *mazl:* Under the leadership of an enterprising businessman named Bruce Slovin, it joined forces with the American Jewish Historical Society, the Leo Baeck Institute, the Yeshiva University Museum, and the American Sephardic Federation to establish a new $54-million Center for Jewish History. Other older organizations are also gaining new ground, including the Workmen's Circle and the resurgent Folksbiene Yiddish Theater.

True, I haven't attended a Yiddish banquet in years—I'm not sure anyone has. But I'm glad many of the older Yiddish organizations are still here. They have knowledge and memory found nowhere else, and even if they won't speak with one another—or with me—surely there is still work enough for us all.

PART FOUR

Ganvenen dem Grenets—

Crossing the Border

19. Squandered at the Concord

M r. Lansky?" boomed the resonant voice on the other end of the line. "Mr. *Aaron* Lansky? You don't know me, but let me assure you, I know *you*! My name is Towers. *Bob* Towers. Does that name mean anything to you?"

"No, I don't think so."

"Well, let me assure you, in my business Bob Towers is a name people don't forget!"

"And what business is that, Mr. Towers?"

"What business? *Talent!* I book talent for the Catskills, the Borscht Belt, the Jewish resorts. A young fella like you, you're too young to remember, but years ago there were dozens—did I say dozens?—there were *hundreds* of Jewish hotels in the Catskills. Today just eleven *giants* remain, and it just so happens that I represent four of them. It's my job to be on the lookout for new talent. That's why, when I read about you in the *Times,* I said, *'He's our boy!'* Whatd'ya say—do you know how to make a speech? Even if you don't it doesn't matter, you can learn. I loved what I read. What a story! What color! What drama! What Yiddishkeit! What *youth*! I'm ready to sign you up right now, *sight unseen,* the Cotillion Room of the Concord, eleven A.M., fourth day of Pesakh. Do we have a deal or *do we have a deal?!*"

I had always thought of the Borscht Belt as the enemy camp: the place where they turned Yiddish into a punch line. So why even consider Mr. Towers's offer? Well, partly out of curiosity—I had never actually seen the place. And partly because I had learned that the best way to garner support for the Yiddish Book Center was to speak to Jews, and in the late 1980s the Catskills was still a place where Jews could be found. So I persuaded my friend and occasional traveling companion Roger Mummert to join me, and late on a rainy night, we pulled up under the front portico of the Concord.

Even at that hour, the Concord was ablaze with light. Up and down the main driveway we passed double- and triple-parked Cadillacs, with New York and New Jersey plates, waiting for harried valets to return them to the multistory garage. Inside, whole families, three and sometimes four generations, were promenading back and forth along a broad, brightly lit concourse in their furs, jewelry, and Pesakh best. Although it was too late for the nightclub acts, other entertainment was still going strong. We passed up the disco (the average age of the writhing dancers seemed to be about sixteen) and headed instead to the Night Owl, the Concord's late-night bar. A tired band, heavy on the wire brush work, played pop favorites of the forties and fifties—a muted version of "Boogie Woogie Bugle Boy" sticks in my mind—while middle-aged couples sat on black leatherette chairs at round tables, each with its own sputtering citronella candle in a red glass bowl covered with white plastic lace. The kidney-shaped bar was made of translucent faux marble, softly illuminated from below. Since the Passover prohibition against *khumets,* leavened food, extends to beer, whiskey, vodka, and all other manner of grain alcohol, the bar list was limited to Carmel concord grape wine, extra sweet Malaga, apricot brandy, and an improbable assortment of mixed drinks all made with Slivovitz, a *kishke*-burning plum brandy from Yugoslavia: Slivovitz on the rocks, Sliv and soda, Slivovitz sour, and Sliv and Coke. I downed a Sliv straight up and, my eyes bleary, stumbled off to bed.

At 10:30 the next morning I headed downstairs to the Cotillion Room to set up for my eleven o'clock lecture. In my years as a public speaker I had lectured at many lavish—if not to say garish—synagogue social halls, but none could top this. The Cotillion Room was shaped like a half moon, with the audience seated in tiers looking down on an expansive, jet black stage. The décor was a cross between Louis XIV and classical Greek. Heavy draperies, crystal chandeliers, six-foot-tall plaster-cast urns at either side of the double doors, and standing in ornate, fluorescent-lit alcoves along the walls, a dozen larger-than-life alabaster Greek goddesses with bared breasts and missing limbs. As I set up the slide projector I was watched by two naked Venuses balancing water jugs on their heads.

At ten to eleven they let in the audience. They entered talking. Roger stood by a Grecian urn, handing out Yiddish Book Center brochures, while I, still fiddling with wires on the stage, was fending off a widening circle of well-wishers.

"Mr. Lansky? Mr. Lansky? I have books for you back in Canarsie. When can you come get them?"

"Excuse me, young man, maybe you have Jewish books in large print?"

"Yungerman, yoo-hoo yungerman, I come from Cleveland, I read about you in *Hadassah*."

"Read, shmead, what does he care what you read? Mr. Lansky, do you know who I am? I'm Mrs. Simkin, I'm a member . . ."

The din had grown deafening when, out of the corner of my eye, I spied a tall, tanned, vigorous man in his seventies striding from the wings and heading straight for me.

"Which one of you is Lansky?" he demanded of the milling crowd— a foolish question, I thought, since I was the only one in the circle under seventy. "I'm Towers," he announced, pumping my arm up and down, "Bob Towers. Welcome to the Concord. Now let's go somewhere quiet where we can talk business before you go on."

Wearing a brightly colored jogging suit, with a heavy gold chain around his neck, exuding health and good cheer, Mr. Towers led me past the throng to a small, curtained area at the side of the stage.

"Okay, first things first," he said with no further introduction. "How much did it cost you to get here?"

I was scheduled to speak in five minutes and would have preferred to spend the time reviewing my notes, not discussing pecuniary details. "Actually, we drove here," I said, "so it didn't cost very much."

"Never mind!" he boomed. "When Bob Towers invites a guest, Bob Towers pays for him to get here. You know the Exxon station at the top of the hill?"

"Uh, no, not exactly, it was pretty dark when we arrived."

"Dark, shmark, you may not know the Exxon station, but one phone call from me and that Exxon station will know *you*! You pull in there and tell 'em Bob Towers sent you. They'll fill you right up to the top— premium, high test, the best—whatever you want."

My car, a diminutive Honda Civic wagon, had a ten-gallon gas tank and was still half full, but I managed some small expression of grati- tude as my fingers anxiously leafed through the folded notes in my pocket.

"No, no, don't thank me," said Mr. Towers. "After all, you're the speaker. You're the *star*. You call the shots around here. Now tell me, how much do want for this performance?"

"Performance?"

"That's right, no need to be shy. I've been in this business more than thirty years, I've seen it all. Now, how much is it gonna be?"

I had received honoraria before, but the directness of the question, three minutes before I was scheduled to speak, caught me off guard. Before I could respond Mr. Towers had pulled a five-inch wad of cash from his pocket and was peeling off bills: "Five, ten, fifteen, twenty . . . " He went on to $65. "That'll do for now," he said, folding the bills and deftly stuffing them into my jacket pocket. "We'll talk again after the show."

The "show" was drawing nigh—two minutes to go—but Bob Towers wasn't through yet.

"Okay, how long are you planning to speak for?" he asked.

"I don't know, probably about an hour, then time for questions—"

"An hour? *An hour?* Kid, you're new to this business; you don't have the benefit of my thirty-plus years of experience. Take it from me, *no one* speaks for an hour. Let's face it, we've got old people out there, their plumbing's not what it used to be, it doesn't matter what's happening on stage, they can only sit so long before they've got to get up and scram—straight to the john. I've seen it happen to the best of them. They got up on Abba Eban. They got up on Bella Abzug. And let me assure you, young man, they're gonna get up on you too if you try to speak for an hour. Remember what I'm telling you, *keep it short, short is golden, short is beautiful.* Okay, let's go!"

And with that he pushed me out of the wings and onto the stage. Not counting the Greek goddesses, there were about three hundred people in the room, and they were definitely not young. While I squinted into the spotlights, Bob Towers was already at the stand-up microphone (there was no podium), launching into his introduction:

"Three weeks ago," he thundered, enunciating every word like a boxing announcer at Madison Square Garden, "three weeks ago, I read an article in the *New York Times*. It was an article about a young man. A young man who knows Yiddish. The *mame loshn!*" At this first Yiddish utterance the audience was already laughing. Despite his admonition to me to be brief, his introduction went on for fifteen minutes. He covered the Old Country, Second Avenue, Isaac Bashevis Singer's Nobel Prize, and a rousing pronouncement that "Yiddish will not be consigned to oblivion!" before finally coming back around to me. "When I read the story in the *Times,* I decided to get in touch with this young man and bring him here to you. He was born in New Bedford, Massachusetts, known to the history books as a famous whaling town, and as we say in Yiddish, *Fun vanen kumt a yid?* How does it happen that a boy from New Bedford, still young, still wet behind the ears, should become so enthused about Yiddish? Let's let him tell us himself. Ladies and gentlemen, without further ado, Aaron Lansky!"

As I walked toward the microphone, Bob Towers reached out with another bone-crushing handshake, pulled me close, and whispered into my ear, "Go ahead, kid, knock 'em dead!"

Given the age of the audience, I was afraid to take his charge too literally. I lowered the microphone to my own height, looked out at the audience, and offered a tentative *"Sholem aleykhem."*

"Aleykhem sholem!" thundered the crowd in the proper Yiddish response.

"Un ver redt a Yidish vort?" I continued in Yiddish. ("Who here speaks Yiddish?")

"Vu den? (What else?)*"* came the response, and already I had my first round of applause. This was clearly a different audience—and a different pacing—than I was used to. I spoke for forty-five minutes, showing slides and telling about my adventures on the road. I told about saving books from basements and Dumpsters, I told a lot of funny stories, but I also spoke seriously about historical continuity and cultural preservation, about the need to transcend nostalgia and lachrymose fixations and develop a practical program to convey historical consciousness to the next generation. I ended, of course, with an appeal for the Yiddish Book Center.

The audience loved it. Before the applause could die down Bob Towers bounded onto the stage and grabbed the microphone from my hand. "Ladies and gentlemen! Ladies and gentlemen!" he yelled, hugging me to his side like a bar mitzvah boy. "Ladies and gentlemen, Aaron Lansky!"

The crowd was going wild, Towers waving them on with his right hand while his left hand held me tight, my face pressed sideways against his nylon jogging suit. And then, when the applause finally subsided, he released me and stepped to the front of the stage.

"Ladies and gentlemen, I've been in this game we call show business for more than thirty years. *Thirty years.* I've seen the best of them, I've seen them come and I've seen them go. And I want to tell you that never—*never*—in all that time have I seen a performance like this one. No, not since a young man named Cha-im Weiz-mann spoke from this very stage here in the Cotillion Room. This is the real thing. This is culture. This is an undiscovered talent." He paused to catch his breath. "Ladies and gentlemen, I've known you for a long time now, and I don't mind telling you—this young man just knocked me on my *arse!*"

Again the crowd was clapping, louder and louder, and then some of them were on their feet. I thought it was a standing ovation until, one by one, they turned around and began pushing one another in a mad dash for the door. Bob Towers was right. These were old people; they had to go to the bathroom.

The lunch that followed my lecture almost defied description. There were five full courses, each with a half dozen selections. When I hesitated in choosing my "cold fish" appetizer—I couldn't decide between the pickled herring, smoked herring, matjes herring, herring in cream sauce, gefilte fish with horseradish, smoked sable, and pickled whitefish in aspic—the woman next to me jumped in and ordered for me. "He'll have one of everything," she instructed the waiter, "and while you're at it you can bring two more plates of gefilte fish for the table." I was just digging into my second dessert, stewed prune compote topped with six inches of whipped cream, when the voice of Bob Towers came bellowing over the PA.

"Today, three hundred people were in the Cotillion Room for a lecture by a certain young man," he informed the assembled diners, "and two thousand and three hundred others were cheated. *Cheated!* I don't mind telling you: this young man was *squandered* here at the Concord this morning."

As though to make amends, after lunch Mr. Towers packed me and Roger into his Cadillac Eldorado and took us to see Murray Posner, the owner of a nearby resort. I thought I was there to ask Mr. Posner for a contribution; he thought he was interviewing me for a new act.

"Where else have you performed?" Murray asked me from behind a copy of *Variety*.

"Well, I don't perform, exactly," I answered, "but I have spoken at synagogues, and I lecture from time to time at colleges and universities—"

"Universities?" Murray sputtered. "Did he say universities? Worst audience in the world. I spoke at a university once. They invited me to speak about the hotel industry. Believe me, I've got a pretty good routine on this, I've used it many times before, and I know where I'm supposed to get reactions: chuckles, laughs, applause. Son of a bitch, I stand up there and it's a grim audience! All these young people in jeans and sneakers. I opened it up for questions. These bastards are dead serious—they're taking notes! I realized later, they weren't an audience, they were *students*. They take notes and get grades. They're not there to laugh. Who wants to perform for an audience like that?"

"Look, Murray," said Mr. Towers, "he didn't come here to listen to your sob stories. Give him a chance to talk."

"Bob, will you shut up. I know you're in pain, but *I'm* conducting this interview. Let me do it my way. Okay, Lansky, you're on, tell me some stories."

I took a deep breath and began describing some of the collection adventures I had related that morning at the Concord, in hopes they would underscore the urgency of collecting books and the need for stable funding.

"Tell him the Philadelphia story!" shouted Towers, asking for a particular tale from the morning's repertoire.

"*The Philadelphia Story?*" said Murray. "Wait a minute, wait a minute . . . Cary Grant and Katharine Hepburn. Wasn't Jimmy Stewart in that one too? I thought so. Forget *The Philadelphia Story,* I already saw the movie. What else you got?"

I earnestly related story after story, hoping to convince Murray of the importance of the cause. When I finished, rather than pulling out his checkbook and making a contribution, he turned to Roger, whom he assumed was my writer, and offered a long list of suggestions. "Overall it's great material," he said. "I like the realism, the detail, but you're going to have to play it up more for our audience. You know, a little flourish, a little polish, a little shmaltz. Take that Bronx routine for example: Your timing's good, but maybe you could introduce another character to . . ."

I did my best to set things straight, but I don't think he or Bob Towers ever really understood. As we were leaving, Murray followed us to the door. "I have just one more question for you," he called after me, "What's all this about collecting Yiddish books? I mean, the stories are good, it's definitely a new act—but can't you find an easier way to get your material?"

It was quiet when we got back to the Concord. The couches outside the dining room were full of snoring guests too *ongeshtupt* from lunch to make it back to their rooms for an afternoon nap. Presumably when they awoke four hours later they would be first in line for dinner.

For our part, we decided to head down to the health club to work off our lunch before starting for home. This was the Borscht Belt idea of exercise: one weight machine, two stationary bicycles, and four cavernous *shvitz* baths: two steam and two sauna.

The particular steam bath we chose was crowded, so we had to settle for seats on the lower bench. Above us, on the much hotter upper bench, a tough old Jew with a big smile and a great overhanging belly sat stark naked, presiding over an endless round robin of off-color Jewish jokes, most of them about the sex lives of Yiddish-speaking Jews in their eighties. Before each one, the unclothed impresario would look at me and Roger and a few other younger men on the lower bench and proclaim, "Now, you young fellas aren't gonna understand this one." Every time the door opened and a new person entered, someone would yell, *"Er iz an antisemit, redt Yidish!* (He's an anti-Semite, speak Yiddish!)"

At the end of the day, as the bellhop was loading my rucksack into the Honda, the Concord's owner approached me. He wanted me to sign a contract to perform every Jewish holiday—six times a year. "You're new, you're refreshing!" he assured me. "No one else is doing this particular material." I was flattered, but I also knew that if I spent my *yonteyvim* at the Concord I wouldn't stay refreshing for long, so I politely declined, explaining that my real work was rescuing Yiddish books. The owner nodded, but before I drove away he called after me, *"We'll be in touch!"*

He was as good as his word. Every February for the next several years he called to invite me back for Pesakh. Each time I said no, and each time he responded, "No problem, I understand, you already *have* a booking for Pesakh."

Even if I had agreed, my show-business career would have been short-lived. In 1998 the Concord, like the other giants before it, closed its doors as a Jewish hotel. (It later reopened as a golf resort.) Still, I'm grateful to Bob Towers for the chance to speak there when I did. I went expecting to see Jews denigrating Yiddish, and instead I found them reveling in it: on stage, in the *shvitz,* at meals, in a thousand private jokes and conversations. They enjoyed dropping Yiddish words the way they enjoyed stuffing themselves with *flunken* and *ptsha* (jellied calves' feet): It was a forbidden pleasure, a chance to come out of the closet, if only for a week, to be themselves in a mountain redoubt where there were no *goyim* to hear. True, the Concord *shvitz* was hardly the reading room of the Bodleian, and there's a difference between laughing at Yiddish jokes and reading Yiddish books. Still, here among their own, these English-speaking Jews seemed to enjoy Yiddish a lot more than I expected. On the ride home I started thinking, What if those who proclaimed the death of Yiddish were wrong? What if the patrons of the Concord weren't the only ones? What if all across America there were Jews who still held a closeted affection for Yiddish? All I had to do was figure out a way to reach them, and I just might stand a chance of signing up enough members to save the world's Yiddish books after all.

20. Kaddish

If it took a certain optimism to think I might find support for Yiddish among the denizens of the Concord *shvitz,* at the home of Sam and Leah Ostroff the language remained as natural as breathing. Through the first half of the 1980s, as the pace of book collection quickened, Sam and Leah remained our staunchest allies. Every few weeks we made the pilgrimage to Sea Gate for a ten-course breakfast, followed by a busy day of zamlering. When I'd phone ahead to ask what we could bring, Sam always gave the same answer: "The holes for the bagels."

We weren't the only ones to enjoy the Ostroffs' hospitality. In the summer of 1983 a young *New York Times* reporter named Doug McGill was assigned to accompany me and Sharon on a day of book collecting in New York, and we agreed to begin with a 7:00 A.M. breakfast at the Ostroffs' home. Poor Doug: twenty-nine years old, not Jewish, recently transplanted from Minnesota, he never knew what hit him. After welcoming him with kisses, the Ostroffs immediately launched into a heated discussion about his name. In Hebrew the word *dog* (or *dag*) means fish. "I just don't understand," Mrs. Ostroff said, "such a nice-looking boy, he doesn't look like a fish, why do they call him Dog?"

Once we cleared up the confusion Doug tried to pull his notebook from his pocket in order to ask a few questions of his own, but the Ostroffs were aghast. "Oh no, mister," said Sam, "a car doesn't go without gasoline, a reporter doesn't go without eating. First you'll eat, then we'll talk."

The Ostroffs led us into the living room, where they had laid out their usual repast, only this time it wasn't just a meal, it was an ethnographic experience. Sam started from square one. "Now, Doug," he explained, "this first dish, you probably don't have it in Minnesota, it's called lox, L-O-X. It comes in two kinds, Nova and regular, we bought both today, you should be able to try them. You eat it with this hard role with the hole in the middle, that's called a bagel. Some people like to shmear a little cream cheese first. Me, I'm a Litvak, that means I come from Lithuania, so I put on a little onion too—okay, Leah's right, maybe a *lot* of onion—but *you* don't have to if you don't want to, as long as you take plenty of lox."

Doug was game, sampling everything from the matjes herring with onion to the cucumber, scallion, and radish salad with sour cream. But Mrs. Ostroff still wasn't satisfied. When she cleared the table and saw there was a little food left on Doug's plate, she shook her head and said in Yiddish, "It's no wonder they call him Dog—he *eats* like a fish!"

After breakfast Sam, Doug, Sharon, and I climbed into the van to begin the day's rounds. Mrs. Ostroff stayed home to cook the next meal. Sam had phoned everyone the day before to let them know when we'd be coming, which gave them all ample time to prepare their own "real Jewish meal" in Doug's honor. Surprisingly, they took his presence for granted: After all, they were handing over their Yiddish libraries, a lifetime of books, so why *shouldn't* the *Times* send a reporter?

At six foot three, Doug towered over these elderly Jews, but that didn't stop them from addressing him in the diminutive: *"Nu tatele* (So, little father)," they'd say, "maybe just one more piece of *kugl?"*

Presumption knew no bounds. "McGill, McGill," mused one old man when they met, "there used to be a writer for the *New Masses*, A. B. Magill, maybe you're related?"

At the next apartment Doug took out his notebook. "Do you mind if I ask a few questions?" he politely inquired.

"You want to ask *me* questions?" the hostess replied. "First I have to ask *you* a question: Do you want your cake with ice cream or with whipped cream from the can?"

"Neither, please," said Doug, "you see, we just ate—"

"Nonsense," the woman interrupted, "a big boy like you, you need to eat! Now *zets zikh*, sit!"

Doug remained standing. The woman, who barely came up to his waist, grabbed his belt and pulled him down hard onto a dining room chair. "Such a big boy, *kaynehore* (no evil eye), for you I'll give both: the ice cream *and* the whipped cream!"

At the next apartment, in a high-rise building on Coney Island, our hostess greeted us not only with food but with song. As soon as we walked in the door she dropped the tone arm on her record player, launching a full-blast rendition of *"Di grine kuzine* (My Greenhorn Cousin)"* by the Barry Sisters:

"S'IZ BAY MIR GEKUMEN A KUZINE . . ."

The sound was deafening.

"EXCUSE ME," Sharon shouted over the music, *"But it's a little LOUD! Maybe you could turn it down so we can talk?"*

"OH NO," the woman shouted back, *"a reporter from the* New York TIMES *is here, it's important he should listen to our Yiddishe music, he'll write about it in the paper, everyone should know how GOOD it sounds!"*

Doug didn't need to write about it in the paper—the music was so loud they could hear it in Manhattan.

Only one woman was unprepared for our arrival.

"GEY AVEK! (GO AWAY!)"* she yelled.

"I think you don't understand," I politely explained to the closed door. "We're here for the books, the Yiddish books."

Vos? Vos vilstu fun mir? Ganovim! Gazlonim! Gey avek fun danet! (What? What do you want from me? Thieves! Robbers! Get out of here!)"

"Yiddish books!" I repeated, more loudly this time.

"Gey shoyn avek! Loz mikh tsuru! (Go away! Leave me alone!)"

"Maybe she doesn't speak English," Sharon suggested.

"Let me try," said Sam, whereupon he began pounding on the door and yelling at the top of his lungs, *"Bikher! Mir kumen far di bikher! YID-ISH-E BI-KHERRR!"*

Up and down the hall people were peering out through the chained doors of their apartments. Suddenly the door before us swung open.

"Yidishe bikher?" said a frail-looking woman in a quiet voice. "So why didn't you say so in the first place?"

Doug remained patient and good-natured through it all. He listened respectfully, looked at albums of family photographs, and even helped carry books. When Sam invited him and his girlfriend to return a week later for dinner, he accepted on the spot. Sam asked his girlfriend's name, so he could make her a pin of her English name in Hebrew letters, cut from an old silver spoon.

"I'll tell you the truth," Doug confided at the end of a long day of shlepping. "I'm a young reporter, I usually get the worst assignments. They send me to New Jersey because someone's dumping toxic waste, and when I get there no one wants to talk to me. But today . . . today every person I interviewed fed me first and kissed me afterward. It's an experience I'll never forget."

IT WAS MIDWINTER when Sam summoned us to the Beth Am building, an old Labor Zionist center in Brighton Beach. The organization had fallen on hard times in recent years and was forced to sublet its space to an ultraorthodox yeshiva. When the yeshiva moved in, the first thing the teachers did was to remove every last one of the eighteen thousand Yiddish books in the Beth Am library and throw them down the cellar stairs, locking the door behind them! No doubt they thought they were doing a mitzvah, a good deed, protecting their students from the corruption of modern literature. Luckily the building's custodian, a recent Soviet Jewish immigrant, did not share their sentiments: Having tipped us off, he was now on hand to let us in and help us remove the discarded books.

The basement was filled with huge, untidy piles of books, like coal heaps in a bunker. Many had landed with their covers bent backward. We borrowed a shopping cart from a nearby grocery store and set to work. When the *rosh yeshiva,* the principal, and his teachers arrived, they didn't apologize for what they had done; instead, they stood at the top of the stairs and glowered at us: *"Apikorsim!* (Heretics!)" they muttered as we passed, *"Shkotsim!* (Non-Jews!)"

Apikorsim? Shkotsim? Considering that they had just given the heave-ho to thousands of Jewish books that didn't even belong to them, and considering that they were now standing there with their arms crossed, not so much as raising a finger to help, while Sam Ostroff, at eighty-three and with a bad heart, puffed up and down the stairs, their epithets struck me as a bit thick. And misdirected. While it's true that some modern Jews turned to Yiddish as a substitute for religion, Sam, as it happened, was far more inclusive. He kept kosher, observed Shabbos, and went to shul, and unlike the black-hat crowd, he did so without forswearing the outside world in the process.

I had learned just how worldly Sam and Leah could be when Doug McGill asked them about their favorite writers:

"Do you like Sholem Aleichem or I. L. Peretz?" he inquired.

"Well, yes, I like Peretz *and* Sholem Aleichem," Leah answered, "but I'll tell you the truth, I also like Meller."

"Meller?" asked Doug, figuring his background research had failed to turn up this important Yiddish writer. "*Meller?* I'm not sure I've heard of him."

"Oh, of course, Meller, he's a very big writer," said Mrs. Ostroff. "Wait, I think I have one of his books here." With that she walked into her bedroom and returned with a dog-eared paperback of *The Naked and the Dead.* "You see," she said triumphantly, "here he is: Meller, *Norman* Meller."

For Sam and Leah, tradition wasn't ossified, a brittle relic that had to be guarded behind yeshiva walls; rather, it was alive, organic, resilient, the warp and woof of daily life. Their daily conversation was full of traditional references brought back down to earth. The summer before, when we all came for breakfast and Doug asked Sam why he kept kosher, he had a ready answer: "So when *Meshiekh* (the Messiah) comes he'll have where to eat." When I suggested that Sam stop serving long enough to sit down and join us, he said, "Today I don't have to sit down, it's not Pesakh." (On Pesakh, or Passover, Jews are commanded to sit casually at the festive table, to show that they are no longer slaves.) When Leah brought out one course too many, Sam said, "It's only July, and already she thinks it's time for *bdikes khumets*" (the ritual removal of the last crumb of leavened food before the spring festival of Passover). When, in the back of the van, Sharon began speaking to Doug about modern Yiddish literature, Sam leaned over to inform me that "*Shurn lernt im a kapitl tilim* (Sharon is teaching him a chapter of Psalms)."

But unlike the ultra-orthodox, the Ostroffs were not fundamentalists, they were not focused on the *pitshevkes,* the minutiae, of religious observance, and they preferred to adapt Jewish law as events warranted. Reasonably observant ourselves, we usually avoided travel on Friday, when Shabbos, the Jewish Sabbath, begins at sunset. But one day there was an urgent pick-up in New York that left us no choice. We set out before dawn that Friday morning, but there were more books than we expected and we fell further and further behind, until we were afraid we wouldn't make it back to Amherst in time. Leah offered to put us up for the night, but we had to get back. "It's all right," she said, "I have a better idea: I won't *bentsh likht* (light the Shabbos candles) until you get home; that way Shabbos won't be able to start, and you won't be *mekhalel Shabbos* (in violation of the Sabbath)." We arrived home well after dark; when we called the Ostroffs to tell them we were safe, Sam breathed a sigh of relief. "I'm so glad you're home," he said. "We couldn't eat until Leah *bentshed likht,* and to tell the truth we were starting to get a little hungry."

Sea Gate was changing in the early 1980s: As older, modern Jews died, young Hasidic families moved in. "Is that your shul?" Roger asked Sam one day as we walked together past a large synagogue. "God forbid," said Sam, "that's the *khsidishe* shul, the Hasidic shul. We go to the *Mentshishe* Shul." The Mentshishe Shul—I think Sam coined the phrase— means literally, the "human" shul: not "humanist," as in Ethical Culture, but "human," as in the kind of old-fashioned orthodox synagogue where tradition was important but people still came first.

Sam's version of orthodoxy was not without precedent. In his memoir, the Yiddish writer I. L. Peretz recalls how he grew up in Zamość in a home that had no running water: Every drop they used had to be carried from the well by a poor water carrier named Ayzikl. A particular guest used to come to their home who, to show how religious he was, performed the ritual handwashing before meals with far more water than was necessary. *"Frum af Ayzikls kheshbn,"* Peretz's mother observed. "Pious at Ayzikl's expense."

My friend Kenneth Turan, film critic for the *Los Angeles Times,* tells a similar story from his own childhood. One time a guest inadvertently mixed up a *milkhig* (dairy) fork with a *fleyshike,* one used for meat. "It's all right," his mother said. "God is too big a person to worry about things like that."

So there we were at the Beth Am Center in Brighton Beach, carrying load after load of books up from the basement while the *rosh yeshiva* and his minions looked at us with contempt, certain that they were the better Jews. By day's end our diesel truck — at Sam's insistence, we had rented the biggest one on the Ryder lot — was loaded floor to ceiling and stem to stern with nine tons of neatly stacked Yiddish books. I'm no mechanic, but I do know that we had far exceeded the truck's weight limit. We pulled away from the Beth Am with a shudder and trailed smoke down Mermaid Avenue until, not two blocks from the Sea Gate entrance, the truck broke down.

The mechanic at a nearby garage, a friend of Sam's, came to the rescue, but not before he made us promise, for safety's sake, to offload half the books in New York before heading back to Massachusetts. Leah walked over to meet us, and we all stood kibbitzing on the street while the mechanic did his work. Two hours later we were ready to go.

"Good," Sam said to us, "now you'll come to our house for dinner."

"I'm sorry," I said, "but we're already hours behind schedule, it's getting dark, and we've still got to unload half the books — there's no way we have time for dinner."

"You *must* come to dinner!"

"We *can't* come to dinner!"

"You must!"

"We can't!"

It was Leah who broke the impasse.

"Sam, don't make a big deal. *Kinder,* children, if you don't have time, it's okay, you'll come to my house, I'll *peck* you a *sneck.*"

It's a forty-minute drive from Sea Gate to the Lower East Side of Manhattan, where we were staying; with her "snack" we could have made it to California. Among the highlights I remember were challah and cream cheese, gefilte fish and *khreyn* (grated horseradish) wrapped in tin foil, egg salad sandwiches, three cans of sardines, marble cake, and halvah. There were also two tea bags and a plastic spoon, though what we were supposed to do with them in a moving truck was never quite clear.

Offloading half the books took a lot longer than we expected, and by the time we were through we had actually managed to eat most of Leah's snack. It was midnight before we pulled up in front of my friend Roger's apartment, padlocked the back of the truck, trudged upstairs, opened a few bottles of beer, and collapsed at the kitchen table. Then the phone rang!

"Aaron, I think it must be for you," said Roger, "because he's not speaking English."

I picked up the receiver with understandable trepidation.

"Hello?"

"Lahnsky? Ostroff! Sea Gate!"

"Khaver Ostroff," I said, *"s'iz a bisl shpet* (Mr. Ostroff, it's a little late) . . ."

"Never mind," said Sam, "we've been worried sick ever since you left our house!"

"What are you worried about?" I asked.

"Well," he said, "after you left we realized *az mir hobn fargesn ayntsupakn dos lokshn kugl, hobn mir gehat moyre, ir zolt nisht zayn hungerik!* (we realized that we forgot to pack the *lokshn kugl,* and we were afraid you might be hungry!)"

ALTHOUGH THE OSTROFFS' health was never great, they didn't let it stop them. When Sam went to the hospital for cataract surgery, he told me that he felt *"azoy vi a bild* (like a painting)."

"Like a painting?" I asked.

"Yo, ikh bin gevorn an eyn-eygiker, un ikh fil azoy vi a bild fun Picasso! (I've become a one-eyed person, and I feel like a painting by Picasso!)"

Even with a patch over one eye he kept on working: hanging posters, answering phone calls, scheduling pickups, and hopping in and out of our truck. Then one day in the fall of 1984 Leah spoke to me in confidence. "Don't tell Sam," she whispered, "but I think his health is not so good anymore. Maybe we should move to the Arbeter Ring Home, where they can take better care of him."

A month later it was Sam who pulled me aside. "I love it here in Sea Gate," he confided, "but you can see what's doing with Leah: She's becoming sometimes a little *oyverbotl*, a bit senile. Maybe it will be better for her in the nursing home."

So I wasn't altogether surprised when, in January of 1985, Sam called to say he had "one more bit of business" for us:

"We've picked up everyone else's books," he said. *"Itst zolstu kumen nemen* mayne *bikher* (Now it's time for you to come pick up *my* books)."

We agreed not only to pick up their books but to help them move out of their apartment and into the Workmen's Circle Home in the Bronx. And so the ritual Sam and Leah had helped us perform countless times — the passing of a *yerushe* from one generation to the next — now took place in their own apartment. We arrived on a slushy winter morning with a crew of five, the Center's van, and a rented diesel truck. Sam insisted that the Center take not only the books but their artwork and furniture. "Don't worry, whatever you don't need you'll sell, you'll use the money to save someone else's books."

They began, naturally, with their books, handing them to us like fine china, one volume at a time. Because they'd been friends with so many Yiddish writers, many of their books were personally inscribed. When their bookcases were empty they led us to an overflowing closet and pulled down a battered, black leather case. Inside was an antique, portable Yiddish typewriter, its platen and paper support folded neatly atop the keys. According to Sam, the machine had belonged to Lamed Shapiro, a writer whose stories of pogrom violence in the Ukraine in 1919 are among the most shockingly realistic in all of Yiddish literature.

"How did you get Lamed Shapiro's typewriter?" I asked in amazement.

"*Vu den?* He was a friend. For years, after the First World War, he lived in Hollywood, trying to invent some process for color film. It never worked. When he got older he went to Israel, it was a long trip in those days, so he left his typewriter with us, we should take care of it for him. What more can I tell you? He died and the typewriter's still here. He'd want better that you should have it now."

For us it was as though we had just been handed Shakespeare's pen.

And so the morning continued: books, magazines, artwork, original photographs of Yiddish writers—one treasure after another, each with a story all its own. My young colleagues and I listened attentively, acolytes at the Ostroffs' feet, until suddenly the spell was broken by a loud knock at the door, followed by the entrance of their forty-six-year-old son, his wife, and their teenage son. I'd never met the Ostroffs' son before. All I knew was that he had a Ph.D. in engineering, worked for a large corporation, and lived in the Connecticut suburbs with his wife and four children. But it didn't take long to see that he harbored little affection for his parents' world.

Which, to be fair, should not have been all that surprising. Intergenerational conflict is, after all, nothing new; I for one am not exactly a paragon of equanimity in my own parents' home, and neither was the younger Ostroff that day. He chose a few pieces of furniture (which he asked us to truck to Connecticut), bundled his parents into the backseat of his car, drove away, and did not look back. Sam and Leah, who had lived in the same community for sixty years, would never see Sea Gate again.

Without Sam and Leah, the apartment, which just that morning had been an oasis of culture and learning, was reduced to a few small, shabby rooms with sooty ceilings and faded walls. We loaded the van and the diesel truck, and four hours later arrived at the Workmen's Circle Home, a massive, yellow brick building that occupied almost a whole block in the Bronx. Sam had prevailed on the director, an eighty-year-old *landsman* from Zabludow, to let him take his tools and art supplies to the communal crafts room. But there was so much more than the director had bargained for that when we actually started unloading, he had to open an empty patient room for the overflow.

When we finished we found our way down a wide corridor to the Ostroffs' room. Like the rest of the building, it was immaculately clean, the tile floor polished to a high sheen. The single window looked out over a low roof to an inside courtyard; it was clear that the sun would never shine here. In one corner was a chrome-framed chair upholstered in baby blue Naugahyde that looked as if it had come from a doctor's waiting room. The only other furniture consisted of two metal hospital beds (each with its own commemorative plaque), two metal nightstands, and two brown metal bureaus. Having been delivered there by their son, the Ostroffs were sitting tentatively on the edge of their respective beds, looking older and more forlorn than I had ever seen them before.

"Lahnsky, we need you to help us," Mr. Ostroff said, speaking Yiddish (which hardly afforded privacy, since it seemed to be the predominant language of the entire home). "The room comes with two single beds. In sixty years Leah and I have never slept apart. How can I leave her alone now?"

I promised to see what I could do. While Sharon stayed with the Ostroffs, I went off to find a social worker, who explained that there was nothing to be done, since these were the only beds they had.

"How about if I drive back to Sea Gate and bring their old double bed?"

"No, I'm afraid not, old beds are made of wood, and wood isn't sanitary."

"Well, what if I buy a new double bed that's made out of metal?"

"No, that won't do either, all the sheets in the home are standardized for single beds. I'm afraid your friends are just going to have to adjust."

I returned to the Ostroffs' room to convey the bad news, but by now Leah had a new worry.

"What's wrong?" I asked.

"You and Sharon are our first guests," she said softly in Yiddish, her eyes filling with tears. "This isn't like in my apartment. Here I have no stove, no pots and pans, no table, no dishes. How can I welcome you to our new home if I can't give you what to eat?"

SAM DIED LESS than two months later. It was his son who called with the news and who invited me to deliver a *hesped,* a eulogy at his funeral. Sharon and I drove down together, stopping along the way to pick up Gella Fishman, a prominent Yiddish educator who had first met the Ostroffs when she was a young teacher in Sea Gate almost forty years before.

"The Ostroffs were like my parents," she said. "Leah was always *eydl* (refined), but Sam was a true *folksyid*. His hands were rough and strong, the hands of a worker. He reminded me of Chaim, in the story by Peretz."

It was the perfect tribute. In Peretz's story *"Sholem bayis*—Peace in the Home,"* Chaim is a *treger,* a poor Jew who makes his scanty living hauling heavy burdens on his back. One Shabbos an itinerant preacher speaks in the study house, extolling the virtues of *Oylem habo,* the World to Come. Chaim is enthralled.

"Tell me, Rebbe," Chaim beseeches after the sermon, "what can *I* do to earn a place in Paradise?"

"Study Jewish Law, my son," answered the teacher.

"I can't."

"Study the commentaries, religious legends. . . ."

"I can't."

"Recite the Psalms!"

"I haven't time!"

"Pray with devotion!"

"I don't know what the prayers mean!"

The teacher looks at him with compassion:

"What are you?" he asked.

"A street porter."

"Well then, do some service for the scholars."

"I beg pardon?"

"For instance, carry a few cans of water every day toward evening into the house of study, so that the students may have something to drink."

"Rabbi," he inquired further, "and my wife?"

[The rabbi answers in accordance with Jewish tradition.] "When a man sits on a chair in Paradise, his wife is his footstool."

Chaim thinks about this. He is very much in love with his resourceful and virtuous wife, Hannah. When he gets home and sees her reciting "God of Abraham," the Yiddish woman's prayer at the end of Shabbos, he decides to disregard tradition and take matters into his own hands.

"No Hannah." He flung his arms around her. "I won't have you be my footstool! I shall bend down to you and raise you and make you sit beside me. We shall sit both on one chair, just as we are doing now. We are so happy like that! Do you hear me, Hannah? You and I, we are going to sit in a chair together. *Der Rabeynu-shel-oylem vet muzn bashteyn!*—the Almighty will *have* to allow it!"

In other words, when the dictates of justice collide with those of tradition, tradition must give way. Even the most humble Jew has the right and the responsibility to change the world, and if he acts justly—as Sam Ostroff surely did—even God will have to accede.

Sam's funeral took place at the Parkside Chapel, a modern building on Flatbush Avenue near Avenue U. Fran and Roger were already there waiting for us. Although the rabbi was a cousin, he knew little about Sam's life. Fortunately there were other speakers who did. Sam's nephew, Harold Ostroff, was himself deeply immersed in the Yiddish world. He had spent years building union housing, and he was now a leader of the Workmen's Circle and general manager of the *Forward*. He spoke at length about Sam's character, his commitments and accomplishments, and informed us that at Sam's request copies of the *Forward* and *Pakn Treger* (*The Book Peddler*), the Yiddish Book Center's magazine, had been placed with him in the coffin. "I want I should have what to read when I get there," Sam had told him.

I, too, spoke that day, sharing stories of our adventures together during the last five years of Sam's life. And then, as the room hushed, his son got up to speak. To my surprise, he spoke movingly, respectfully, and most astonishingly he spoke in Yiddish—the first time he had done so in public, he said, since he was fourteen years old. We embraced each other afterward, and every unkind thought I had harbored since moving day melted away. *Gey zay a novi*—Go be a prophet. Go predict how things will turn out.

If it had been up to me, I would have buried Sam next to Sholem Aleichem, in the Workmen's Circle cemetery in Queens. Sam was, after all, precisely the sort of Jew the great writer celebrated and for whom he wrote. But there was no room left in the Workmen's Circle cemetery, so we drove an hour and a half to Paramus, New Jersey, for the interment. I helped carry the coffin and set it down by the open grave. The skies were gray, as it seems they always are over cemeteries. Three black crows circled overhead. Leah, looking frail, cried bitter tears. The cantor chanted the *"El moley rakhamim* (God of Mercy),"the rabbi led the family in the recitation of Kaddish, the ancient Aramaic prayer for the dead, and then the plain pine box was slowly lowered ground. Since it was an orthodox service, only men were allowed the honor of shoveling dirt into the grave. I shoveled with all my heart, again and again and again. When I finally looked up, the rabbi was gone, the mourners had returned to their cars, and only Sharon and I were left. Without hesitating, Sharon took the shovel from my hands, dug into the soft earth and, in contravention of Jewish tradition, threw in a shovelful of her own.

"Sam would have wanted it that way," she said firmly.

"*Un der Rabeynu-shel-oylem vet* muzn *bashteyn*," I thought. "And the Almighty will *have* to allow it."

21. A Job for the Young

When we first began collecting Yiddish books, in the early 1980s, 90 percent of the volumes we recovered came from the homes and hands of older, Yiddish-speaking Jews. Ten years later, most of our stops were in the suburbs, at the homes of American-born children and grandchildren who had inherited books they couldn't read. A generation was literally passing before our eyes.

One day not long after Sam Ostroff's funeral, we were summoned to a sprawling, modern mansion on Long Island. A West Indian maid in a black-and-white uniform answered the door, and not only did she not offer to feed us, she didn't even invite us inside. Instead she directed us around back to a four-car garage, where, stacked inside built-in wooden cabinets, were several hundred Yiddish books. According to the maid, they had belonged to the mother of the woman of the house.

As we set to work, a sullen teenage boy, probably thirteen or fourteen years old, came out of the house and sat down on the stoop to watch. His manner was aloof, but eventually curiosity got the better of him and he asked what we were doing.

"Picking up Yiddish books," we explained.

"No kidding," he said. "Whose are they?"

"Your grandmother's, apparently."

"What are they about?"

We picked up a random pile and showed him. The titles were impressive: world literature in Yiddish translation, social history, political theory, ethnography, literary criticism. The teenager was amazed.

"My grandmother's still alive, in a nursing home," he explained, "but she speaks with such a heavy accent, I didn't even know she could read."

He vowed then and there to visit her, to ask her where she came from and try to understand what her life was all about.

Encounters like this inspired us to reach out more actively to young people. In 1986 the Center introduced a summer internship program for college students. Our motivation was not entirely altruistic. The mountain of unopened boxes in our Holyoke warehouse had reached alarming heights, and given the nature of the work—unpacking and sorting dusty books in the ninety-degree heat of an un-air-conditioned factory loft—we decided it was definitely a job for the young. Since it was virtually impossible to find young people with prior Yiddish knowledge, we decided to entice students with a combination of work and study: intensive early-morning classes in Yiddish language, followed by a full day of shlepping and evening seminars in Jewish history and Yiddish literature in translation.

The schedule was demanding, and the response was astonishing. That first year we received a hundred applications for eight positions. Once our Web site was up and running, the number of inquiries increased to almost a thousand. It was harder to become an intern at the Yiddish Book Center—to be allowed to spend one's summer shlepping old books—than it was to get into Harvard. Why did so many students apply? "Because it's the closest you can get to a junior year abroad in Yiddish," one young man told us. "Because it's like an archaeological dig," observed another, referring to the thrill of excavating books from boxes that had lain unopened for thirty years or more. Almost every student we accepted was inspired by the experience, and a remarkable number went on to further study, until today our alumni are among the most promising, up-and-coming leaders of the field. Jeremy Dauber, who came to us straight out of high school, went on to study Yiddish literature at Harvard, continued his studies as a Rhodes Scholar at Oxford, directed our Great Jewish Books program, and is now professor of Yiddish literature at Columbia. Naomi Seidman became a professor of Jewish literature at Union Theological Seminary, in Berkeley, and wrote a provocative first book called *A Marriage Made in Heaven: The Sexual Politics of Yiddish and Hebrew.* Sarah Benor completed a Ph.D. in Yiddish linguistics at Stanford. Caraid O'Brien, a non-Jew, staged a popular production of Sholem Asch's *God of Vengeance,* an early-twentieth-century Yiddish play with lesbian themes that takes place in a bordello, and is now a leading authority on Yiddish theater. Andy Ingall studied Yiddish at Columbia and now runs the film and television program at the Jewish Museum in New York City. Leah Strigler earned degrees in Jewish education from the Jewish Theological Seminary and Bank Street College and now runs educational programs for a major Jewish foundation. Four former interns returned as members of our permanent staff: Jeffrey Aronofsky and Abra Greenberg were successive directors of our Yiddish Book Department. Lori McGlinchey, who wrote her Amherst College honors thesis on the Center, helped enlist thirty Hollywood actors and coproduced our thirteen-hour NPR radio series, *Jewish Short Stories from Eastern Europe and Beyond.* Gabe Hamilton, who began as an undergraduate fellow, became a Yiddish cataloger and, at the age of twenty-three, the director of our Steven Spielberg Digital Yiddish Library, responsible for the electronic preservation of most of modern Yiddish literature.

But no matter how successful our alumni are today, I remember them best as they were when I met them: in their cut-off shorts and

T-shirts, steel-toed work boots, leather gloves, and colorful headbands, reporting for their first day of work at our Holyoke annex. What with intensive classes and hands-on experience, they learned Yiddish extraordinarily quickly, although not without a few snags along the way.

One day we set up pallets for each of the most prolific writers—Sholem Aleichem, I. L. Peretz, Avrom Reisen, Sholem Asch—and left the students to open boxes and sort their contents accordingly. When I returned several hours later, I found a new pallet, piled to overflowing. "Guess what, Aaron? We discovered a really important writer that you didn't even know about. He wrote so many books we had to set up an extra pallet just for him!" one of the students informed me.

"No kidding," I said, "what's his name?"

"Gezamelte Shriftn," said the student.

It was an understandable mistake: With less than a week of Yiddish under their belts, the interns had set aside a tower of books by a new writer named Collected Works.

SOMETIMES IT SEEMED that Yiddish was a Rorschach test: Young people, especially, saw in it what they wanted to see. For atheists it was Jewishness without religion; for feminists, Judaism free from patriarchy; for those uncomfortable with Israeli politics, nationalism without Zionism; for socialists, the voice of proletarian struggle; for more contemporary radicals, a *shtokh* to the establishment. Although there was truth in each of these characterizations, they remained fragmentary at best; those who espoused them had rarely read deeply in what was, after all, an incredibly rich and multifaceted literature.

Not so our interns. Whatever their motivation for coming to the Center, they soon learned to appreciate Yiddish literature on its own terms, in all its unexpected glory. We trained them to spot especially valuable volumes, such as those published in the Soviet Union before World War II. The more Yiddish they learned, the more treasures they found. One warm summer evening, for example, they brought me a massive tome entitled *Leksikon fun politishe un fremdverter (Dictionary of Political and Foreign Terminology in Yiddish)*, edited by Dor-Ber Slutski and published in Kiev in 1929. Nearly eleven hundred pages long, the book was a scholar's dream: a lexical snapshot showing exactly how Jews perceived the world around them at a moment of great social and political change. In fact, the book was so significant I couldn't understand why I had never heard of it before. At that time, in the days before the Internet, we maintained duplicate card catalogs of two of the world's most important Yiddish research collections: those of the YIVO Institute, in New York, and the Hebraic section of the Library of Congress, in Washington, D.C. I found no card for Slutski's dictionary in either catalog. Next I searched the standard reference works. Nothing. It was well after dark before I finally found, in an obscure Yiddish volume, a mention of Slutski himself: "Slutski spent the entire decade of the 1920s working on a comprehensive dictionary of foreign and political terminology. The book was published in 1929. However, the authorities deemed it politically unacceptable and destroyed the entire print run. No copies survive."

My heart started thumping—I didn't know what to do first. I hid the book, locked the door, and turned on the burglar alarm. That night I could hardly sleep. Early the next morning I phoned Zachary Baker, one of the world's foremost authorities on Yiddish bibliography. He confirmed what I had begun to suspect: The book our interns discovered could well be the last copy on earth.

How had it survived—and how did it end up at the Center? We placed a query in *Pakn Treger,* our English-language magazine, asking for information. Two days later I received a phone call from a woman on Long Island. The book, she said, had belonged to her father, who in 1929 had traveled to the Soviet Union to visit his cousin, Slutski. They were together at the printing plant in Kiev when the first copies of the dictionary came off the press, and his cousin had handed him one as a gift. The American had placed it in his luggage and carried it home to New York, never knowing that just days or maybe even hours after he left, the NKVD, the secret police, had burst into the factory and destroyed the entire run. This one copy had remained in his private library until his death, whereupon his daughter mailed it to the Center, and our interns discovered it in an otherwise unassuming box of Yiddish books.

BOOKS WEREN'T THE only treasures we found. During our first internship program, in the summer of 1986, we received an urgent call from Arye Gottlieb, a rabbi in Paramus, New Jersey. He had just heard rumors, he said, of a two-car garage in Boro Park, a Hasidic neighborhood of Brooklyn, that was "literally filled to the rafters" with Yiddish and Hebrew sheet music. I was skeptical. By that point we had collected more than six hundred thousand Yiddish books, and in all that time had found fewer than one hundred fifty intact folios of sheet music. It wasn't because immigrant Jews didn't like music; to the contrary, they liked it too much. The sheet music they bought was in almost constant use, leafed through at the piano (a surprisingly common fixture even in poor immigrant homes), passed around for family sing-alongs, opened and closed and opened again until few copies remained.

Or so we thought. As Rabbi Gottlieb explained, much of the Yiddish and Hebrew sheet music in America was published by a company called Metro Music, located in the heart of the Yiddish theater district on New York's Second Avenue. The company sold the scores of the latest Yiddish theater hits, as well as cantorial music, art songs, folk songs, socialist anthems, and work songs of the *halutzim,* the Jewish pioneers in the Land of Israel. Metro Music went out of business in the early 1970s and sold its entire back stock—an astonishing *eighty-five thousand* brand-new, unsold folios—to a group of private investors, who hoped to resell the music on the commercial market.

The investors were ahead of their time: The klezmer revival hadn't yet begun, and demand for Yiddish sheet music was limited at best. This remarkable treasure trove might well have been lost were it not for the heroic intervention of a young, religious Jew named Sidney Rimmer. A part-time cantor, Mr. Rimmer realized that there was a great deal of *khazones,* cantorial music, mixed in with the Metro Music stock, and he saw it as a mitzvah, a good deed, to save it all, regardless of its commercial value. So he made the necessary business arrangements, cleared out a two-car garage behind his Boro Park home, filled it with secondhand steel shelving, and carefully stored all eighty-five thousand pieces. Many were still packed in the publisher's original brown-paper bundles, the oldest sheets dated to the 1890s, and virtually all were in mint condition.

And there they lay. Occasionally a local cantor would hear of the collection and come to Mr. Rimmer in search of a particular piece of liturgical music. For the most part, though, the existence of these folios—the largest single collection of unsold Yiddish and Hebrew sheet music in the world—remained largely unknown.

When Rabbi Gottlieb explained all this to us, we immediately phoned Mr. Rimmer. He was thrilled to hear from us, eager to have the music returned to active use, and more eager still to get his garage back after all these years. "Come as soon as you can," he said. "It's all yours."

Two days later, on a hot, muggy morning in late July, two interns, Elliot Glist and Jennifer Luddy, joined me in the cab of a big, yellow rental truck. Mr. Rimmer, who was standing in the middle of the street waiting for us, turned out to be a friendly, clean-shaven, relatively modern man in a short-sleeved shirt and small black yarmulke. He directed us down a narrow alleyway beside his house. The truck was so tall it necessitated the removal of the *eruv,* the ritual Sabbath boundary wire stretched overhead. When he pulled open the double doors to his detached brick garage, we understood just what a mitzvah he had done.

We set up a ramp, brought out the hand trucks, and began loading. The day was *hot,* ninety-two in the shade, and the humidity was palpable. Elliot and I were wearing cut-off shorts and T-shirts; Jennifer had on gauzy pastel shorts and a matching sleeveless top, with a generous display of *pupik* in between. Although this was not exactly regulation dress for Boro Park, Mr. Rimmer, his wife, and two children could not have been less judgmental. In fact, the only problem came at noon, when it was time to break for lunch.

"Is there a restaurant nearby?" I asked.

"Yes," said Mr. Rimmer, "but I'm afraid it's closed. You see, today is the Seventeenth of Tammuz."

It took a moment for the significance of the Hebrew date to register. Of course! Sheva-esrey Tammuz was an obscure Jewish fast day . . . obscure for us, that is. We realized with sinking hearts that there'd be no lunch here in Boro Park that day—which was not a great problem, since it was too hot to eat anyway. What was a problem was thirst. We had depleted our own water bottles long since, and we were sweating so profusely that the Rimmers finally concluded it was *pikuah nefesh,* a matter of life and death—a Jewish legal concept that trumped most other commandments and allowed them to bring us a welcome pitcher of ice water.

After working all day we spent the night in Great Neck, where Sidney and Ruth Berg treated us to a huge dinner in an air-conditioned restaurant. The next day an excited crew of interns was on hand in Holyoke to help us unload. It took months to sort and catalog all eighty-five thousand folios, which boiled down to roughly eleven hundred discrete titles, most with wonderfully ornate covers. There were old favorites, such as "'*Rumania, Rumania'*—The Sensational Song Hit Starring Aaron Lebedeff!" and "That Tremendous Success of the People's Theater, '*Der Idisher Yenke Dudl*' (The Jewish Yankee Doodle)!" by Boris Tomashevsky, the grandfather of the conductor Michael Tilson

Thomas. *"Di Yidishe shikse"* by Dora Weisman is about the travails of a newly arrived Jewish immigrant. Zionist favorites included *"A folk on a heym* (A People Without a Home)," *"Erets-Yisroel iz undzer land!* (The Land of Israel Is Our Home!)," and *"Prezident Artur Tsions shif* (President Arthur, Zion's Ship)," a celebration of the S.S. *President Arthur* of the American Palestine Line, which had delivered Jewish pioneers to "Zion's Gate." Of course, there were arrangements by all the great cantors: Moyshe Oysher, Joseph Rumshinsky, and Yossele Rosenblatt. There were many love songs—all of them sad. Thirty or forty titles concerned themselves with immigrant mothers: "A Letter to Mama," "A Mother's Heart," "A Mother Is the Best Friend," "When There Is No Mother," "Mamenyu, Buy Me That!" "Can a Mother Be Guilty?" "A Mother's *Nakhes*," and "A Mother's Tears."

Father songs? There were only two: *"Narishe tates* (Foolish Fathers)" and—though it wasn't until I had children of my own that I was able to appreciate it—*"A tate iz nisht keyn mame* (A Father Is Not a Mother)."

22. The Four Corners of the Earth

When Merriam-Webster published its dictionary of "the world's seven most widely spoken languages" in 1966, Yiddish was one of them. That's not because so many people spoke the language (at its peak, the number never exceeded one half of one percent of the world's population) but because those who did speak it were so widely scattered. Fleeing persecution in Eastern Europe, Yiddish-speaking Jews found refuge in *arbe kanfes ha'orets,* the four corners of the earth, and wherever they went they brought, bought, or published Yiddish books. When those Jews died or, as sometimes happened, when new political upheaval forced them to flee yet again, it fell to us and our *zamlers* to track down the books they left behind.

Not long ago, on a warm spring morning, a tractor-trailer backed up to the loading dock of our Amherst building. On board was a huge wooden crate with the improbable return address of Bulawayo, Zimbabwe. Zimbabwe was once the British colony of Rhodesia, where some five thousand Jews took refuge before World War II. Successful in business, they created Jewish schools, synagogues, and cultural centers, but in the 1970s, as colonialism unraveled, most took flight, abandoning large numbers of Yiddish books. It was a local rabbi named Bryan Opert, our only zamler on the African continent north of Johannesburg, who rounded them up, packed them into this homemade crate, and dispatched them by ship to Amherst, by way of Harare, Capetown, and Boston.

The crate was so big that it took most of our staff to wrestle it off the truck and two crowbars and a stepladder to open it. Inside were hundreds of volumes, many of them exceedingly rare, such as prewar imprints from Vilna, a Zionist pamphlet published in Tel Aviv in 1938, and various *yizkor* books and Holocaust memoirs. But most interesting by far were Yiddish books written and published in Africa. One, *Unter afrikaner zun (Under the African Sun),* sounded like a Jewish version of Hemingway. Another, *Udtshorn: Yerushalayim d'Afrike (Oudtshoorn: The Jerusalem of Africa),* was the chronicle of a commune of Yiddish-speaking ostrich farmers who, before styles changed, supplied the lucrative market of feathers for women's hats. Most of these African imprints were titles we'd never seen before, and we immediately set them aside for cataloging and scanning. A short time later, the day before Yom Kippur 2003, we received word that the Bulawayo synagogue had burned to the ground. Had Rabbi Opert not sent us the books when he did, they would surely have been lost.

I MADE MY first attempt to organize book collection in Israel in the late 1980s, when I accepted an invitation to address the Veltrat, the World Council on Yiddish. A thousand delegates from around the world crowded into the ballroom of a faded beachfront hotel in Tel Aviv for the three-day conference. When they rose to sing the *Hatikvah,* the national anthem, at the start of the first session, they used the opportunity to get better seats, jostling one another and pushing their metal chairs forward like so many mechanical walkers, so that by the time the anthem was over the neat rows were in shambles and the entire audience was jammed together as close to the stage as they could get. I was seated on the stage, at a long head table with delegates from two dozen countries, each of whom was supposed to speak for five minutes. Instead, they spoke—or rather shouted—for a half hour each, invoking over and over again the familiar refrain, *"Vu iz undzer yugnt?—* Where are our youth?" Although the chairman pounded away with his heavy rubber mallet (the sort used to bang hubcaps onto a car), some speakers refused to relinquish the microphone, giving rise to several onstage scuffles. My scheduled 3:00 P.M. lecture—an hour-long slide show and appeal for books—finally took place at 7:30 in the evening. It wasn't enough that I had to address a thousand people in Yiddish; the whole time I spoke, the chairman was whacking me from behind with a rolled-up newspaper, loudly whispering, *"Gikher! Gikher!* (Quicker! Quicker!)" I spent the next two days hanging out in the back of the hall with the Israeli sound crew (the only other young people I could find), or else lying by the hotel's empty swimming pool reading Henry Beston's *The Outermost House*—about as far from Yiddish as I could get. This was not the organization that was going to help us collect Yiddish books in Israel.

Then in 1991, UNESCO passed a resolution—over the objection of its Arab members—declaring Yiddish "an endangered language" and calling for immediate steps to assure its preservation. I was invited to join delegates from Canada, France, Holland, Hungary, Israel, Mexico, Poland, and the United States (the Soviet delegates had been denied visas) for three days of intensive deliberations in Israel to decide what the world should do. The scholar Chone Shmeruk presided as chairman, and Avrom Sutzkever, arguably the greatest living Yiddish writer, lent a certain gravity to the proceedings. We labored conscientiously for three days. On the last night I was assigned the task of drafting the final resolutions—in English, since despite UNESCO's sudden embrace of Yiddish, no one there could actually read it. Working in my

Jerusalem hotel room on a then state-of-the-art, fourteen-pound laptop computer, I finished at midnight and, without thinking, plugged in my brand-new portable printer. *Kaboom.* Apparently the printer wasn't wired for foreign current, because it blew its main circuit board, along with every light on the floor. Not knowing where else to turn, I phoned a young Yiddish performer named Mendy Cahan, whom I had met earlier that evening. A native Yiddish-speaker from Antwerp, where his Hasidic family worked in the diamond trade, Mendy was now a student of Yiddish literature at Hebrew University. As I suspected, he owned a printer, he and his girlfriend were up late anyway, and they invited me over. The espresso was already steaming when I got there, we talked for hours, and by the time I left, proposal in hand, he'd accepted my invitation to serve as a faculty member and *tumler*-at-large (a sort of all-purpose emcee and entertainer) at our upcoming "Winter Program in Yiddish Culture" in San Diego.

Mendy was even younger than I and nothing if not charismatic. What's more, his Yiddish was perfect. As part of our program we had scheduled a guided tour of the San Diego Zoo, and we enlisted Mendy to offer a simultaneous Yiddish translation. Of course all languages reflect the concerns of those who speak them, and Yiddish is therefore not exactly rife with biological terminology. So before we headed west, we asked Dr. Mordkhe Schaechter, a leading Yiddish linguist and a master of neologisms, to prepare a glossary for us. He accepted the challenge and outdid Adam himself in giving names to all the animals, beginning with aardvark *(dos erd-khazerl)* and boa constrictor *(di boa-shlang)* and continuing through hornbill *(der shoyfer-shnobl)*, koala *(dos zekl-berele)*, panda *(der ketsisher ber)*, porcupine *(der shtekhl-khazer)*, rattlesnake *(di klapershlang)*, rhinoceros *(der noz-horn)*, yak *(der yak)*, and zebra *(di zebre)*.

Mendy took his place in the front of the bus, ready to render into *mame loshn* the running commentary of our two young, khaki-clad,

English-speaking guides. Microphone in hand, he managed to keep up with them sentence for sentence, *vilde khaye* for *vilde khaye* (wild animal for wild animal), adding enough Yiddish commentary of his own to convulse our passengers with laughter, turn the head of more than one startled Jewish pedestrian, and make ours the loudest and most uproarious bus in the zoo. It wasn't until we got to the snake house that the official guides, who'd been playfully trying to stump Mendy from the outset, were sure they finally had him. "Over there are the boa constrictors," one guide explained. "We used to feed them live rats. But snakes don't eat very often, and if they weren't hungry, then instead of the snakes eating the rats, the rats would eat the snakes. That's why we now feed them dead rats instead." She then turned to Mendy and said with a wide smile, "Okay, translate *that!*"

Mendy didn't miss a beat. *"Raboysay,"* he said in his folksy Yiddish, *"vos ken ikh aykh zogn? S'iz geven a gantser 'Khad Gadyo' do!* (Friends, what can I tell you? The feeding practices here were something right out of *'Chad Gadyah!'*)" a familiar Aramaic song about serial death cheerily if uncomprehendingly sung by Jews every year at the Passover seder. Sholem Aleichem himself could not have done better.

In short, Mendy was a thoroughly modern young man who understood Yiddish culture from the top of his head to the tips of his toes, and I decided then and there to give him a new and even more challenging assignment: to open an office for us in Israel. The truth be told, the Israel office of the National Yiddish Book Center was never quite as grandiose as its name implied. It was located, in fact, in a Jerusalem basement that Mendy and his friends cleared out, painted, and fitted with homemade shelves. But they did collect books. Mendy traveled the country, speaking at Yiddish clubs and cultural centers, appearing on radio and television, even winning an official handshake and congratulations, in Yiddish, from the country's president—no small feat when you consider how energetically most of the early Zionist pioneers had rejected their native Yiddish. Because Yiddish was no longer a threat (it was now being taught in most Israeli universities and even some high schools), Mendy's efforts met with more enthusiasm than derision, and before long he was shipping thousands of volumes to Massachusetts.

Unfortunately, they weren't exactly the unique titles we were looking for, since most of Israel's Yiddish readers had arrived straight from the liberated death camps and displaced persons camps of Europe, and they had no books to carry with them to their new home. Virtually all the books Mendy found were new imprints, published in Israel after the war, all of which we had seen before. Eventually we spun off our Israel office into an organization of its own, which Mendy dubbed *Yung Yidish,* Young Yiddish. The basement storeroom was transformed once again, this time into a Yiddish cabaret and coffeehouse. Mendy did much to make Yiddish fashionable among a certain cadre of young Israelis; but as for one-of-a-kind titles, it was apparent that the Jewish homeland was not the place to find them.

OUR ZAMLERS HAVE shipped us priceless volumes from Costa Rica, Uruguay, Chile, and Brazil. With the help of a professional translator named Jacqueline Tornell, we traveled to Mexico City and returned with several thousand volumes. But nowhere in Latin America did we find more—or more important—Yiddish books than in Argentina, where, despite (or perhaps because of) widespread anti-Semitism, Yiddish flourished among its estimated five hundred thousand Jews to a degree unknown in most other countries.

As with Mendy Cahan in Israel, in Argentina, too, we had an indomitable ally. Mark Swiatlo was a Polish Jewish refugee who fled to Argentina after the war and lived there for many years before finally resettling in southern Florida. Well past the age when others were content to spend their days golfing in the sun, he set out single-handedly to build one of the world's great Yiddish research collections at Florida Atlantic University in Boca Raton. It didn't matter that FAU then had relatively few Jewish students and no courses in Yiddish or modern Jewish studies. If he built it, they would come. With the backing of the library director, Dr. William Miller, Mark began traveling back and forth to Buenos Aires, calling on his many friends and contacts and returning each time with thousands of Yiddish books.

By the time Mark and I met, in the late 1980s, the situation was out of control. Having opened the flood gates, Mark, like the Sorcerer's Apprentice, could hardly be expected to close them, and soon enough FAU's Yiddish collection had taken over an entire floor of the university's five-story library. There were thousands upon thousands of duplicates, many of them valuable South American imprints, and there were also lacunae: titles published in Europe and North America that Mark had been unable to find south of the River Platte. So we decided it was time for a *shidekh* — to exchange his proliferating duplicates, which he didn't need, for selected titles from our collection that he could find nowhere else.

Appearances are often deceiving. At first glance Mark looked like someone's *zeyde,* a little old Jewish man from the Old Country. But beneath his mild-mannered and disarmingly charming exterior, he was one of the smartest and toughest negotiators I have ever known. At first I thought we had won the better half of the bargain: For every Yiddish or Hebrew title he chose from our collection, he would send us three duplicates from his, including rare imprints from Buenos Aires, Montevideo, Santiago, and Rio de Janeiro. What we underestimated in our negotiations was Mark's tenacity: For the next ten years he was constantly on the phone with our staff, *haking a tshaynik* (literally, banging on a tea kettle) to get them to drop everything and scour our warehouse for one or another title. But over the years we developed a strong mutual respect, and eventually he began sending us more titles than we expected: literature, memoirs, essays, and scholarship—an entire Yiddish universe from the far side of the world.

Without a doubt, Mark's greatest coup was the discovery of thousands of brand-new, long-lost copies of *Dos Poylishe yidntum* (Polish Jewry): a 175-volume series published in Buenos Aires between 1946 and 1966. Conceived in response to the Holocaust, some of the series' titles—such as *Malka Ovshiani Tells Her Tale,* one of the first Holocaust memoirs by a Jewish woman; or works by survivors such as Hillel Seidman, Jonas Turkow, Shlomo Frank, and Szmerke Kaczerginski— were among the most significant first-person accounts published in any language in the years immediately following the catastrophe. Other titles—memoirs, novels, poems, dramas, Hasidic portraits, and ethnographic and historical studies—chronicled not the Holocaust itself, not the process of destruction, but rather the rich, complex, multifaceted tapestry of Polish Jewish life that the Nazis sought to destroy. Many of these are now regarded as classics: Yehoshua Perle's *Yidn fun a gants yor (Everyday Jews);* Menachem Kipnis's *One Hundred Folksongs;* Chaim Grade's *Pleytim (Refugees)* and *Shayn fun farloshene shtern (The Glow of Extinguished Stars);* Rokhl Korn's *Heym un heymlozikayt (Home and Homelessness);* novels by Sholem Asch, Y. Y. Trunk, and Mordkhe Strigler; and Elie Wiesel's *Un di velt hot geshvign (And the World Kept Silent),* better known through its later incarnation as *Night.*

When they first appeared, the successive titles of Polish Jewry were instant best-sellers, both in Argentina and abroad. Avrom Novershtern, who grew up in Argentina and is now professor of Yiddish literature at the Hebrew University in Jerusalem, recalls that "in hundreds of Jewish homes throughout Argentina one could immediately recognize the shelves of volumes standing back-to-back in their distinctive black bindings—a modern type of *Zeykher Likhurbm* (Holocaust Memorial)." The books proved so popular that, as early as 1950, a list printed in the front of each volume indicated that many of the titles were already *oysfarkoyft,* sold out. It wasn't until Mark Swiatlo smoked them out in 1991 that the world learned of the existence of thousands of brand-new copies—including every one of the purportedly sold-out titles—that had been misplaced and forgotten in a Buenos Aires warehouse since the late 1940s!

We raised the money for shipping, and in the spring of 1991 Mark packed the lost copies of the Polish Jewry series into big waxed cardboard boxes, tied them with manila rope, and shipped them by sea to Amherst by way of Boston. Forty-five years after the first titles appeared, we are finally able to distribute them to eager readers and libraries around the world.

Over the years we've heard rumors of other Yiddish treasures in Argentina—in remote parts of the country, far from Buenos Aires, beyond even the long reach of Mark Swiatlo. The reports are credible. Beginning with an experimental Jewish agricultural colony in Tierra del Fuego—the last, windswept stop before Antarctica—Yiddish-speaking refugees from Eastern Europe eventually settled throughout Patagonia and across the pampas. There were Jewish gauchos and Jewish farmers who founded rural utopian communities. Here, as everywhere, they read Yiddish books, and when they died or when they or their children finally forsook those distant climes for the cities, as they inevitably did, they often left their books behind. Undoubtedly yet another adventure awaits—but first we had to finish saving other endangered books a good deal closer to home.

IF EUROPEAN-BORN, Yiddish-speaking Jews were gradually fading from view in the United States, they were still surprisingly active just north of the border. Canada, a bilingual country, prided itself on being a "mosaic" rather than a melting pot, which meant the

Jewish community felt no need to limit itself to religion alone, as it had in the States. Here my colleagues and I were mavericks; in Canada we coordinated our efforts through the Canadian Jewish Congress, the country's most important national Jewish organization.

Our liaison at the congress was Sara Rosenfeld, head of its National Committee on Yiddish. A teenage firebrand in pre–World War II Warsaw, Sara had fled to no-man's land on the Soviet frontier, eluded the border guards, suffered in Siberia, escaped to Kazakhstan, and after the war, made her way to Canada by way of Sweden. When I arrived as a graduate student in Montreal in 1977, she immediately recruited me as a teacher at a local Jewish high school. In 1980, when I founded the National Yiddish Book Center, she became one of our first board members and most energetic volunteers. Unlike most zamlers, who organize a building, a neighborhood, or at best a small city, Sara mobilized a country. She signed up zamlers in Toronto, Calgary, Winnipeg, Edmonton, Regina, Saskatoon, and Vancouver; she prevailed on the Jewish owner of a trucking company to transport collected books for free as far as Montreal; and she persuaded her employers at the Canadian Jewish Congress to allocate temporary storage space in their basement parking garage. Every six months, when the pile in the garage grew high enough, Sara would phone us in Massachusetts to schedule a pickup.

Despite the obvious difficulties—snow, cold, language—our door-to-door collection trips in Montreal yielded a disproportionately large number of treasures. Many of the people we met were intellectuals who, having arrived after the war, kept abreast of the latest Yiddish literature. Along with copies of Sholem Aleichem, Morris Rosenfeld, Avrom Reisen, and other writers popular in the early decades of the century, they also donated works by more contemporary authors, such as Chaim Grade, Avrom Sutzkever, and Isaac Bashevis Singer. We were thrilled to meet the surviving spouses and children of some of the major figures of modern Yiddish literature, including the widow of Melekh Ravitch and the daughters of Rokhl Korn and I.M. Weissenberg. We even helped distribute the latest works by contemporary Canadian Yiddish writers, such as Yoysef Heilbloom and Yehudah Elberg.

One day Sarah sent me to the home of a ninety-year-old widow who wanted to give us ten boxes of books that had belonged to her late husband. Born in London, England, the woman confided that she had always been somewhat contemptuous of her husband, a Yiddish-speaking refugee from Poland. Still, when he died, she felt she owed it to him to see that his books were cared for. "I'm curious," she said in her proper British accent as we carried his library out to a waiting truck; "I've always assumed my husband was an unsophisticated man. Just what was it he was reading all these years?"

I opened one of the boxes, expecting the usual authors. Instead what I found were dozens of hand-bound volumes, each of which contained ten to twenty pamphlets published in London and Geneva in 1905 by the Press Abroad of the Jewish Labor Bund in Russia and Poland. Most of the pamphlets were printed on tissue paper in crowded six-point type, and it took me a moment before I realized what I was looking at: compact political tracts designed to be smuggled into Russia to fan the flames of the 1905 Revolution. How her husband had come into possession of these treasures his widow couldn't say, but even she was impressed. Many of the pamphlets proved to be the only surviving copies, and they are now in the permanent collections of the YIVO and the Library of Congress.

In all the years I knew Sara Rosenfeld, I don't think I ever saw her sitting still. She was the only person I ever met who could speak on the phone, dictate English letters to her secretary, type Yiddish letters herself, read mail, and greet visitors, all at the same time. When she was seriously injured in a car accident in Florida several years ago, the doctor ordered her to stay in bed for three months; she was back at work in three weeks. Her disregard for her own health was evident in her eating habits. Being a bit self-righteous about my own commitment to organic food, I once chided her about a jar of instant chicken soup mix on her desk, the first four ingredients of which were sugar, starch, salt, and MSG. "*Akh,*" she replied, "who has time to cook when there's so much work to be done?"

In 1982, at Sara's invitation, three thousand delegates from two dozen countries descended on Montreal for the Veltrat, the World Council on Yiddish and Yiddish Culture. This was the Yiddish equivalent of the Olympics, and the logistics were enough to flummox a general — but not Sara. She reserved the biggest hall at the biggest shul in town for the opening session, and persuaded Elie Wiesel to deliver the keynote address — in Yiddish, no less. Sara was not one to look for *koved,* for recognition, or to stand on ceremony. The next day, when the Veltrat reconvened at the congress's headquarters and the speakers, as usual, pounded the podium and bellowed, "*Vu iz undzer yugnt?*" we, the elusive *yugnt,* were in the basement with Sara, on our hands and knees, sorting her latest haul of Yiddish books.

As the years passed, the Canadian Jewish Congress began to drift closer to the model of the American Jewish establishment, eschewing culture in favor of a narrower agenda — and trying to cut Sara's budget in the process. She fought back every step of the way. I was once in her office when she was approached by a particularly pompous executive in a three-piece suit.

"Sara, Sara," he said condescendingly, "why do you spend so much time worrying about a dying language?"

"*Nu,* and you're *not* going to die someday?" she shot back. "I don't see how that stops you from worrying about yourself!"

If the Jewish establishment failed to appreciate Sara's contribution, the government of Canada did not. In Ottawa she was hailed as a national hero for her role in preserving the country's multicultural heritage. In the summer of 2002, barely eighteen months before her death, she was appointed to the Order of Canada—making her the closest thing to a Yiddish knight the world has ever seen.

For all Sara's efforts, there was one problem she could not solve: helping us transport the books we collected in Canada across the U.S. border. Historically speaking, Jews have had little use for national boundaries. Countless Jewish refugees made their way to the United States and Canada by hiring smugglers to lead them across the frontiers of Europe. Their historical disregard for borders was not their fault. There were, after all, Jewish families on both sides of the frontiers— prompting a World War I cartoon of Russian and Austrian soldiers in opposing trenches: *"Reb Yid,"* shouts one soldier to another, "how about joining us in our trench—we need a tenth man for the minyan!" Even when Jews stayed put, the borders themselves kept changing. Between the two world wars there were Jews who never left their *shtetlekh* yet found themselves living in Russia, Poland, and Lithuania, all in quick succession. Not surprisingly, then, the most common way of saying "crossing the border" in Yiddish is *"ganvenen dem grenets,"* which translates literally as *"stealing* the border."

Of course, most law-abiding people do not need to *ganvenen dem grenets* when crossing between the United States and Canada. The border is relatively open, and before September 11 at least, one could generally cross with little more than a driver's license and a smile. But not us. After days of book pick-ups in Montreal, we would invariably arrive at the American border with our clothes grungy from attics and basements, our eyes bloodshot from days of insufficient sleep, our rented trucks the cheapest we could find, and our cargo a disordered heap of hundreds of torn and dusty cardboard boxes. In the early days, when we were still in our twenties, the customs agents mistook us for drug smugglers: They'd make us pull over, get out of the truck, and stand against the wall while their German shepherd sniffed around in the back of the truck, presumably in search of a stray joint stashed inside a volume of Sholem Aleichem. All the dogs ever got was a snoutful of dust.

As we got older and began arriving in a more respectable truck of our own, the agents backed off on the drug searches. But now they had a new demand: They wanted to charge us duty on the books we were transporting. The first time it happened they made us pull up to a low cinderblock building and report to a gray-haired officer standing behind a gray metal counter.

"Manifest?" he asked, perfunctorily, fitting a form onto his clipboard.

"Excuse me?"

"Manifest. Where's the warehouse ticket for your load, the bill of lading?"

"Well, sir, we don't have a warehouse ticket. You see, we didn't go to a warehouse, we collected these books door-to-door and loaded the truck ourselves."

This was apparently highly unorthodox, and it took a good fifteen minutes before we could make the customs man understand that the load came not from a warehouse but from the basement of the Canadian Jewish Congress building and dozens of individual homes.

"*Yiddish* books, you say?"

"Yes, sir, Yiddish books" I repeated.

"Hmmm," said the customs man, "we don't see many Yiddish books coming through here. What's the commercial value?"

"There is no commercial value," I replied. "You see, we're a nonprofit organization; our job is to rescue old Yiddish books and—"

"Look, son, don't give me a lot of malarkey, you've got to have a value, any value, it doesn't matter what it is, otherwise I can't let you across."

In the end we settled on a token $100, which was low enough to exempt us from duty altogether. Before we left, the customs agent made it clear that next time he wouldn't be so lenient—either we came with a proper manifest and a confirmed valuation or else our cargo stayed in Canada.

Next time came sooner than we thought. While still in Montreal I had recorded a national radio interview with one of Sara's many friends at the CBC. Now, just two months later, Sara was back on the phone: The broadcast had done its job, and boxes of Yiddish books were pouring in from Halifax to Vancouver.

This time I took no chances. I phoned our congressman, Sylvio Conte, and asked for advice about crossing the border with used Yiddish books. Conte's office checked with the customs service in Washington and got back to us the same day. Under customs law, *all* books are exempt from duty. Nonetheless, there was no way to avoid the complicated process of manifests and bonded brokers unless we could show that the books we were carrying were "American Goods Returning"—items manufactured in the United States that, by law, could be brought back into the country without duty or undue delay.

That seemed fair enough. After all, about two-thirds of all Yiddish books were published in New York City. The only problem was the remaining third, most of which were printed in Warsaw, Vilna, and the other great Jewish cultural centers of eastern Europe. *Meyle,* no matter. They were all in Yiddish anyway—written in a Hebrew alphabet—and the next time I arrived at the border I proceeded with confidence.

"No sweat," I told the customs man as he hoisted himself onto the running board and peered into the cab, one hand resting on the .45 on his hip. "Just a load of American books, sir, printed in the USA, bring-ing them all back home."

The customs man was not impressed.

"Okay, buddy, pull it over."

I pulled up to the same cinderblock customs shed, and this time an-other, younger agent came out to meet me.

"You say all these books were printed in the United States?" he asked.

"Yes, sir."

"Well, I'm going to have to perform a spot check to confirm that."

He opened the back of the truck, rummaged through the boxes, and pulled out three books at random. The first two were safe; both were published in New York and had English copyright information on the verso of the title page. The third volume had no such English in-formation. Peering over the customs man's shoulder I saw to my hor-ror that it was published by Farlag Emes, the Yiddish state publisher in Moscow.

"All right, where's it say here this book was published in the United States?" the officer demanded, carefully scrutinizing the volume. He was holding it upside down.

I took the book, turned it right-side up, and opened to the title page, where it said in *kidish-levone-oysyes,* big Hebrew letters: *Aroysgegebn in Moskve,* meaning "Published in Moscow."

I swallowed hard, pointed to the Yiddish letters, and affecting my best Borscht Belt accent, pretended to read the Yiddish word for word: "Look, it says right here: 'Pooblished in Nyu Yoorrk.' "

The customs man sagely nodded his head. "All right," he said, "in that case, you can take 'em across."

The strategy worked, and we've been *ganvenen dem grenets* ever since.

. . .

IT TOOK TWENTY years to arrange a collection trip to Cuba—
and a twenty-minute flight from Miami to actually get there. Of the
fifteen thousand Jews who lived on the island before the revolution, all
but a handful had left. As in Zimbabwe, they departed so quickly that
many left their Yiddish books behind. We first tried to retrieve them in
1985, but between the U.S. embargo and Cuban intransigence, we
made little headway. The situation looked more promising in 1999,
when Bob Schwartz, a political activist who regularly delivered medical supplies to the island, led a celebrity delegation that included Ed
Asner and Mohammed Ali. Cut off from American television, few
Cubans recognized the actor; but no one failed to cheer Ali. One government minister was so grateful for the boxer's appearance that he
asked Bob what he could do in return. "Let us have the Yiddish books,"
Bob replied. The minister agreed on the spot, and I was already packing my bags when the head of Cuba's Jewish community, a retired oral
surgeon, intervened at the last minute and said no. True, the books had
lain untouched and unread for decades; but for the Jewish leader, it was
a matter of pride: "As long as a communist Jew remains in Cuba," he
decreed, "the books will, too."

So again we bided our time until, in the winter of 2002, I received
a phone call from Stephen Rivers, a publicist who had just returned
from Cuba with California's congressional delegation. "Since September 11," Stephen explained, "Castro has been bending over backward
to accommodate Americans and distance himself from terrorism. If
you still want the books, now's the time."

Although the embargo was still in place, pressure was clearly easing,
and thanks to a special exemption for scholars, it took just two weeks
to obtain permission from the U.S. government to travel there. Three
days later I flew to Miami with Gabriel Hamilton, the twenty-seven-
year-old director of our Steven Spielberg Digital Library. We proceeded to the airport's lower level, past the last baggage carousel,

around a No Admittance sign, under a rope, and down a corridor, un-til—like Harry Potter arriving at Platform 9¾—we found the un-marked gate for the charter flight to Havana.

An American diplomat wrote of Cuba in 1888: "You are only ninety miles from the winking lighthouses and sandy shore of Florida, but you have entered dominions as foreign, as different, as full of strangeness, as though you had sailed around the world to find them." His observa-tion was doubly true now. Isolated from the States for forty-three years, Cuba was bursting with contradictions: green cane fields, white sand beaches, good-natured people, and lovingly maintained vintage American cars (where else can you hail a Desoto taxi?), alongside crumbling, overcrowded houses, renovated Mafia-built hotels (for for-eigners only), pulsing music, ubiquitous sensuality, and rationed food. In the words of one guidebook, "Sex, music and dancing are Cubans' greatest pleasures, since none is rationed and all are free."

Our mission in the country seemed straightforward enough: Track down the surviving Yiddish books, identify important titles, and secure permission from the head of the Jewish community to bring them back and digitize them. But no sooner had we landed than we realized the job would be anything but straightforward. Despite the six e-mails and twenty-three faxes we sent to the Cuban Jewish community before we left, there was no one at the airport to meet us and no message waiting for us at our hotel in downtown Havana. Gabe and I were on our own until the next morning, when we went looking for La Gran Synagoga, the Ashkenazic shul that serves as headquarters and library for Cuba's roughly five hundred remaining Jewish families.

Fortunately the shul wasn't hard to find. Located at the end of a shady street lined with crumbling colonial mansions, the building would have been more at home in a New Jersey suburb, save for a bright blue arch that towered over the front entrance, giving it the ap-pearance of a tropical McDonald's.

Our only contact at the shul—our only contact in the entire country, for that matter—was Adela Dworin, the head of the library and
vice president of the official Cuban Jewish community. We found the
Biblioteca, a narrow, windowless, book-filled room in the synagogue
basement, but to our dismay, Adela wasn't there. *"Donde está Adela?"* we
asked one of the half dozen people in the room (contrary to what we
had read in the tour books, almost no one in the country spoke English,
and our Spanish was limited to what we had been able to cram from a
phrase book the night before). "In a meeting," we were told. We waited,
ten, twenty, forty minutes, until Adela finally appeared, accompanied
by Dr. José Miller, the seventy-eight-year-old president of the Jewish
community—the man who had stood in the way of our removing Yiddish books three years before.

This time we tried to soften the opposition by bearing gifts: expensive books in English, CDs of Jewish music, videos of classic Yiddish
films, and more. But as we slowly laid them out, we received our first
lesson in the harsh realities of daily Cuban life. Adela picked up one of
the brand-new books we had brought—Joan Nathan's *Jewish Holiday
Kitchen*—and asked with a sad smile, "So tell me, did you happen to
bring the ingredients to go with this?" Gabe and I shrugged sheepishly.
We agreed to speak again that afternoon, after we had had a chance to
examine the library's Yiddish holdings.

Over the years, I had heard rumors that there were "thousands upon
thousands" of abandoned Yiddish books in Cuba. If that was true, we
didn't find them. According to Adela, most were probably lost when
Castro confiscated Havana's Zionist Center in 1978 and turned it over
to the local Arab League. No one knows for sure what the new tenants
did with the center's Yiddish books, but Adela felt certain that the few
hundred volumes in the synagogue library were all that remained.

I picked a random volume off the shelf—a copy of *Habana lebn
(Havana Life),* a Yiddish magazine—and, just leafing through the pages,

began to understand how rich Cuba's Jewish life had been before the Revolution: Yiddish schools, libraries, publishing houses, literary journals, lectures, cultural centers, and three kosher restaurants, one of which went by the irresistible name of Moyshe Pipik's (Moses Belly-button's). Was it really possible, forty-three years after the Revolution, that of that whole rich, teeming Jewish life, only these few hundred books survived? And if so, imagine how valuable they must be!

With Adela's help, Gabe and I squeezed between the stacks and set to work. I'd like to report that Cuba's few hundred remaining Yiddish books were in good shape. They weren't. Relegated to the bottommost shelves, many had grown *farshimlt,* covered with mold from the heat and humidity of the Caribbean climate. Stuck to one cover was a dead cockroach the size of a mouse. It wasn't long before Gabe and I were sneezing from the dust and spores, our hands black, our clothes filthy, our backs and knees aching.

But it was worth it. Some of the volumes were the same New York imprints we had seen a hundred times before: Yehoash, Sholem Asch, Sholem Aleichem, even a Yiddish translation of *Uncle Tom's Cabin*. But there were also rare books we had never seen: an 1872 imprint from Stuttgart, and another from Palestine dated 1947; a Yiddish translation of Isaac Babel's short stories published in Odessa in 1925; Holocaust memoirs published in various D.P. camps right after the war; and just as we'd hoped, hard-to-find Latin American imprints, including three printed in Havana before the Revolution. By the time we had finished, we were more eager than ever to get these precious volumes back to the States.

Ober vi kumt di kats ibern vaser? (How was the trick to be done?) Gabe and I discussed strategy over lunch, and that afternoon we presented Dr. Miller with what seemed to us a reasonable offer: Instead of actually taking the books, we proposed *borrowing* them long enough to dig-

itize them. They were moldering anyway; in their place we would return brand-new, digitally generated, acid-free reprints.

Dr. Miller didn't agree, exactly, but he didn't say no, either. So that
night Adela, who cared deeply about the books and wanted to see them
saved, let us load two bags with the most valuable titles and take them
back to our hotel. We returned the next morning, and this time the library staff not only greeted us warmly, they led us to a stash of additional Yiddish volumes hidden in a closet. But the key to success still lay
in Dr. Miller's hands. So at noon, we offered to take him, his wife, and
Adela to lunch. In a country where good food is scarce, Dr. Miller
didn't have to be asked twice. He suggested we go to "the best fish
restaurant in Cuba," a waterfront establishment run by the Ministry of
Fisheries that, outside of the tourist hotels (where Cubans were not allowed), was one of the most expensive eateries in the city. We were
driven there in style, by a native Cuban driver in a brand-new van donated to the Jewish community by our good friends at the Kaplen
Foundation of New Jersey. (Larry Kaplen, a young screenwriter and a
trustee of the foundation, was a member of our board.) On each door
of the van was a Jewish star, and on the back, in large block letters, the
English words "Kaplen Van," which apparently was the Cubans' idea of
an acknowledgment. "People think it's Hebrew for 'Hyundai,'" Adela
quipped.

From the outside, with its large neon sign, Cuba's "best fish restaurant"
reminded me of the Cape Cod of my youth, but inside it was straight out
of the Soviet Union: more waiters than customers, and huge, multipage
menus with only a single item, red snapper, actually available.

"Why only one kind of fish?" I asked Adela.

"What does it take to go fishing?" she asked in return.

"I don't know," I answered, "what does it take?"

She raised an eyebrow, as though marveling at my naïveté. "It takes
a *boat!*"

She didn't have to spell it out: If the government started supplying boats, how long would it be before the entire Cuban fishing fleet was docked in Miami? So we settled for the snapper, along with lox, Coca-Cola, and ice cream—unimaginable luxuries in a country where even rice and beans can be hard to come by. When we returned to the library, Dr. Miller informed us that the books were ours. Adela sadly conceded that she was one of the last Yiddish-readers in all of Cuba, and she asked for nothing, not even reprints, in return.

Carrying two suitcases packed full of Yiddish books, we returned to the States the same way we came, unhindered by officials from either side. Regrettably, several hundred volumes had to be left behind (there was a limit on how many we could stuff into our luggage), but Adela graciously agreed to put them aside until we could send someone to pick them up. I wrote a letter to our members asking for help, and among the scores of responses was one on behalf of Jimmy Carter, who was planning to be in Havana in June, the first visit there by a former U.S. president since the Revolution. We were honored, of course, particularly in light of President Carter's role in freeing Cuban prisoners. But other members and friends were able to go even sooner, and within a month of our return, every one of Cuba's known Yiddish books was safe and sound in Amherst, ready to be digitized and shared with the world.

23. Back in the U.S.S.R.

Ladies and gentlemen, we are now entering Soviet airspace . . ."
Kenneth Turan, our translator Kevin Lourie, and I crowded around
the small window. All we could see was winter far below: frozen tun-
dra, vast solid lakes and marshes, and evergreen forests shrouded in
snow. We stared for an hour, maybe more, as our plane rushed on.
There was only snow, ice, and emptiness as far as the eye could see. If
Napoleon had been on this flight before he ordered his troops to advance on Moscow, he surely would have called the whole thing off.

What, then, were *we* doing, advancing on Moscow at the end of November 1989? After distributing Yiddish books to students and scholars in twenty countries, we had, for the first time, begun receiving
requests from individuals and organizations in the Soviet Union, where
most Jewish books had been illegal for fifty years or more. As one man
wrote from Estonia,

> During the decades of Stalin's murderers they stuffed our mouths
> and cut off our tongues, and we were unable to speak Yiddish,

forbidden to read or write or learn about Jewish history and literature. Two generations have grown up knowing nothing about Yiddishkeit; they are strangers to the sound of *mame loshn,* strangers to Sholem Aleichem, Mendele, Peretz, Opatoshu and the other bearers of our culture. You cannot imagine the fate of those of us who tried to do something to further Jewish knowledge. But now, at last, the times are changing. . . .

Gorbachev's policy of glasnost, liberalization, had opened unprecedented opportunities, and all over the country scattered Jews were looking for Yiddish books, determined to reclaim the language of their parents and grandparents, the culture that prevailed before the repression began. Our initial response was to ship books by post, but they never arrived. We sent two more trial boxes six weeks later, two more a month after that, two more the next month—much like Noah sending out his doves after the flood, except that our books neither arrived at their destination nor returned. Officials in Washington surmised they had been confiscated by overzealous customs agents or, more likely, waylaid by thieves—corrupt postal workers who routinely intercepted foreign parcels, looking for items to sell on the black market.

So we decided to go to the Soviet Union ourselves, to figure out firsthand a way to get large numbers of Yiddish books into the country. It's hard now to convey the sense of urgency that informed our travels. Today we think of the fall of the Soviet Union as inevitable; back then no one knew for sure if glasnost was the precursor of deeper change or merely a window that would be slammed shut at any moment. We moved quickly. My friend Kenny Turan, a noted film critic and seasoned journalist who had traveled in the Soviet Union before, agreed to accompany me. We left right after Thanksgiving and didn't return until Christmas Eve. During that eventful month—it felt more like a year—we attended the founding conference of the Vaad, the first-ever gathering of Soviet Jewish organizations; we shivered with thousands of other mourners at the outdoor funeral of Andrey Sakharov; and we were present at the Lithuanian Embassy in Moscow on the night the Lithuanian Communist Party declared its independence. But mostly we were on the move, traveling unofficially by train, asking questions, making contacts, laying the groundwork for a second trip in the spring, when we would return with the books themselves.

To call most of Russia's one-and-a-half million Jews assimilated doesn't begin to capture the reality of their lives. Although their internal passports clearly marked them as Jews, most lacked even the most rudimentary Jewish knowledge. In Minsk, the capital of Byelorussia (now Belarus), we met the granddaughter of a rabbi who had never heard the words "Torah," "menorah," "Pesakh," or "Shabbos." In Moscow, the Mikhoels Jewish Cultural Center—the opening of which had warranted a front-page picture in the *Times*—turned out to be a sham, a Potemkin village for the deception of American Jewish officials.

It wasn't always that way. The founding document of the Russian Social Democratic Workers' Party (the precursor of the Bolsheviks)—a document roughly equal in significance to our Declaration of Independence—first appeared in Minsk in 1898, in a bilingual text of Russian and Yiddish. During the Kerensky regime, the official Russian currency was trilingual, printed in Russian, Ukrainian, and Yiddish. The early Bolsheviks, many of them Jews themselves, embraced Yiddish, as opposed to Hebrew, as the authentic language of the Jewish proletariat. After the Revolution the government supported secular Yiddish schools, newspapers, journals, publishing houses, and perhaps most important, Yiddish sections of the major Soviet research academies, where scholars conducted first-rate research in Jewish history, ethnography, and linguistics. State-run theaters produced experimental Yiddish plays, and avant-garde artists explored Jewish themes. As a counterpoint to Zionism (and to strengthen their own borders), the Soviets established Birobidzhan, a Yiddish-speaking "Jewish autonomous region" in the Soviet Far East, near the border with Manchuria. But it was not to last.

By the early 1930s, as official anti-Semitism intensified, Yiddish schools and research academies across the country were closed, books burned, and finally writers imprisoned or killed. Solomon Mikhoels, the director of Moscow's Yiddish art theater, perished in a suspicious automobile accident in 1948. The best writers—Dovid Bergelson, Peretz Markish, Moyshe Kulbak, even the poet Itsik Fefer, who wrote, "When I say sun, I mean Stalin"—all were executed in a final purge on the night of August 12, 1952.

Even in 1989, this history was still uncomfortably close at hand, as we learned on our second day in Moscow when we were introduced to a Yiddish poet named Chaim Beyder. In 1949, Beyder had been in Birobidzhan when a directive came from Moscow denouncing Yiddish writers as "enemies of the people" and ordering that all Yiddish books be destroyed. Even now, forty years later, Beyder's voice trembled as he told us how he was forced to watch as soldiers emptied the Jewish library, doused the books with kerosene, and set them ablaze—an experience he captured in a Yiddish poem called *"Der shayter* (The Pyre)":

> With what anguish those Yiddish books burned
> and trembled in the smoke's stationary vortex,
> their very pages upturned
> like lifted limbs
> writhing in pain amid the flames

This was not ancient history. Gennady Estreich, the assistant editor of *Sovetish heymland (Soviet Homeland),* the country's only Yiddish literary journal, a man not much older than I, told us that his mother had been a Yiddish librarian in a small Ukrainian city from the 1930s through the 1950s. "Every week Moscow would send the librarians a list of the latest banned books they were supposed to destroy. Every library had a special fireplace in the courtyard just for this purpose, and every week my mother had to join her colleagues all across the country in burning another batch of Yiddish books."

Even worse than the fate of Yiddish books was the fate of those who wrote them. In Minsk we were visited by an elderly woman named Dina Zvolovna Kharik—the widow of the Yiddish poet Izi Kharik. "What I have lived through!" she sighed as she settled into a chair in our hotel room and poured forth her tale. She was just fifteen, she said, and Kharik thirty-four when they met. They married a year later, in 1932. "The government married us; I was in Komsomol, he was in the Party, we didn't believe in a *khupe* [the traditional Jewish wedding canopy]. We got congratulations in Yiddish from France, from Argentina, from all over the world. I took everything I owned to his apartment in one little suitcase. One dress, that's all I had."

Kenny Turan, who was taking careful notes, picks up the story from there:

> For a time, life was sweet. The Khariks had two sons. Dina Zvolovna remembers with glee the many new experiences which awaited her, including a 1937 trip to Moscow. . . . But by the time the Khariks returned to Minsk, life started to unravel. "They began taking people, arresting them all over the city," Dina Zvolovna remembers. "At first, we thought that because the people were arrested, they must be guilty. We knew Kharik was innocent and besides, what could we do?"
>
> Then a close friend was arrested. "Kharik was very upset, he said, 'I know he's innocent.' It was a horrible situation and Kharik

was afraid. I said to him, 'Why don't you go away and rest.' So he went to a small town near Minsk, a little bitty place where the Writers' Union had a rest house. And soon after that, I got a message: 'Dina, they've arrested Izi Kharik.'"

A month later, she received a letter from Kharik. "He had to write all the bad things he'd done, sign that he was an enemy of the people, to be able to write that letter. 'I'm not guilty,' he wrote, 'they must have mixed me up with someone else. I'm coming back—don't marry anyone else.'" It was the last communication from him she was ever to receive.

There was worse to come. "A month later, at night, someone came for me. They were taking all the wives. My oldest son, three years old, and his brother, a year and a few months, were lying in their beds. I had to leave them where they were. They took me and I never saw them again."

Dina Zvolovna ended up in a women-only prison camp in the Soviet Far East. She was assigned to a forced labor brigade, and nearly died from drinking contaminated water after exhausting herself fighting a grass fire. "We fell on this water like animals," she remembers. "Afterwards, I was so sick, I couldn't stand for a year. There were no medicines, no remedies. One woman carried me everywhere. Without this woman, I would have died."

Dina Zvolovna spent ten years in this camp before a doctor gave her a certificate saying she should be released for health reasons. She spent most of the next decade living clandestinely, without proper papers, fearful of renewed police sweeps, before Khrushchev's 1956 speech denouncing Stalin began the process of Kharik's rehabilitation. Eventually, she was able to return to Minsk, where she was given an apartment and a small pension. "I found out recently," she says quietly, "he was shot in 1937 together with other Russian writers." And the children? "No one," she says, "knew where the children were." To this day she had not found them.

After politely but very firmly refusing to be photographed, Dina Zvolovna stood up, shook hands, and expressed regret that we hadn't given her enough notice of our arrival to allow her to cook something for us. As she prepared to leave she mentioned that all her own copies of her husband's work had been lost. Aaron asked if she would like us to send her copies. "With all my life," she said, emotion suddenly in her voice. "With all my heart!"

The murder of writers, the burning of books—after decades of such depredations, only scattered pockets of Yiddish culture remained in Russia proper. But the situation was very different in areas that had come under Soviet rule during and after the Second World War: the western Ukraine, Moldavia, and the Baltic republics of Estonia, Latvia, and Lithuania. There, despite the best efforts of Germans and Soviets both, there were still people alive who had been trained as Jewish teachers before the war, who still spoke Yiddish fluently and remembered its literature clearly, and who were now eager to teach what they knew to a new generation. We headed for the Baltics.

In Estonia we met Moyshe Michelson, who for twenty years taught Yiddish illegally in the university town of Tartu. Now that his classes were permitted, more than two hundred students had enrolled, and he desperately needed books.

In Riga, the capital of Latvia, eighty-two-year-old Avrom Barmazl, a professor in that city's Yiddish Teachers Seminary before the war, had called together all his surviving students. Prohibited for almost half a century from practicing their chosen profession, many had gone on to excel in other fields: one was an engineer, one an actor, one an editor, one the principal of a Russian school. But even after all these years, the moment they had the chance they gave up secure positions elsewhere to return to their old profession as teachers in a new Jewish school.

Opened just ten weeks before we arrived, the school they founded already had four hundred students. With the exception of a home-made, handwritten Yiddish primer and exactly one copy of an anthology of Yiddish folk songs printed in New York, there were no Yiddish books.

In Vilna (now Vilnius), the capital of Lithuania, members of the local community had just reopened the first Jewish school in fifty years. The day we arrived parents and other volunteers were busy removing Soviet propaganda posters from the walls and replacing them with flowered wallpaper and Jewish art. Here, too, we found experienced teachers, eager students, and no books.

At these and other newly opened schools and libraries, Kenny and I promised to return soon with all the Yiddish books they needed. Each time we made this pronouncement some in the audience would clap, some would cry, but most remained coolly skeptical. When, in Riga, I asked why, a teacher showed me a guest book in which were written the names of a hundred or more representatives of Jewish organizations in the United States, Canada, and Israel who had visited the school in the ten weeks since it opened. "You should excuse me, but you are not our first visitors," the teacher explained. "They all make promises, but we have yet to receive a single Jewish book."

I knew that with an intrepid staff and more than a million books in our warehouse, we had a far better chance than most of making good on our promise, and I vowed to return by spring. But I also harbored no illusions: Important as it was to support these schools, I didn't believe for a second that many young Jews would remain here once the doors of emigration were opened and they had a chance to leave. The threat of renewed anti-Semitism was never far from anyone's mind. Already, in Moldavia, a local nationalist movement was organizing with the slogan "We will drown the Russians in the blood of the Jews." But as Boris Kelman, the forty-two-year-old head of the Jewish community in Leningrad explained, "Even if *all* the Soviet Union's one-and-a-half million Jews decide to emigrate, and even if one hundred thousand a year—a figure we've yet to attain—can be resettled abroad, full emigration will take at least fifteen years to complete. In the meantime, we must do something for those who remain."

How exactly we were going to get thousands of Yiddish books into the country and distribute them from city to city, we weren't quite sure. But any doubts we may have had that it *could* be done were quickly allayed once we returned to Moscow and boarded our SAS flight for home. The moment we were airborne the pilot came on the intercome to announce that, while we were in the Soviet Union, the Berlin Wall had fallen. If that was true, Kenny and I agreed, all things were possible.

The plan we hatched was this: We would ship eight thousand books to Sweden, load them on a truck, cross the Baltic by ferry, and deliver them in person to waiting Jews in Estonia, Latvia, and Lithuania. But then, in March, just weeks before our scheduled departure, Lithuania formally declared its independence, and all hell broke loose. By late March, Soviet troops were massed at the Lithuanian border and tanks were rolling through the streets of Vilnius. It was definitely not an auspicious moment to be arriving with a truckload of Yiddish books.

That's when we set to work on Plan B. Among the various groups seeking Yiddish books was the National Library of Estonia, which was authorized to import Estonian books from abroad. They agreed to serve as a go-between for our Yiddish shipments as well. In late spring we sent an urgent appeal to our members, who responded with unprecedented generosity. In May and June we pulled books from the shelves, affixed commemorative Yiddish-and-Russian book plates, and carefully packed the books into coded boxes, each labeled on the outside "Estonian Books." We then delivered them to Port Elizabeth, New Jersey, where they were loaded into a watertight container and hoisted

aboard a freighter bound for Helsinki, whence they would be transported by a Finnish trucking company to Estonia.

It was not until July 12 that we finally received a telex from Tallinn
informing us that the books had arrived. Two days later, at five in the
morning, I was standing in Stockholm-Arlanda International Airport,
waiting to rendezvous with Kenny Turan and Janice Rubin, an old
friend and freelance photojournalist from Houston, Texas. The two
would be covering the trip for *Smithsonian* magazine. It was almost fifty
years to the day since the Soviet occupation of the Baltics, forty-nine
years since the Nazi invasion, and eighteen months since we had received the first letters from Soviet Jews requesting Yiddish books.

Thanks to advance work by leaders of the Stockholm Jewish community, we had no difficulty renting a van and booking passage on the
Nord Estonia, a trans-Baltic car-passenger ferry that had begun regular
service to Tallinn just six weeks before. The sea voyage lasted
sixteen hours. After a good night's sleep we awoke in time to see a
weatherbeaten pilot boat with a faded hammer and sickle on its stack
plowing through the waves to meet us. An hour later, standing on the
windy deck of the *Nord Estonia,* we caught our first glimpse of the medieval spires of Tallinn rising in the distance.

Due to mechanical problems, once we had docked it took more
than an hour to open the main door to the car deck. (The successor to
the *Nord Estonia* had similar problems: Not long after our voyage, the
ferry's door accidentally opened in stormy seas. The ship sank with
all nine hundred people aboard.) Customs was harrowing. Armed
soldiers in blue coveralls swarmed over each car in turn, pulling up
carpets and removing door panels in an energetic search for contra-
band — though what it was they were looking for was not entirely
clear. Although we had sent most of our books ahead, we were carrying one large box of late arrivals: newly commissioned reprints of
Dubnow's *Idishe geshikhte far shul un heym (Jewish History for School and*

Home), a Jewish history text for children, originally published in Riga in 1937.

"What is in box?" asked the chief customs officer.

I swallowed hard and answered as matter-of-factly as I could, "Jewish books."

"Religious books?" he asked.

I thought for a second. The books were, of course, social history, written by a secular historian. But guessing that the Soviets might be eager to demonstrate their newfound embrace of religious tolerance, I decided to respond in the affirmative. It was the right answer. The officer turned to his men and said something in Russian, which sent them to the next car in line. After they were gone he turned back to us and asked, "So tell me, are they in Yiddish or *Ivrit?*"

His use of the word *"Ivrit,"* the modern Hebrew word for "Hebrew," was clearly intentional. Surprised, I looked up at him, and under his official visor I suddenly recognized an unmistakable *yidishe ponim,* a Jewish face. Our eyes met and his stern expression softened into a warm smile. We smiled back, he nodded, closed the back of the van, stamped our papers, kissed each of us on both cheeks, and signaled to a soldier to open the gate. We restarted the engine and, with a friendly wave, made our triumphant entry into the USSR.

Waiting for us on the other side of customs was Moyshe Michelson, the indomitable seventy-year-old Yiddish teacher from Tartu. He hopped into the truck, directed us to the hotel, stopped traffic so we could back into a parking space, and then showed us how to remove the van's windshield wipers (a necessity in the Soviet Union, where rubber was in short supply and windshield wipers a favorite target of thieves). He stayed with us illegally that night in our hotel (a pack of Marlboro cigarettes—brought for just such an occasion—was enough to persuade the floor monitor to look the other way). I gave Mr. Michelson a new Yiddish Book Center T-shirt to sleep in, but he declined to put it on.

"*Aza min hemdl trogt men nor af yontef!* (A shirt like this one should wear only on holidays!)"he explained.

The return of Yiddish books to Tartu was one of the greatest moments in Mr. Michelson's life, he said, and he had persuaded the Tartu Public Library to designate a special room just for them. He had already transported many of the boxes himself, traveling back and forth to Tallinn by train. He was a strong man, a veteran of World War II with shrapnel still lodged in his leg; but as he showed us the familiar books, which had been sitting in our Holyoke warehouse just a few months before, tears began flowing down his cheeks. "When you count the books you'll find that several volumes are missing," he hastened to explain. "My friends and I have already checked them out—we couldn't wait to read them."

IN MIDSUMMER THE sun in the Baltics rises at four o'clock and doesn't set until just before midnight; our own working day was almost as long. After a brief night's stay in Tallinn we got up at dawn, reloaded the van, met our volunteer guide, a Jewish university student named Lena Beckergoun, and shoved off for Riga, three hundred kilometers to the south. The day was beautiful, and we sang and talked as we rolled past fields of beets and rye. At lunchtime we stopped in Pärnu, an old Jewish resort town, where we ate rich, creamy ice cream and drank kvass, a fermented grain drink dispensed from a tank-trailer and served in dirty glasses by a twelve-year-old street vendor. The scene could have been straight from Sholem Aleichem's *Motl the Cantor's Son,* the story of an exuberant orphan boy who, among other misadventures, peddles diluted kvass on the streets of his shtetl—except there were so few Jews around. "Most have left for Israel already," Lena explained.

I'm not sure anyone in Riga really believed us when we announced in December that we'd be back with enough Yiddish books for all the students in the school, but here we were, barely seven months later, pulling into the courtyard with a truckload of three thousand school texts and a complete five-hundred-volume reference collection for the school library. The first job was to get the boxes out of the truck and into the third-floor auditorium, where the books could be unpacked, sorted, and shelved. Luckily we had plenty of volunteers. Although most of the students were away for the summer (some were at Jewish camps in the countryside, others in Israel), some thirty young people, most of them members of a Jewish chorus, showed up to help. The excitement was palpable. In a mixture of Yiddish, Hebrew, and English, with frequent translation into Russian by the teachers, we organized the students into a bucket brigade that wended its way up three circular flights of stairs. It took less than half an hour to unload the truck, and then the real excitement began. Wielding knives and scissors, some students began cutting open the boxes, while others pulled out the books and stacked them by title on long tables set up all around the room. Professor Barmazl and the other teachers were beside themselves, examining every volume. "Even in the best of times we didn't have such books here," Professor Barmazl told us. Sema Gassel, a teacher who had studied under Professor Barmazl fifty years before, came over and kissed my cheeks. "My eyes want to cry in happiness," she said. "Perhaps you don't understand, we are hungry in our hearts for this. Seeing all this reminds us of our childhood, our Jewish teachers, our Jewish homes."

The young students, of course, had no such memories — most had never seen Yiddish books before — but they were no less enthusiastic. They crowded around as I went from pile to pile, introducing each title in turn. Many of the books came from the former Sholem Aleichem Schools, the only politically independent Yiddish schools in America; we had retrieved them, in brand new condition, from the basement of a Queens apartment building several years before. There were also new Yiddish primers and song books donated by the Workmen's Circle, and dictionaries and reference works donated by the YIVO. But the books that made the biggest impression were the reprints we had carried with us across the border: Dubnow's *Jewish History for School and Home,* originally published right there in Riga. The author, Simon Dubnow, was murdered in the city in 1941, and as far as anyone knew, no copies of his book had been seen there since. For the teachers the title's return to Riga was a vindication; for the students it was history come alive.

By now we were all happily conversing in a mélange of languages. I told the students about Yiddish literature and the history of Jews in their own city, and they reciprocated with an impromptu concert of Yiddish and Hebrew songs. When our work was finally done, the students celebrated by taking handfuls of Styrofoam packing bubbles, an American novelty that they had never seen before, and throwing them into the air as confetti. They made a big mess, but even the teachers agreed it was worth it.

OUR LAST STOP was supposed to be Vilna. Although tensions had eased somewhat since the declaration of independence in March, gasoline was still embargoed and entry by foreigners forbidden. Our applications for special visas, submitted to the Soviet Embassy in Washington before we left, had been rejected, and now here we were, stuck in Riga with twelve hundred Yiddish books bound for new Jewish schools in Vilna and Kovno (Kaunas) and no way to enter Lithuania to deliver them.

Our contact in Lithuania, Emanuel Zingeris, was, at thirty-two, the chairman of the Jewish Cultural Association, a member of the newly formed Lithuanian parliament, and the head of the nascent government's Foreign Affairs Committee. "*Zay ruik, zay ruik, Lahnsky* (Calm down, calm down, Lansky)," he repeatedly admonished me during 2 A.M. phone calls in advance of our trip, "*Alts iz in ordnung* (Everything is under control)." Sure enough, just hours before we were scheduled to leave Riga for Vilna, his personal courier showed up with an official letter of passage written on the letterhead of the as yet unrecognized Lithuanian Parliament, and signed and sealed by none other than Zingeris himself. I placed a hasty call to Vilna.

"*Fraynt* Zingeris," I began, "what are we supposed to do with this letter?"

"*Zay ruik,* Lahnsky," he replied. "Just show it to any Lithuanian policeman who stops you. They will respect the authority of the Lithuanian Parliament."

"And what if the policeman is not Lithuanian? What if we get stopped by the Red Army or the KGB?"

To this Zingeris had no answer. Fortunately Kenny Turan, who as a reporter was more experienced in such matters than I, insisted we check with the U.S. Consulate in Leningrad before trusting ourselves to Zingeris's safe conduct. By the time Kenny got off the phone he was shaking his head.

"What did they say, what did they say?" I asked.

"They said that Zingeris's letter is a one-way ticket to the gulag," he replied.

Salvation comes from unexpected quarters. Our phone calls and subsequent conversation took place in the office of the head of the Riga Jewish community, an elderly woman named Esther Rapina. We had assumed she couldn't understand us, but after Kenny spoke she stepped forward and said in perfect English, "I think perhaps I could be of assistance." She explained that there were sometimes ethnic Latvians working in the local office of the Soviet Interior Ministry. "They hate the Russians so much they might be willing to help."

With that Mrs. Rapina picked up her cane and led us to an impressive government building, past a prominent sign that said Closed (*"Blote!* Mud!" she opined as she pushed her way inside), and proceeded straight to the office of a high Latvian official she thought might be sympathetic to our plight. She guessed right. "I do not have the authority to give you a visa to Vilna," the official explained, "but I can issue a visa to Minsk in Belarus, which will grant you a one-day transit through Lithuania. As long as you can deliver your books and be out in twenty-four hours, you will not be arrested."

We phoned Zingeris to make the final arrangements. He promised to have forty liters of bootleg gasoline waiting for us, so that *"ir vet nisht darfn blaybn in Vilne af eybik* (you won't have to remain in Vilna for eternity)." He also agreed to dispatch two *shtarkers,* tough Jewish bodyguards, on the overnight train to Riga, who would meet up with us first thing in the morning and return with us by truck.

We left on schedule, the *shtarkers* asleep in the back of the van. Shortly after noon, ready for lunch, we pulled off the road into a small Lithuanian city called Ukmerge, seventy kilometers north of Vilna. Our *shtarkers* were awake by now, and the larger of the two, Sasha, who spoke halting English (but no Yiddish), explained that before the war Ukmerge was a shtetl called Vilkomir, which was home to more than seven thousand Jews. The birthplace of M. L. Lilienblum, an important nineteenth-century Hebrew writer, the town once boasted a well-known yeshiva, secular Hebrew and Yiddish high schools, a Jewish trade school, numerous synagogues, study houses, and a full complement of Jewish social and religious institutions. The rabbi, who was born in Palestine, was considered one of the leading Jewish scholars in Lithuania. Driving down the main street, it was possible even now to imagine that nothing had changed: tin-roofed houses, goats tethered in the yards, chickens underfoot, women washing their laundry by the river, and horse-drawn wagons passing us on the street. Yet as much as we wanted to think otherwise, Ukmerge was not the town that time forgot: Though the streets were full of people, no matter how hard we looked there was not a single Jewish face to be seen.

It's funny. In America people sometimes think I'm Irish; in Eastern Europe they could tell from a hundred yards away that Kenny, Janice, and I were Jews, and as a result no one in Ukmerge wanted to talk to us. They were afraid, Sasha explained, that we were descendants of the town's earlier inhabitants, come to reclaim the empty homes their neighbors had expropriated after the war.

And where *were* the Jews of Vilkomir? Dead, dead, every man, woman, and child, rounded up and shot by German soldiers on a single summer day in 1941. The only remnant of Jewish life we could find was the old cemetery, an empty field on the outskirts of town, overgrown with weeds, with a children's playground at the far end. Strange, but there was only one *metseyve,* one tombstone, marking the graves of the tens of thousands of Jews who must have lain buried there. It bothered us, and we asked about the missing grave markers later that afternoon, when we arrived in Vilna.

"Until last month there were no *metseyves* at all in Vilkomir," our host told us. "The one you saw, we put it there as a memorial."

"And what happened to the rest?"

"Kumt mit mir (come with me),"said our host, and he drove us to the base of a monumental stone staircase leading to an imposing Soviet building called the Palace of Trade Unions. Looking closely at the stairs, we could just discern carved Hebrew letters. The entire staircase—like retaining walls, streets, and other staircases throughout the Soviet Union—had been made of Jewish *metseyves.* Not enough that the Nazis murdered the Jews of Europe; after the war, the Soviets were determined to eradicate the memory that they had ever lived.

But that was later in the day, in Vilna. We were still in Ukmerge, in Vilkomir, and next to that lone *metseyve,* the Jews of Vilna had placed a boulder on which they carved a Jewish star and below that a simple inscription in Lithuanian and Yiddish: "The Old Jewish Cemetery: Hallowed Is the Memory of Those Who Died." I tried to read the Yiddish out loud, but my voice choked with tears before I could finish. Kenny put down his notebook, Janice her camera, and for the only time during all our travels, the three of us stood there and wept. We wept, of course, for the forgotten dead—Jews no different than ourselves except that our grandparents had had the prescience or the *mazl,* the blind luck, to leave when they did, and theirs did not. But even more, I think, we wept out of futility, for the lost illusion that the Yiddish books in our little van, parked at the curb, could somehow make amends for Vilkomir and a thousand other cities and *shtetlekh* like it, where, like memory itself, even the *metseyves* are no more.

Humbled, we delivered our books in Vilna. Zingeris did not have the gasoline he promised, and, at two A.M., with no other choice, we turned to the head of the Vilna underworld for help. Not much older than I, he spoke fluent Yiddish, and eight hours later, just as he said he would, he showed up in the parking lot of our hotel with three jerry cans of purloined fuel. When I asked, not without some trepidation, how much we owed him, he waved his hand with all the noblesse oblige of Isaac Babel's Benya Krik. *"Gornisht,* nothing,"he said. "Consider it my small contribution to the cause."

Two days and eleven hundred kilometers later we were back in Tallinn, where we reboarded the *Nord Estonia* for the start of our long journey home. The ship's whistle sounded, and the tugboats, puffing great black clouds of smoke, pushed us into open water. I stood on deck for a long time, reflecting on all we had seen and done. Hundreds of eager Jewish students now had Yiddish books, and I'll never forget the wonder and delight with which they received them. Still, it was only a matter of time before most of those students left for Israel or the States, where for better or worse they would have new languages to learn and new books to read. As long as Yiddish books were needed in the Soviet Union, we would continue to send them (with Communism gone, we now do so via UPS). But that night, standing alone at the taffrail as the Old Country dropped astern, it was as achingly clear to me as it had been to my grandparents eighty years before that the future waited across the sea.

PART FIVE

Bringing It All Back Home

24. *Der Oylem Redt* — The World Takes Notice

It was a ramshackle life I was living: half my time on the road and the rest at the Center, working fourteen hours a day, eating left-over rice and beans, sleeping on a cold futon, and waking early each morning to start again. True, there was Shabbos off, friends, and sometimes girlfriends, but working for peanuts, I was too broke even to think of settling down.

Then late one day in 1989, while fund-raising in New York, I stopped at a pay phone to check in with my office and learned that Adele Simmons, the outgoing president of Hampshire College, soon to be installed as the new president of the MacArthur Foundation, wanted to see me in Amherst first thing the next morning. "She says she wants to introduce you to a big donor," my assistant, Maria Magliochetti, explained.

So at the end of the day I raced back to New England, arrived home at midnight, slept as long as I dared, skipped breakfast, and had time to iron just the two front panels of my Oxford shirt; I'd be okay as long as I kept my jacket on. I then sped up the highway in my sorry Civic wagon, grabbed a handful of brochures from a stash in back, and, right on time, rang the doorbell of President Simmons's gracious country home.

"Do come in," she said, leading me to the living room. "I'm so glad you could make it on such short notice. The person I'd like you to meet will be with us shortly. But first there's another matter I'd like to discuss. The board of the MacArthur Foundation met yesterday, and they've asked me to inform you that you have been awarded a MacArthur Fellowship."

My jaw dropped. The MacArthur — commonly known as a "genius grant" — is awarded to fewer than thirty people a year, President Simmons explained. You can't apply for it. The nominators are anonymous. And although the amount of the grant is (or at least was) determined by age — and I would be one of the youngest recipients — I would still receive almost $250,000, payable over the next five years.

My head was spinning. I didn't know whether to laugh or cry. Then a dozen of my closest friends and colleagues, summoned under the strictest secrecy by our former board chair, Penina Glazer, came streaming in from a side room, along with a public relations officer from Hampshire College, who stood there, pen at the ready, to record my reaction. I'm afraid I disappointed her: My mouth remained open, but not a single sound came out.

Oh, what a difference that grant made! It bestowed much needed credibility on the nascent Yiddish Book Center — and on Yiddish itself. It opened closed doors. It paid off a mountain of personal debt accumulated during the nine years I had worked for next to nothing. And, slowly, it made settling down seem not quite so inconceivable after all.

I think it was two months later that my former teacher, Leonard Glick, handed me a small sheet of paper with a handwritten name and phone number. "I met this young woman at a book group at her parents' house," he explained. "I think you know them: Arnold and Anita Sharpe, lovely people. Their daughter Gail was home for the weekend. She's pretty, she's fun, she's single, she's Jewish, what more do you need? So I asked her parents if I could give you her number, and they said it would be okay."

"And what did *she* say?"

"She?" Len stammered, "Well, to tell you the truth, I'm not quite sure. 'Yes,' I think she said 'yes.' And I almost forgot—she's about to move to California, so you'd better call her right away."

The match hardly seemed auspicious. I crumpled the paper and stuck it in the pocket of my jeans. Eventually it ended up in a basket on top of my bureau, and I didn't give it a second thought until six weeks later when, on a bleak November night, I returned from a long trip to a stone-cold house where the wood stove was out, not a single light was burning, and the few edible items in the fridge were covered with mold. "This is no life," I remember thinking as I dragged my suitcase upstairs and wriggled out of my traveling clothes. And there it was, on top of my bureau, that crumpled piece of paper with Gail Sharpe's phone number. So I called her in Boston and explained who I was (she had completely forgotten about Len's intervention). She was different from other women I had gone out with: not political, but forthright and funny, and after twenty minutes of conversation we agreed to get together in Boston on Saturday night. The day arrived cold and rainy. She met me at the door of her apartment with permed hair, red fingernails, and a short skirt. I was momentarily encouraged by a framed Diego Rivera print on the wall behind her, until I learned that it belonged to her roommate. I, for my part, was admittedly no paragon of sartorial splendor: an army surplus parka (still sporting a hole from the battery acid spilled the day we saved the books from the Dumpster in New York), a well-worn Harris Tweed sport jacket sticking out below the parka, corduroy pants smooth in the knee, and a visored wool stocking hat (left over from the Korean War) that barely contained my untamed hair. Standing there, facing each other across the threshold, neither of us could keep from staring. "Oh my God," we each thought, "I'm about to spend the evening with a date from another planet."

If Gail was put off by the *hefkeyres*, the chaos, of my car — books, papers, brochures, empty juice bottles, beach rocks and shells — she was too polite to say. She chose a funky Italian restaurant in the North End. Unpretentious — I liked that. She ate more than I did — I liked that, too. We sipped Chianti and talked and talked and talked, until halfway through the spumoni I was thinking, This woman is great! and then, So how come I never meet women like this in *my* world?

We went back to her apartment and talked till two. For people from different planets, we seemed to have an awful lot in common. I floated the hundred miles back to Holyoke. The next morning I split a cord of firewood, then sat down and wrote Gail a letter, inviting her to join me for Thanksgiving weekend. She did, and we had a great time. Okay, we had a GREAT time. My mother once told me that the reason I should marry a Jewish girl was so she would get Jewish jokes. I told Gail a Jewish joke and she laughed and laughed, all the way from her sparkling blue eyes to her glossy red toes.

But to what avail? I was leaving in two days for my first, month-long trip to the Soviet Union, and Gail was already packed, set to depart in ten days for Marina del Rey. *Bashert iz bashert,* the saying goes: what is meant to be is meant to be. The night before I left for Russia I phoned her and, on the basis of an Italian meal and a single weekend, asked her to postpone her move out West until I returned. She agreed. I wrote her a half dozen very long letters from Russia. On Christmas eve I returned. The airport was empty — except for Gail, who, to my delight, had come out to meet me. She later told me that she probably wouldn't have recognized me were it not for the fur hat and balalaika. A friend had given her a key to my house, and when we got home there was a fire in the woodstove and a festive meal on the table. That was Christmas eve. We were engaged on New Year's eve and got married three months later. Smart, spirited, resourceful, Gail was immediately swept up in the swirl of Yiddish books, and in that and so much more we've been partners ever since.

IT WASN'T BY choice that the Yiddish Book Center became, in the words of *Esquire* magazine, "the most grassroots Jewish organization in America." We were too young, and Yiddish was perceived as too marginal, to raise money any other way.

I tried the conventional route first. Shortly after starting the Center I went to Brooks Brothers, bought a suit on credit, and took the train to Chicago to meet with a former U.S. Secretary of Commerce who had grown up in a Yiddish-speaking home. Maybe it was my vegetarian canvas boots or my bandana handkerchief that gave me away, or maybe it was his own ambivalence about his Yiddish past. Whatever the case, the first words out of his mouth were, "You dress like my son." Apparently it was not a compliment, because I left empty-handed. In that and so many other encounters, I was reminded of the eighteenth-century German Jewish philosopher Moses Mendelssohn, who characterized his native Yiddish as "a wild and barbarous tongue that contributes not a little to the impropriety of the common Jew." For many Jewish philanthropists, Yiddish was worse than dead; it was a specter, an unwelcome reminder of the immigrant culture they had worked so hard to forget.

Fortunately there were other donors who enjoyed Yiddish precisely because it did foster impropriety, because it stood outside both the Jewish and non-Jewish mainstream. Arnold Picker, for example, was the former head of United Artists and number one on Nixon's "enemies list." When I went to see him and his wife, Ruth, in Florida, they greeted me with open arms, invited me to dinner, assured me they never spoke anything *but* Yiddish with their friends in Hollywood ("Take Edward G. Robinson—oy, could he speak a good Jewish!"), regaled me with Yiddish jokes, and offered to help in any way they could.

"Don't you want to visit first so you can see the books for yourself?" I asked.

"Why do I need to shlep to Massachusetts to see the books?" Arnold answered, "I can see them right here in your eyes!"

There were other major donors in those early years: Joe Newman was a real estate developer in New York who loved to read Yiddish poetry. Harris Rosen was an ex-Marine who grew up on the Lower East Side and became one of the most successful hotel owners in Orlando, Florida. Working out of a modest office and driving an old Ford Taurus, he funded innovative educational programs for the poor and helped support student interns at the Book Center.

These were people who "got" Yiddish, who understood in their bones what we were trying to do. Others took a bit more persuading. I once paid a cold call on a Florida businessman who promptly informed me that he wasn't going to give me a penny. "This isn't the time to save Jewish books," he insisted. "Whatever money I have I send to Israel for guns and bombs. Let's take care of survival first. Then we can worry about books."

I responded by telling him a story I'd read about a prominent physicist who testified before Congress in support of a new particle accelerator. A sympathetic senator asked about its defense application. "It has nothing to do directly with defending our country," the scientist replied, "except to make it worth defending."

The donor was amused but unmoved. But I didn't give up. When I returned home I sent him a note quoting a passage from a two-thousand-year-old Hebrew text called *The Ethics of the Fathers:* "'Im eyn kemekh eyn toyre,' the rabbis taught, 'Where there is no bread there is no learning.' But then they continued, 'Im eyn toyre, eyn kemekh. Where there is no learning, there is no bread.'" His response came by return mail: "You win. I surrender. My check for $500 is enclosed."

The trouble was that large donations were few and far between,

while our expenses—staff, truck, rent, heat, phones, computers—
were growing fast: $50,000 in 1980, $500,000 in 1985, $1 million in
1990, $3 million today. I tried public speaking to drum up support,
hitchhiking from city to city and speaking at every synagogue that
would have me. I lectured in old urban shuls that looked like Moorish
temples and new suburban ones that looked more like spaceships. In
one synagogue the rabbi pushed a button on the bimah and the doors
of the ark slid open with a soft *whoosh,* as surely as if we'd been standing on the bridge of the Starship *Enterprise.* At another, in front of eight
hundred people, the rabbi's podium was so imposing I had to stand on
the stool usually used by bar mitzvah boys just to see over the top.
Once, during a lecture in Sarasota, Florida, the electricity went out; I
kept on speaking while the congregants surrounded me with every
menorah and candelabrum they could find, until I finally had to say,
"*Genug*—enough, I'm starting to feel like Liberace up here." In the
course of twenty-four years I delivered well over a thousand lectures,
sometimes (especially in Florida) speaking as many as four times in a
single day. I became a popular speaker, I took standing ovations in stride,
but only rarely did applause translate into significant financial support.

"How about direct mail?" asked my coworker Sharon Kleinbaum.
"You know, write a letter, mail it to all the Jews in the country, tell
them what we're doing. They won't be able to send their checks fast
enough!"

Maybe, but how? In the early 1980s we were a small staff, still typing
and stuffing our envelopes by hand. There was no way we could produce
and mail hundreds of thousands of appeal letters on our own. A professional direct mail company offered to help, but they wanted $100,000
up front plus a hefty monthly retainer. That's when we met Ken Coplon.
Then in his mid-thirties and living in Santa Monica, California, Ken jokingly referred to himself as "the direct mailer of the fringe Left." Smart,
forceful, funny, honest, and utterly unpretentious, he had, at the time,

no particular interest in Jewish culture or Yiddish books—but he did have two adopted children living in our area and he was looking for a local client so he could deduct the airfare when he came out to see them. In short, it was strictly a marriage of convenience.

But it took. The first time we met, in 1983, Ken confirmed what the other company had told us: Returns on "prospect mail," the mass appeals that most of us know as junk mail, are usually less than 1 percent, which is why it typically takes three years just to recoup costs. But Ken is a gambler by nature, and there was something about the Book Center that he found promising. "The mantra of direct mail is 'Life-Death-Urgent,'" he explained. "You've got all three, except that instead of saving people you're saving books. If you can make your case you've got a good chance of cracking one-and-a-half percent, and if you do that you'll actually make money on the prospecting, which will give you a large membership that you can rely on for ongoing support. If you're willing to take a chance, so am I." Naturally we had no upfront money of our own, so Ken raided his kids' college fund and put his own $30,000 on the line, then persuaded an elderly non-Jewish couple he knew to lend us another $5,000. Our old friend from Greenwich Village, Sonya Staff, always the visionary, gladly wrote a check for the rest.

Ken hired a professional writer living on a houseboat in San Francisco Bay, to write the initial appeal. I had assumed the letter would be signed by Isaac Bashevis Singer, who was then the honorary chairman of our board. Instead, it began, "My name is Aaron Lansky. I'm 29 years old, and I urgently need your help." When I protested, Ken quickly put me in my place. "Relax," he said, "you've got a good story, so the writer decided to use you. It's nothing personal—for him you're just another can of soup."

Flattering. Meanwhile Ken was busy tracking down lists: Jewish organizations such as the Jewish Publication Society and *Moment* magazine, along with lists of donors to liberal causes (back then, one could still assume that most Jews were liberals). Ken ran these against a "Jewish dictionary," a computer program that identified Jewish-sounding names. Our first test consisted of 108,000 pieces, and I was alone in the office when the first returns arrived. I opened the envelopes and *s'iz mir gevorn finster far di oygn* (the world went dark). Instead of checks, they were stuffed with hate mail: anti-Semitic tracts and handwritten diatribes, festooned with swastikas and crosses. My hands shaking, I dialed Ken in California.

"Don't worry," he assured me, "sometimes the Jewish Dictionary has a hard time distinguishing between Jewish names and German ones. The anti-Semites have nothing else to do, so they're always the first to respond. Give it another day or two, you'll start seeing checks."

He was right. By the second day the checks and the hate mail were running neck and neck. By the third day the checks were in the lead, and by the fourth the anti-Semites were through and the post office was delivering our mail in trays. By the time the first test was complete we had received almost two thousand contributions, more than doubling our existing membership. More important, we had reached an astonishing 1.8 percent return—thereby turning a profit on our prospecting, just as Ken had wagered. We identified the lists that had performed best and continued mailing. Those who responded stuck with us. Unlike most organizations, which hire professional letter writers to compose their routine "house" appeals, I insisted on writing subsequent letters myself, breaking every rule of direct mail fund-raising in the process. Who was it that said "Forgive me for writing such a long letter; I didn't have time to write a short one"? Instead of short, punchy letters with loads of underlining, indentions, and bullets, mine generally ran four to six pages, single spaced. I spoke to our members as friends, letting them know what we were doing and why. In addition to an annual renewal letter there were frequent emergencies: to recover those eighty-five thousand folios of forgotten sheet music, to preserve the world's last Yiddish Linotype, to hire interns, or to rescue the latest treasure trove of Yiddish books in the Soviet Union, Argentina, Mexico, or Cuba. Our members broke every record in the generosity of their response. Along with their contributions they'd send personal notes about their children or their health; Nansi Glick and I would try to answer every one personally.

It's now twenty-one years since Ken and I met. He's become one of my closest friends, and the Center's membership has reached 35,000. Not long ago, in New Bedford, a friend approached my father at shul. "You know, Sid," he said, "when most kids need money, they write home to their parents. When your kid needs money, *he* writes to *everyone!*"

STOPPING OFF IN Stockholm in the winter of 1989 to plan our return to the Soviet Union, we were surprised by how helpful everyone was—so much so that I commented on it to our liaison, an official of the Swedish Parliament. "Well, of course we're helpful," she said. "After all, haven't we just read about you in this week's issue of *Time* magazine?" That evening, at a Stockholm newsstand, Kenny Turan managed to track down a copy. On the cover was a photo of Tom Cruise, whom, with my imperfect grasp of popular culture, I failed to recognize. "Don't worry," said Kenny, "I'm pretty sure he doesn't know who you are either."

For all that, there were, over the years, many press stories about our work. A young radio reporter named Doug Berman won the AP Broadcasters Award for his coverage of our fifth-anniversary celebration—before going on to greater fame as the producer of NPR's *Car Talk*. But the only medium I could not seem to master was television. Maybe, since I didn't own a TV myself, I didn't understand its pacing. Maybe the medium and the message, TV and books, are intrinsically incompatible. Whatever the case, I just couldn't figure out how to tell the Center's story, explain its historical context, issue a call for Yiddish books, and appeal for financial support—all in twenty seconds or less. The best I learned to do was to be unresponsive. If a reporter asked me "How old is Yiddish?" I had two choices: I could say, "Yiddish is a thousand years old," and *cut,* that would be my sound bite on the evening news; or I could ignore the question, point to the books behind me, and say, "As you can see, we here at the National Yiddish Book Center have already rescued one million endangered Yiddish books. Now we're looking for help to save the rest."

On average, an article about the Center in the *New York Times* would bring two hundred letters, an NPR piece three hundred. Television appearances brought none. But that didn't mean TV viewers weren't watching. Not long after the Center opened, a local television station came to cover our first big public event. We rented a coat rack for the occasion, and when I went to return it the next day, I realized I was already several hours late, and I was afraid they'd charge me for an extra day. Instead, when I dragged the coat rack through the door, I was immediately surrounded by the smiling owner and his crew. "I saw it!" the owner shouted. "Last night I'm lying in bed watching the news and all of a sudden I says to the Missus, *'That's our coat rack!'* Our coat rack is famous. Don't worry, son, you don't owe me an extra penny, it's on the house."

Which is the only way to explain why, when I was invited in 1991 to appear on a network television show with Leo Rosten, author of *The Joys of Yiddish,* I readily agreed.

"What's the show?" my wife asked when I told her about it over dinner that evening.

"Nightwatch," I informed her. "I think it's a big deal."

"Are you sure you don't mean *Nightline?"*

The next day I phoned the network to find out.

Nightline, the producer sniffed, was a late-night news show on ABC. *Nightwatch* aired on CBS, from two to four in the morning.

"Who watches television at two o'clock in the morning?" I asked, incredulous.

"Who? Two million insomniacs, that's who!" the producer replied.

Several days later I flew to Washington and, at the network's expense, checked into a hotel room so luxurious it would have made an ambassador blush. The next morning I walked the short distance to the CBS studio, where I was taken directly to makeup. A young woman scoured my face with witch hazel and then labored over me for ten minutes with various goops and powders. "What would happen if I didn't wear all this makeup?" I asked. "Then you'd look like Richard Nixon," she replied.

The studio itself was less grand than I expected. On one wall was a composite of the Washington skyline: Capitol, White House, Supreme Court, Washington Monument. On another was a bookcase filled with a dozen random books. The floor was of painted plywood, covered by a small oriental rug. The guests sat on a couch; the NPR journalist John Hockenberry was the host. "How long have you been on television?" I asked him when we met. "Do you want that in hours or minutes?" he replied. It was his first week on the job.

And Leo Rosten? He was there, too, albeit in an incorporeal sort of way. Elderly, in imperfect health, he had decided not to travel to D.C. and was sitting instead in the CBS studio in New York. I could observe him on a large television monitor off camera to my right. "Just look at the TV when you speak to him," the engineer instructed me; "we'll mix in the feed from New York, and the audience will never know the difference."

The audience will never know the difference. It seemed a fitting tag line for the exchange that followed. Rosten's magnum opus, *The Joys of Yiddish,* is a compendium of several hundred colorful Yiddish words and expressions, defined by anecdotes and jokes. First published in 1968,

the book sold 500,000 copies and was still the first title most journalists turned to when they needed to translate a Yiddish word. "According to Leo Rosten . . . ," they'd write. Not that other, more definitive
dictionaries weren't available. Since the 1950s, for example, a small but
committed group of scholars had been painstakingly compiling one of
the most ambitious works of Jewish lexicography ever conceived: the
Great Dictionary of the Yiddish Language, the Yiddish equivalent of the *Oxford English Dictionary.* After decades of Herculean effort and the publication of four massive volumes, the *Great Dictionary* had finally reached
beys, the second letter of the alphabet. In fairness, those two letters account for roughly one-third of the language, since so many compound
words begin with alef. Be that as it may, day after day these scholars
continued to pore over citations and debate definitions, and meanwhile
the rest of the world was praising—and what's worse, quoting—Rosten's "dictionary." In the eyes of Yiddish scholars, *The Joys of Yiddish* was
a travesty, a trivialization of a vast lexical universe that Rosten, who
himself was largely unread in Yiddish literature, could not begin to
comprehend.

Me, I'm not such a *faynshmeker* (stickler). I remember laughing aloud
when I read *The Joys of Yiddish* in junior high. I believe that populariza-
tion has its place. If Rosten didn't know much about Yiddish literature,
he did know how to tell a story, and what's more, he knew what stories
American Jews wanted to hear. So my intention in appearing with him
on national television was not to argue with him, but rather to accomplish something a good deal more practical: to use his populist approach as a starting point, a way to whet viewers' appetites for the
great literature that lay beyond. The message I intended to convey was,
"If you liked *The Joys of Yiddish* you'll *love* Yiddish literature, and if you
love Yiddish literature, you'll want to sign up right now as a member
of the National Yiddish Book Center."

The show was loosely structured. "You've got a half hour," the producer told me before I left for Washington. "Let Mr. Rosten hold forth first, and then you come in halfway through with stories about Yiddish books and what you're doing to save them."

Fair enough. I watched the big clock on the wall as Leo Rosten leaned back in his chair and poured on the shmaltz, all in an affected English accent. He told cute jokes and anecdotes. At one point he actually referred to Yiddish as "a darling little language." *Darling?* The language spoken by some of the most intensely literate people the world had ever known was darling? The language in which millions of Jews lived and died and affirmed their dignity in the face of cataclysmic violence and oppression, the language in which they cried out to God and man for justice, was darling? I had to remind myself that this was television. I bided my time, eyes on the clock. Fifteen minutes past the hour and I made my move, changing the subject from nostalgia to books. Rosten didn't like being upstaged, but Hockenberry was intrigued. I launched into my first story, and I could see on the monitor that even Rosten looked interested. I was rolling now, picking up steam, pacing myself by the clock, when suddenly, out of the corner of my eye, I could see lights flashing, the engineer waving, and then John Hockenberry was smiling, interrupting, saying, "I'm sorry, but I'm afraid that's all we have time for tonight." And *"Cut!"*

"What happened?" I asked, "I thought we had half an hour?"

"We did," Hockenberry explained. "In television a half hour means twenty-two minutes. The rest is for commercials."

If fame eluded me, famous people—a surprising number of whom were enamored of Yiddish—did not. In the mid-1990s the Yiddish Book Center teamed up with KCRW in Santa Monica to produce a thirteen-part series for National Public Radio called "Jewish Short Stories from Eastern Europe and Beyond." My partner, KCRW's station manager, Ruth Seymour, once studied Yiddish literature with Max Weinreich (it

was to her that Weinreich made his prediction that Yiddish would outwit history). Together, we were determined not to "ghettoize" Yiddish
literature, not to present it in isolation, and we therefore chose thirty-
two Jewish stories from Yiddish, Hebrew, Russian, and English, all of
which would be read aloud in English translation. Our director, Joan
Micklin Silver (whose feature-film credits included *Hester Street* and
Crossing Delancey), and our two producers, Lori McGlinchey (the Center's twenty-five-year-old program director) and Johanna Cooper (a
Los Angeles radio producer), approached a veritable who's who of
famous actors, virtually all of whom readily signed on as readers: Alan
Alda, Lauren Bacall, Jeff Goldblum, Elliott Gould, Leonard Nimoy,
Walter Matthau, Rhea Perlman, and Jerry Stiller.

My grandmother never used to tire of enlightening me as to which
Hollywood stars were Jewish. What she didn't know was how many of
them grew up speaking Yiddish or had strong Yiddish roots. Walter
Matthau, for example, who told us so many stories about his Jewish up-
bringing that it took him six hours to record a forty-minute story, actually began his professional career in a Yiddish theater on Second
Avenue. "I wasn't an actor back then," he remembered. "I was a teenage
kid peddling ice cream during intermission. I had a loud voice, and I'd
walk up and down the aisles yelling, 'Get your Federal Ice Cream
here!' One day one of the actors took sick and they didn't have an un-
derstudy, so someone says, 'What about that tall kid with the loud
voice who sells the ice cream?' They sent for me, stuck a beard on my
face, gave me three lines in Yiddish, and pushed me out on stage. I liked
it so much I decided then and there to become an actor."

Leonard Nimoy, the series' host, grew up in a Yiddish-speaking home
in Boston, left for California, and began his career under none other
than Maurice Schwarz, the legendary Yiddish actor and director who
was then making his first forays onto the English stage. "My parents

were worried about me," Nimoy recalled, "a Jewish boy alone in Los Angeles. So every week Schwarz would write them a long letter in Yiddish. That's how they knew I was all right."

Even Alan Alda, a non-Jew, had Yiddish roots. "As a young man, I landed a part in an English-language production of *Yoshe Kalb* by I. J. Singer," he told me. "The director was Maurice Schwarz, who also played the role of a Hasidic rabbi. He was always telling the actors to speak louder. When his character died early in the second act, he stayed on stage covered by a sheet. If you looked closely, you could see the sheet over his face rising and falling. *'Hekher! Hekher!'* he was yelling, 'Louder! Louder!'"

The *Jewish Short Stories* series was a huge hit. It aired in every major market in the country and went into three rounds of reruns. Tape sales brought in almost a half-million dollars, enough to keep our operating budget afloat while we were out raising money for our new building. We learned an important lesson: Yiddish was famous already; all we had to do was make it accessible and the world was ready to listen.

25. A Home of Our Own

It was a beautiful spring day in 1991 when the sky came crashing down: The town of Amherst, faced with a growing school-age population, announced plans to reopen the redbrick schoolhouse that had been our home for the past eleven years. The Yiddish Book Center would soon be homeless.

I'll admit, for the first few minutes our predicament seemed hopeless. But then I got to thinking: Maybe it wasn't so much a calamity as an opportunity, a chance to build a permanent home of our own, a modern, state-of-the-art, fire-protected, climate-controlled building where, for the first time, we could consolidate our books and a growing agenda of cultural and educational programs under a single roof. What's more, it was a chance to give to Yiddish what Yiddish so urgently needed: *an adres,* an address, a physical presence, a destination where people from around the world could come to see the books they'd helped us save and celebrate the culture they contained. Within hours of the town's announcement I was already drafting a plan. As I saw it, all we needed were an architect, land, and money. Whether or not we could actually find them was not yet clear, so our board chair, Myra Fein, and I decided to find out.

We began with land. Unfortunately for us, a local real estate boom was in full swing, and the only acreage we could find in reasonable proximity to the area's colleges was in a cornfield or a strip mall, neither of which possessed quite the dignity we were looking for. "Maybe," Myra mused, "instead of building *near* one of the college campuses, we could build *on* one." It seemed unlikely, but Myra was determined, so we went to see the presidents of several of the local schools. To my amazement, they all wanted us. Mount Holyoke made an outright offer of an eighteenth-century house; all we had to do was restore it. In the end it was Hampshire College, my alma mater, that carried the day. The president, Gregory Prince, was looking to develop what he called a cultural village. The idea was to ring the campus with interesting nonprofit organizations. They would benefit from the infrastructure of the college, and the college in turn would gain unique resources for its self-directed students. He invited us to come in as the "anchor" institution.

It seemed like a *shidekh,* a good match. The only problem was that Greg wanted to lease us land for a dollar a year for the next ninety-nine years, and we didn't think that was nearly long enough. "Colleges never sell land," Greg informed us. "That may be true," I answered, "but Yiddish has known enough impermanence as it is; we have no choice but to own." Greg was nothing if not persevering. That summer he and his wife, Toni, traveled four hundred miles to visit me and Gail at our summer house, a tumbledown fisherman's cottage perched above a saltmarsh in an Acadian fishing village in Nova Scotia. For two days Greg and I tromped the beach. He explained the subtleties of academic politics, and I explained the vagaries of Jewish history and our consequent need for permanence. Greg understood. It took another three years before he was able to bring his board around, but in the end they relented, and we became the proud owners of the most magnificent piece of land that Yiddish has ever known: a ten-acre apple orchard at the southeast corner of a New England campus, with its own woodland pond and an open view of the Holyoke Range.

There was a bonus prize, too. Even though we had decided not to locate at Mount Holyoke, the college graciously provided us with a twenty-room mansion, free of charge, until our own building was complete.

We had less luck, at first, in finding the right architect. Myra and I interviewed a dozen firms. We spent a year working with one of the leading architects in Boston, to no avail. We were getting ready to launch a national competition, a costly proposition, when board member Hillel Levine gave us the name of Allen Moore. Unlike most of the architects we interviewed, Allen was not Jewish. In fact, he was *very* not Jewish. He fished. He hunted. As a young man he had opted out of the family business, the Stanley Tool Company in New Britain, Connecticut. Instead he studied architecture at Yale and went on to a singularly public-minded career, building imaginative cultural and educational buildings in the U.S. and Europe, planning a yet-to-be-built biblical study center in Israel (a collaboration with Hillel Levine), and teaching local craftspeople in the West Indies to build innovative workers' housing. Although he once ran a large architectural firm in Cambridge, he was now sixty years old and working largely on his own out of a small storefront office in Newburyport, Massachusetts. The first time we met he arrived in a secondhand Ford Taurus station wagon, wearing a waxed-cotton jacket, a wool sweater, a flannel shirt, and khaki pants. His architectural vocabulary was unlike any I had heard before: it included words like "honesty," "courtesy," and "respect." We hadn't spoken five minutes before I knew he was the one.

Myra was a bit more cautious: She liked him, too, but first she wanted to see something he had built. So in the middle of a wild snowstorm she, Gail, and I bundled into her private plane and flew to Martha's Vineyard to see a summer house Allen had just completed.

Unlike most of the island's newer homes, it was neither palatial nor ostentatious. Rather, it was just *right*. Both Myra and Gail were ready to move in on the spot, and Allen got the job.

His first stop was Harvard's Widner Library, where he researched Jewish architecture of East Europe. He was particularly taken with photos of the old wooden synagogues of Russia and Poland, virtually all of which were destroyed in the Holocaust. "It's going to be a tough challenge," he told me. "On the one hand we want to evoke historical recall. On the other hand we don't want to create a Yiddish Disneyland. We'll have to walk a very fine line."

Next he spent a snowy weekend meeting with our advisory board, a group of national museum directors and other special friends. Early Wednesday morning he came bounding into my office. "I've been up for three days and three nights," he declared. "I think I've designed your building."

And so he had. Scrunched down on his hands and knees on my office floor, he rolled out a simple, elegant plan that integrated a core book collection, extensive exhibits, a hundred-seat theater, and a resource center, reading library, English-language bookstore, offices, and kosher kitchen. The 27,000-square-foot structure would be built of wood and what Allen called "other honest materials" and would be thoroughly modern, bright and airy, with state-of-the-art climate control, fire protection, and security. Yet, remarkably, it still conveyed the impression of a traditional shtetl, albeit a decidedly whimsical one. Although it would take Allen another four years of full-time effort to perfect the details, the basic plan he presented that day never changed. It was truly a work of genius.

Which left only money to go. The price tag for the entire project—land, design, construction, and exhibits—was $7 million. Until then, with one exception, our largest single gift was $10,000. Most contributions averaged between $18 and $36 a year.

We consulted experts, who said it couldn't be done. They said we'd have to raise 90 percent of the goal from 10 percent of the donors. They said we'd need 40 percent in hand before we could announce the campaign to the public.

We took exactly the opposite approach. I wrote a letter to our members, and the response was overwhelming. Several donors who had been sending us $18 a year mailed checks for $50,000. The phones rang from morning to night. Within two months, through direct mail alone, 4,481 members had contributed $2,625,260!

The race was on. During the ensuing years, I traveled hundreds of thousands of miles to visit hundreds of individuals and foundations. Some turned me away empty-handed; many more contributed. We received $250,000 from Steven Spielberg's Righteous Persons Foundation, and $600,000 from the Kresge Foundation (though only after they inquired about "minority representation" on our board; Jews, at 1.7% of the nation's population, didn't count). The National Endowment for the Humanities helped with exhibit development. There were major gifts from some remarkable people: David and Barbara Hirschhorn (Baltimore philanthropists), Max Palevsky (technology pioneer, philosopher, and polymath), Marty Peretz (editor of *The New Republic*), Robert Price (assistant mayor under John Lindsay), Marion Brechner (an intrepid, now nonagenarian, Orlando-based television broadcaster), and Joe Jacobs (civil-rights pioneer and one of the leading labor lawyers in the South). A former Rhodes Scholar named Lief Rosenblatt—then managing director of Soros Fund Management— made a substantial gift in memory of his late wife, Melinda. Not much older than I, brilliant, principled, and a natural leader, he eventually became the chairman of our board.

But we were still several million dollars shy of our goal, with few prospects remaining, when a call came one day from Bernie Siegel, director of the Harry and Jeannette Weinberg Foundation in Baltimore.

He had read one of our direct mail letters and wanted to know more. Fortunately someone recognized the name. The Weinberg Foundation had assets of over $1 billion and accepted proposals by invitation only. When he learned about the building campaign, Mr. Siegel agreed to read "just one piece" of information. A month later he called back to request a formal proposal. Two months after that he called again: "I was intrigued by your proposal," he said. "Tell me, do you ever get to Baltimore?"

This was a question? As it happened, I was leaving that night for Los Angeles, but the second I returned I was on the Amtrak for Baltimore.

"Don't worry," my wife said. "It will all be personal. If you like each other, you'll get the grant."

I liked Bernie Siegel the moment I met him. He was kind and *heymish,* and he had a warm spot for Yiddish. We spoke for two hours in the living room of the late Weinbergs' apartment (which was surprisingly modest). I told him all about the new building. And then I took a deep breath and went for broke.

"What we're looking for," I said, "is a gift of $2 million to complete the campaign."

Bernie leaned back in his chair. "I'm afraid you're whistling at the moon," he said. "A project like this, there's no way we could commit more than $1 million."

I didn't know whether to laugh, cry, or turn a cartwheel. I could barely focus as Bernie explained that the gift would be a challenge grant: We had one year to raise the remaining $1 million on our own.

I prevailed on our board, revisited donors, wrote to our members. Within eight months we had met the challenge. Yiddish would have a home at last.

• • •

BUT LIKE MOSES, I almost didn't live to see it. In the midst of the campaign, after a particularly grueling stretch of travel, I was out walking our dog, Sadie, one cold Monday night when I was stopped in my tracks by a ferocious pain in the back of my head. The next day the doctor diagnosed it as flu and I returned to work. But all week long the pain grew worse, until by Friday night it hurt so bad I was vomiting. Gail called the doctor. "That's good," he said, "the vomiting proves it's the flu." The next day, Shabbos, brought the worst blizzard in twenty years. I drifted in and out of consciousness as the snow lashed against our bedroom window. Again Gail called the doctor; again he said it was just the flu. By evening Gail had had enough. "I don't care what the doctor says," she announced, "I'm taking you to the hospital." A neighbor came over to take care of our one-year-old daughter, Sasha. Gail was three months pregnant with our second. She phoned the ambulance: The drifts were too deep, they said, they'd have to send a civil defense truck instead.

The emergency room doctor took one look at me and knew something was dreadfully wrong. A CAT scan revealed blood on the brain. The neurosurgeon, who arrived the next morning, diagnosed it as an AVM, a rare, congenital vascular malformation in the brain. The only recourse was surgery. The odds weren't good.

They wanted to operate locally, but Gail wouldn't hear of it. She took me to Mass General, where, thanks to a call from Allen Moore (he was friends with the head of the department), I was seen by a gifted young neurosurgeon named Chris Ogilvey. He took my MRIs home, studied them late that night, and perceived a complication no one else had seen. His conscientiousness literally saved my life. The surgery lasted thirteen hours; I went into it knowing that even if I lived, there was a very real possibility of permanent neurological impairment. I of course was under anesthesia; how Gail lived through that day I'll never know. When I came to in the recovery room hers was the first face I saw. From her eyes I knew: The operation was a success. There was no neurological damage. I was going to be okay.

ADDITIONAL FUND-RAISING, PLANNING, and construction took several more years. Despite innumerable problems with weather, contractors, suppliers, unions, and town officials, the completed building was everything we hoped it would be: warm, welcoming, bright, sunny, safe, and secure. Our children, Sasha, then six, and Chava, four, spent hours rolling down the long ramp to the book repository. They never wanted to leave, which Gail and I took as a very good sign, about both our children *and* the building. In March of 1997 we installed more than three miles of donated steel library shelving and moved in the books; they looked right at home. In April we began installing commemorative plaques for each of our ten thousand donors (it took us more than three years to complete the job!). And on a picture-postcard day in June, we opened the building to the pubic. More than three thousand invited guests gathered under a huge white tent for the *khanukes habayis,* the official housewarming and dedication. Reporters were there from most of the country's major papers. A front-page headline in the English *Forward* called the building "A Post-Modern Shtetl." In a moving speech, Kenny Turan told the story about Max Weinreich with which I began this book, and referred to the building as "a Yiddish Atlantis, a lost continent of Jewish culture." I called it a *lebedike velt,* a lively world, and fighting back tears, acknowledged how gratifying it was finally to make good on the faith of all those who trusted us with their books.

But how did Delmore Schwartz put it? "In dreams begin responsibilities." Once the building opened, our small, hardscrabble organization suddenly found itself on center stage, transformed almost overnight into one of most visited and talked-about Jewish tourist destinations in America. Ten thousand visitors a year streamed through our doors, our mail tubs were overflowing, our twelve phone lines were lit from morning to night, our conferences, courses, and public programs were oversubscribed—and our budget was, as ever, stretched to the breaking point. "Either find a way to cut costs or you'll be broke in a year," our board finance committee warned me. Ken Coplon put it more plainly. "It's time to tell your staff that this isn't the food co-op anymore."

I did. It was a painful time. When the dust finally settled, a sprawling homegrown staff of thirty-two had been reduced to eighteen seasoned professionals—smart, well trained, hard-working, friendly, flexible, and resourceful. We've managed to balance our budget ever since.

Not everyone cheered our success, or if they did, their praise was not always unequivocal. Not long after our new building opened, my former teacher, Ruth Wisse, published an article in *Commentary* entitled "Yiddish: Past, Present, Imperfect," in which she contrasted two recent events: the opening of the new home of the Yiddish Book Center, and, three weeks later, in Poland, the death of Chone Shmeruk, one of the world's greatest Yiddish scholars:

> At the opening of the Center there were mistakes in a Yiddish sign and in the few Yiddish phrases with which some participants sprinkled their speeches. Mistakes are surely correctable, and any non-native speaker is likely to make them, but they signify that not even the champions of Yiddish culture in America are truly at home in the language, and this in a civilization that has historically prided itself on literary and intellectual achievement.

For the record, the single misspelled Yiddish sign to which Ruth referred, one among dozens of correct ones on display that day, had to do with parking, not literature, the mistake was typographical, not grammatical, and the young man who made it—at the last minute, after working most of the night—was Catholic, not Jewish. But in a broader sense Ruth was right: We could spend the rest of our lives studying Yiddish literature and never know a fraction of what Chone Shmeruk knew. I'm the head of a major Yiddish organization, yet my Yiddish is still not half as fluent as that of my grandfather, and he was a junkman. Which makes it hard not to worry about cultural continuity.

In her celebrated short story "Envy; or, Yiddish in America," Cynthia Ozick captures the disdain of a Yiddish writer toward those who write Jewish books in English:

He found them puerile, pitiable, ignorant, contemptible, above all stupid. In judging them he dug for his deepest vituperation— they were, he said, *'Amerikaner geboren.'* Spawned in America, pogroms a rumor, *mama-loshen* a stranger, history a vacuum.

Well, I, too, am *Amerikaner geboren,* American born and raised. Like most of my generation, I didn't speak Yiddish at home, I didn't study Torah and Talmud in my youth, I didn't attend Yiddish schools or belong to a Jewish youth movement or grow up with a life-or-death awareness of Jewish identity, and as a result I will never match the native Yiddish fluency or the depth and breadth of Jewish learning of Chone Shmeruk or Ruth Wisse—or of my friend Sam Kassow. Not ten years older than I, Sam is a Russian, German, and Jewish historian who was born in a displaced persons camp in Germany shortly after the war. His mother was a partisan. He knows seven languages, including Yiddish and Hebrew, and is well read in all of them. Our wives are close friends, our children are roughly the same age, and when we get together for *yonteyvim,* Jewish holidays, the kids play while Sam and I drink *shnaps* and talk about Jews. It's an inexhaustible subject, and what I always realize is that Sam, who is not *Amerikaner geboren,* has more Jewish knowledge in his smallest fingertip than I can hope to acquire in a lifetime of study.

That incontrovertible fact is not necessarily cause for despair, though; it does not necessarily mean that we've reached the end of the road, that Jewish knowledge is condemned to dilution with each passing generation, or that America—a land where *mame loshn* really is a stranger and history a vacuum—does not, perhaps for that very reason, possess certain *mayles,* certain virtues of its own. No one is more aware of America's promise than Ruth Wisse (born in Romania, raised in Canada, now at Harvard), as she makes clear in her impressions of our dedication:

> The new building, architecturally evocative of the wooden synagogues in Eastern Europe, is the most beautiful and certainly the most carefully designed dwelling place that Yiddish has ever had. . . . The Yiddish Book Center has enlisted the American spirit to help save the Yiddish heritage. . . . I have learned a lot from this young man about the potential of good ideas joined to an entrepreneurial imagination. . . . Jews are never more American than when they show initiative on their own behalf. All that Aaron was able to accomplish for the Yiddish Book Center derives from his pride and pleasure in growing up Jewish in New England.

Heneini—of the hundreds of journalists and scholars who have written about the Center, Ruth was the most perceptive. Despite our abiding commitment to history, my colleagues and I at the Yiddish Book Center do not pine for the Old Country or for the past. We are who we are, where we are, when we are. And in that sense I prefer to compare us not to Chone Shmeruk, a twentieth-century Yiddish scholar, but to Zushya, a nineteenth-century Hasidic rabbi. "When I die," Zushya foretold, "God will not ask me, 'Zushya, why weren't you more like Moses?' God will ask, 'Zushya, why were you not more like Zushya?'" We American Jews are often ignorant of history, but we are shaped and challenged by it all the same. Here on the free soil of New England, where our permanent home now stands, we have as good a chance as any to outwit it still.

26. Immortality

Everybody's mad at us!" Abra Greenberg, the stalwart director of our Yiddish book repository, informed me one hot day in September 1997. Until our new building opened three months before, most of the books we collected had been stored in our Holyoke warehouse, where the public rarely got to see them. Unless we had at least five copies of a given title, they were reserved for major libraries and never listed in our published catalogs. As a result, visitors never knew what they were missing. But now, in the new building, our stacks were open, visitors were welcome, and they were invariably incensed when Abra refused to sell them the particular book they wanted, especially when they could see extra copies sitting right there on the shelf. "What am I supposed to do?" Abra asked me. "Our customers won't take no for an answer."

It might seem strange, after collecting more than a million Yiddish books, that we didn't have enough to go around, especially when the ranks of many authors—Sholem Aleichem, Sholem Asch, Guy de Maupassant—were full to overflowing. But when it came to other great writers, such as I. J. Singer, Isaac Bashevis Singer, Hirsch Dovid Nomberg, Moyshe Kulbak, Alter Kacyzne, Dovid Bergelson, and hundreds more, for whatever reason—whether too few copies were printed or the editions were too flimsy, whether they weren't read enough or they were read too much—our stocks were woefully inadequate. Even if we did have sufficient numbers, all it took was one professor in one university to assign such a book to her class, and poof, our entire supply would be instantly depleted. Keep in mind that we are the only comprehensive supplier of Yiddish books on the planet, and then imagine an analogous situation in any other literature: Say, for example, that in all the bookstores in all the world there were only five extant copies of *Don Quixote, Great Expectations, War and Peace,* or *Moby-Dick.* We'd be signing petitions, convening commissions, appealing to publishers, universities, governments, the United Nations, somebody, anybody, until the missing titles were back in print. Why should Yiddish be any different?

The problem didn't stop there. Even when we did have sufficient duplicate copies, their condition was often so bad as to render them unusable. That's because modern Yiddish literature holds the dubious distinction of being 100 percent acidic: printed on inexpensive, wood-pulp paper, which, because of its high acidity, gradually breaks down, turning yellow and brittle and, eventually, crumbling into fragments and dust. Although this is not a uniquely Jewish problem—every library in the world struggles with the Herculean task of conserving books printed after 1850, when pulp paper (as opposed to rag paper) came into widespread use—the problem for Yiddish is particularly severe. Even the best of Yiddish publishers were usually shoestring operations, and more often than not they cut costs by using the cheapest paper they could find.

Like all readers of Yiddish literature, I had grown accustomed to the problem. When I turned the pages of a Yiddish book, I pretty much expected them to crumble. My wife, on the other hand, did not. Night after night she'd watch in disbelief as I lay with her in bed, engrossed in one or another Yiddish novel, oblivious to the monsoon of paper crumbs raining down on our new cotton sheets. Some libraries had begun to deacidify their most brittle volumes by treating them with alkaline gases or solutions, but the process was expensive (as much as $100 a volume) and it could only arrest further disintegration, not reverse the damage that had already been done. A brittle book would remain brittle, no matter what they did. As a result, many libraries balked at acquiring Yiddish books from us: Already swamped with millions of brittle volumes of their own, why compound their *tsores* by bringing more coal to Newcastle?

So there we were in our brand-new building, Abra and I and a handful of students, surrounded by crumbling books and angry customers, without a clue about what to do to make them happy.

"How about *reprinting* books?" one of our work-study students suggested.

"We tried," Abra explained. "A few years ago we reprinted a missing volume of the *Lexicon of Yiddish Literature*. It cost us three thousand dollars. Altogether we've got about fifteen thousand titles in our collection. Let's see . . . that would be $45 million to reprint them all."

"Okay," the student persisted, "but there's got to be another way. Have you ever thought of *digitization?*"

We hadn't; the technology was still in its infancy back then. But the idea was intriguing. Using computer scanners (essentially, high-tech Xerox machines), it was theoretically possible to take an electronic "picture" of every page of every book, store the images in a computer, and use them to print brand-new copies on demand. As far as we knew, no one had ever tried to digitize an entire literature before, but we could think of no compelling reason why it *couldn't* be done. So we consulted experts at Harvard and Yale and turned to our longtime friend Peter Lerner, an investment analyst with the Kaufmann Fund, in search of a company to whom we could outsource the labor-intensive work of scanning and production. Peter went straight to the CEO of

Danka, a spin-off of Kodak, who agreed to take on the project at a price 95 percent less than that of a larger competitor. Three weeks later, at a factory in Mechanicsburg, Pennsylvania, the systematic digitization of Yiddish literature began.

The process wasn't simple. First each book had to be "disbound": the spine cut off so that pages could be fed through the scanner one at a time. Danka had to order special machines from Japan that could scan both sides of the page at once, since many were too brittle to go through twice. Most books were so dusty the technicians had to clean the scanners' lenses after every pass. At our end, we had to keep up with selection, cataloging, and proofing. And fund-raising. Steven Spielberg's Righteous Persons Foundation provided a lead gift, in recognition of which we named the project "The Shmuel Shpilberg Digital Yiddish Library," and our friend Max Palevsky, Spielberg's first boss, sponsored the Palevsky Literature Collection. For $360, we gave our members a chance to "adopt" a title, adding their name and commemoration to the title page every time the book was reprinted. Even my wife and I contributed—we couldn't resist the chance to immortalize our parents.

After four years of round-the-clock scanning, our online catalog went live in June 2001 (at www.yiddishbooks.org). Our project director, Gabe Hamilton, worked with colleagues at VTLS, a library automation company, to design an interface similar to that of Amazon.com: You log on, search for books by author, title, subject, or keyword, and click on the titles you want. The order goes straight to the bindery, where it takes only minutes to produce a brand-new acid-free, clothbound copy that looks as good as or better than the original and will last for five hundred years.

Although many individuals still prefer our original "artifactual" books, the reprints are a godsend for libraries, since they require no conservation and can better withstand the rigors of circulation. We're now reaching beyond our own collection. Our Noah Cotsen Library of Yiddish Children's Literature includes almost a thousand Yiddish children's books, many borrowed from the YIVO. And our David and Sylvia Steiner Yizkor Book Collection, a joint project with the New York Public Library, offers on-demand reprints of almost seven hundred memorial volumes chronicling Jewish communities destroyed in the Holocaust—a crucial resource for historical and genealogical research.

In many ways digitization is the fulfillment of our original mission: to preserve Yiddish books and make them accessible forever. Our electronic masters—3.5 million pages and counting—take up less room than a shoe box, and we have secreted duplicate copies in secure locations across the country, including a former Strategic Air Command bunker buried deep inside a mountain not a half mile from our Amherst headquarters. Our next step is the Virtual Yiddish Library, an ambitious plan to place the *content* of most Yiddish books online, fully searchable and instantly available, free of charge, to any computer user anywhere in the world. The day our catalog went online, the *New York Times* reported that "Yiddish is now, proportionately, the most in-print literature on earth." Just as gratifying was a letter from the makers of Trivial Pursuit informing us that an upcoming edition of their popular board game would include the question "What was the first literature to be digitized?" On the flip side of the card, the answer, of course, is "Yiddish."

EARLY ON THE morning of July 18, 1994, a massive explosion ripped through the main Jewish communal building of Buenos Aires, killing ninety-seven people and injuring two hundred, many of them children. The work of Iranian terrorists, it was the deadliest attack on a diaspora Jewish community since the Holocaust. Within an hour of the explosion, Shoshana Wolkowicz-Balaban, an Argentinian Jew living in New York, phoned to inform me that the building was home to the largest Jewish library in South America. The next day I wired the head of the Jewish community in Buenos Aires, offering to replace every volume that had been destroyed. Four months later, our bibliographer, Neil Zagorin, and Zachary Baker, then head librarian of the YIVO, traveled south to make the necessary arrangements. Their report was chilling:

> The scene still resembled a war zone. An immense crater yawned where the front door of the seven-story building once stood; the rear of the structure, open to the elements, leaned cracked and askew, light and plumbing fixtures dangling. Across the street apartment houses gaped, their facades collapsed, skeletal and empty. . . . Deserted rooms with cracked and crazy walls, suspended ceiling beams like broken bones protruding at rakish angles, and the occasional piece of furniture covered with plaster dust were all that remained of the social service agencies on the lower floors. . . . [In the building's auditorium] a grand piano, its veneer warped by exposure to the elements, still stood—on the edge of nothing. . . . In an adjacent conference room stood a table that rescue teams had used for emergency surgery after the blast.

Because the library was in the back of the building, many books survived, but their pages were covered with pulverized plaster and concrete, and some were stained with blood. Workers carried them down rickety ladders to the basement of an adjacent synagogue, where, as Neil and Zak watched, a small group of volunteers, including students from a local Hebrew school, painstakingly cleaned them, one page at a time.

The bombing in Buenos Aires was a reminder that assaults on Jews and Jewish books are not a thing of the past. All over the world there are ominous signs that anti-Semitism is on the rise. And the tragedy this time is that as lies about Jews grow more extravagant and calumnies more outrageous, most of us know too little about our history and culture to refute them.

Historical amnesia is a dangerous malady, especially for a people whose identity is as dependent on historical memory as ours. And the hour is later than many of us think. Two years ago, as part of our annual Summer Program in Yiddish Culture, Moshe Waldoks delivered a lecture on Jewish humor. A child of Holocaust survivors, a native Yiddish-speaker, a rabbi deeply steeped in Jewish learning, Waldoks was riotously funny — so funny that our adult participants, my wife and I included, were holding our sides, tears rolling down our cheeks, and I was beginning to regret our not having a defibrillator on the premises. After one particularly funny Jewish joke, I happened to turn around to look at our eight student interns, all of them between eighteen and twenty years old. They were standing in a row in the back, arms crossed, and except for one young woman whose parents came from Mexico, they were completely stone-faced. They weren't laughing. They hadn't even cracked a smile. Gail and I spoke with them after the lecture to find out why. "We didn't think it was funny," one intern explained. "We didn't get the joke."

This was not a good sign: If our smartest and most Jewishly committed young people no longer get the joke, it means that on the most fundamental level, they don't understand Jewish culture.

That is what makes the books we've saved so important. In their pages lies a civilization, a missing millennium of Jewish history, the knowledge we need to defend ourselves. Moreover they contain a sensibility, born of marginality, that our fractured world desperately needs. After all, nothing heightens one's commitment to social justice more than injustice, nothing hones one's love of peace more than a few thousand years of violence and oppression. Yet at this precise moment, when threats of terrorism, environmental catastrophe, and nuclear annihilation have the whole world feeling vulnerable, when Jewishness has more to say than ever before, what do we do? We disavow our past, jettison our books, and forget to teach our children who they are.

There's a saying that a person who speaks many languages is a polyglot, a person who speaks two languages is bilingual, and a person who speaks one language is American. How many American Jews speak Yiddish anymore, and how many are likely to take the time to learn? Our work at the Yiddish Book Center is more than academic. If Yiddish books are even half as important as we think they are, if they really ought to be read, then our next big job is to translate the best into English—the language most readers understand.

Which reminds me of an encounter twenty years ago, when, after a lecture in Los Angeles, I was approached by a determined, white-haired woman clutching a thick sheaf of yellowed paper.

"*Yungerman!*" she said. "My name is Trafimov, I am a Yiddish poet. Please, you must help me!"

"Of course, Mrs. Trafimov," I replied, "what can I do for you?"

"I brought you my poems," she said, indicating the dog-eared pages in her hand. "I want you should translate them right away into English."

I explained that translation was a laborious process, that I was working fourteen hours a day as it was, and that, regrettably, I didn't have the time to undertake a project of such magnitude.

She shook her head. "You don't understand," she said. "I'm old, I'm sick. I need you to translate me before I die so my grandchildren should know who I am!"

Although I gave her the names of several people I thought could help, I'm not sure whether her grandchildren ever did get to read her poems while she was still alive. Twenty years later, with her generation of Yiddish writers now all but gone, it occurs to me that the imperative for translation has changed: It is no longer a matter of grandchildren knowing their grandparents, but rather of grandchildren knowing themselves.

Granted, there are those for whom the very notion of translation seems an act of betrayal, an insult to the original books we've worked so hard to save. Back when I was a college student, my Yiddish teacher, Jules Piccus, caught me off guard one day by asking if I had ever read *Don Quixote*. In truth, I had barely skimmed the book when it was assigned in high school, but I did own the record of "Man of La Mancha," which I figured ought to count for something, so I answered halfheartedly in the affirmative.

Jules raised an eyebrow. "Oh, really," he said, "I didn't know you could read Medieval Spanish."

"Oh no," I explained, "I read it in translation."

"Translation?" Jules bellowed, *"What the hell is that?"*

It's hard to believe, but he insisted that he had never read a book in any but its original language. If he didn't know the language he went out and learned it. "It's like the Italians say," he vociferated, *"Traduttore, traditore*—all translators are goddamned liars!"

Easy for him to say, with twenty languages under his belt. But he did have a point. The few times I've had occasion to compare a Yiddish original side by side with its English translation, I've been aghast at how sharply divergent the two texts often are. Translators make mistakes, they revise, bowdlerize, or even change endings to suit their own interpretations. I was once at a lecture where Isaac Bashevis Singer told of his own travails:

"There was a line in one of my books," he related, "in which I said that a woman *'hot oysgeshrign azoy vi a froy in kimpet.'* In English, this was translated as, 'She cried out like a woman in labor,' meaning like a woman about to give birth. When the book was translated into Hebrew, the Hebrew translator didn't know Yiddish, so he had to work from the English translation. In Hebrew the line became, 'She cried out like a woman in the Histadrut'—like a woman in the Labor movement."

Of course, when it came to translation Singer was more fortunate than most. His first translator was Saul Bellow, whose masterful rendition of *"Gimpl tam* (Gimpel the Fool)" appeared in *Partisan Review* in 1953. (Bellow told me that Singer never hired him again, afraid that people would attribute his stories' success to their translator and not their writer.) In later years, as his English improved, Singer himself oversaw his translations—perhaps the only real guarantee of accuracy.

Even more dismaying than *how* Yiddish books were translated was *which* Yiddish books were translated. There is an old Yiddish expression: *"Ale kales zenen sheyn, ale toyte zenen frum* (All brides are beautiful, all dead people are pious)." In the decades following the Holocaust, there was an understandable attempt to eulogize a world that had been destroyed. As a result, translated titles were often those that cast the Old Country in a rosy glow, while those that portrayed Jews as real-life human beings with frailties and foibles, conflicts and contradictions— in short, the best literature—were, with notable exceptions, largely overlooked. Even today, only one-half of one percent of Yiddish literature—one Yiddish title in two hundred—is available in English translation.

So in 2001 we teemed up with Neal Kozodoy, editor of *Commentary* and head of the Fund for the Translation of Jewish Literature, to launch "The New Yiddish Library," an international initiative to identify the best Yiddish books and make them available in accurate, literate, and above all, readable English translations. Under the leadership of our

editor-in-chief, David Roskies, the first-ever professor of Yiddish literature at the Jewish Theological Seminary in New York, our editorial
board has identified scores of spectacular titles, virtually all of them unknown to English readers. Forthcoming translations include:

Smugglers (1920). Twenty-two-year-old Oyzer Varshavski's debut
novel about the upending of traditional values in a Polish shtetl
during the "total war" of 1919 when everyone from rabbis to
prostitutes resorted to smuggling.

When All Is Said and Done (*Nokh alemen,* 1913). Dovid Bergelson's
masterpiece about the independent daughter of a traditional, aris-
tocratic Jew, who tries to find meaning in a chaotic, radically
changing world.

Zelmenyaners (1931). Moyshe Kulbak's comic novel about a Jewish
family during the era of Soviet collectivization.

Ordinary Jews (*Yidn fun a gants yor,* 1935). Alternately described as a
biographical novel and an epic, Yehoshua Perle's "book of vanished
life" deploys a unique, naturalist style to tell the story of a Jewish
boy growing up in a provincial Polish city.

The Poetry of Moishe Leib Halpern. Poet, painter, and bohemian,
Halpern led a tormented life on the streets of New York but produced some of the most exquisitely crafted modernist poetry of
the twentieth century. John Hollander, the distinguished American poet and scholar from Yale University, will capture Halpern's
impassioned Yiddish voice in English.

Collected Writings of Rachel Auerbach. With her keen powers of obser-
vation, Auerbach left an incomparable journalistic record of
Polish Jewish life, both before and during the Holocaust. Her
courageous first-person reports from the Warsaw ghetto—
included in the underground Oyneg Shabbos Archive—were

buried in milk cans and recovered from beneath the rubble after the War.

And that's just the beginning. In short, we have no shortage of titles, only of time. It takes a good translator the better part of a year to translate a single book, and thus far, after scouring the United States, Israel, England, Canada, and South Africa, we've identified just a half-dozen first-rate Yiddish translators. But the literature is there, as is the need, as are the English readers, so we're determined to try. Our goal is to publish at least two or three new titles every year. We have every reason to believe that we can continue to dazzle and inspire English readers with newfound Yiddish treasures for decades to come.

27. The Valise at the Bottom of the Sea

My grandmother was sixteen years old when she emigrated to America. She came alone, carrying with her a single cardboard valise packed with all her life's possessions—a few books, clothing, a goose-down pillow, a pair of Shabbos candlesticks, and a photograph of her mother and father, whom she would never see again. At Ellis Island she was met by her older brother, who had preceded her to America. On the ferry to Manhattan he took her suitcase and flung it overboard. "You're in America now," he told her, "it's time to leave the Old Country behind."

I was thirty years old when I heard this story for the first time, and my initial reaction was one of outrage. How could my great-uncle have done such a thing? But with the passage of time, I've come to take a more philosophical view. If checking our baggage at the gate was the price of admission to America—where we are more free, more welcome, and more accepted than in any other place or at any other time in Jewish history—then maybe it wasn't such a bad bargain after all. Nor is it too late to make amends. My grandparents and, to a lesser extent, my parents thought of themselves as newcomers in America. I, on the other hand, am American through and through—so comfortable in my Americanism that I have no compunction about going back to dredge the harbor to reclaim what was lost.

The valise itself, of course, is long gone, buffeted by the currents, buried beneath a century of silt and sand at the bottom of the sea. So I've had to content myself with collecting a million-and-a-half Yiddish books instead. Between their covers the voices of my grandmother's world can still be heard.

I have no illusions, though. I don't believe, because Yiddish books are now safe, that we'll all start speaking Yiddish again. The social circumstances that gave rise to the Yiddish language no longer prevail for most Jews. But I do believe that we have much to learn from Yiddish books, just as Jews have always learned from the texts of the past. Moreover, although Yiddish literature itself is likely finite, I believe that its spirit and sensibility can still inspire new Jewish literary expression, in English and other languages.

Is such continuity really possible? In Philip Roth's 1969 novel *Portnoy's Complaint,* the young American-born protagonist concedes that he has "twenty-five Yiddish words to [his] name—half of them dirty and the rest mispronounced!" For some, that may have seemed the end of the line. But consider this remarkable scene from *Patrimony,* Roth's 1991 memoir, in which his father is slowly dying of a brain tumor, and he, Philip, inquires about his *tefilin,* the leather phylacteries worn by Jewish men at morning prayer:

> "Who'd you give the tefillin to?" I asked him.
> "Who, nobody."
> "You threw them out? In the trash?"
> "No, no, of course I didn't."
> "You gave them to the synagogue?" I didn't know what you did with tefillin when you no longer wanted or needed them, but surely, I thought, there would be a religious policy for discarding them, overseen by the synagogue.

"You know the Y?" he said to me.

"Sure."

"Three, four mornings a week when I could still drive over there, I'd swim, kibitz, I'd watch the card game. . . ."

"And?"

"Well, that's where I went. The Y. . . . I took the tefillin in a paper bag. The locker room was empty, I left them . . . in one of the lockers."

Maybe it was just revealed to him in a flash . . . the understanding that where his tefillin would come to no harm, where they would not be profaned or desecrated, where they might even be resanctified, was in the midst of those familiar Jewish bellies and balls. Perhaps what the act signified was . . . a declaration that the men's locker room at the local YMHA was closer to the core of the Judaism he lived by than the rabbi's study at the synagogue — that nothing would have been *more* artificial than going with the tefillin to the rabbi . . . Yes, the locker room of the Y, where they undressed, they *shvitzed,* they stank, where, as men among men, familiar with every nook and cranny of their worndown, old, ill-shapen bodies, they kibitzed and told their dirty jokes, and where, once upon a time, they'd made their deals — that was their temple and where they remained Jews.

Resanctified at the Y. What Roth's dying father intuitively understood, and what Philip Roth the writer recognized, was that there are two sides to Jewish life, the holy and the everyday, and that our identity resides not in one or the other, but in the give-and-take between the two. Remember the traditional Jewish proverbs, in which sacred Hebrew texts were played off against common Yiddish? Somehow the juxtaposition of the two was more deeply Jewish than the Hebrew alone. The same is true of Roth's father's *tefilin:* Moving them from the synagogue to the locker room creates a scene infinitely richer in its Jewish evocations than would have been the case had the *tefilin* never left the shul at all. It doesn't matter whether the author knows twenty-five words of Yiddish or twenty-five thousand: As long as he can recognize shul and Y for what they are, opposite but equally authentic aspects of Jewish identity, the spirit of Yiddish literature lives on.

It is one of my few regrets that, having passed up a life of scholarship, I've spent more time collecting Yiddish books than I have reading them. Of the titles I have read, my personal favorite remains *Tevye der milkhiger, Tevye the Dairyman,* by Sholem Aleichem—one of the books handed to me by Mr. Levine from his grandfather's bookcase during my first trip to the Lower East Side so many years ago. Published serially between 1895 and 1916, *Tevye* was a perennial favorite among readers, as attested by the scores of pallets loaded with Sholem Aleichem's *Complete Works* in our warehouse. When, several years back, the Yiddish Book Center convened an international panel of scholars to choose the "One Hundred Greatest Works of Modern Jewish Literature," *Tevye* was everyone's first choice. It has been translated into thirty languages, it was the basis of an important 1939 feature film by Maurice Schwarz, and later it gained worldwide fame through its adaptation to stage and screen as *Fiddler on the Roof.*

Which, for better or worse, is where I first made its acquaintance. I was fifteen years old when my parents insisted on taking me and my brothers to see a production of *Fiddler* at the Melody Tent on Cape Cod. It sounded boring (as did most things Jewish when I was that age), and we beseeched them to drop us off at a nearby go-cart track instead—until my mother mentioned that the lead role of Tevye would be played by Leonard Nimoy, so well known to us as *Star Trek's* Mr. Spock. As I recall, Nimoy made a first-rate Tevye—not so surprising when you consider his Yiddish origins. At the time, however, I only knew about his Vulcan *yikhes,* and my brothers and I spent the whole first act elbowing each other and whispering wisecracks: "Hey, where are his ears?" "Illogical, Lazar Wolf." "Beam me up, Golda!" But by the second act we were enthralled. True, *Fiddler on the Roof* is a long way from Sholem Aleichem's original stories; but it was the first inkling I had that Yiddish literature existed, it was the single most Jewish story I had ever encountered, and in a word, I was smitten.

What is it exactly about Tevye, a rural dairyman blessed with five beautiful but rebellious daughters, that strikes us as so quintessentially Jewish? Is it because of his attachment to tradition, as *Fiddler on the Roof* would have us believe? Hardly. Although Tevye is an observant Jew, he is constantly "twisting biblical quotations this way and that" as he struggles to keep up with the changes around him. He finds himself, in fact, breaking with tradition, or at least stretching it, more often than he defends it.

Is it because he's a great Jewish scholar? Tevye would be flattered to hear you say so. He likes nothing more than to quote from high-sounding Hebrew texts. But on closer examination, his sources are mostly rudimentary: the Bible, the prayer book, the *Ethics of the Fathers,* the kinds of things that, in Tevye's day, any *kheyder yingl,* any elementary-school student, would have been expected to know. It's only we, with our even weaker Jewish knowledge, who are impressed. When Tevye does offer up Hebrew quotations, more often than not he *mistranslates* them into Yiddish.

Is it because he lives in Anatevka, a warm, loving, tight-knit shtetl? Only on the stage. In the original stories, he and his family live a long way from Anatevka, in the countryside, where they're surrounded by Ukranian peasants, with no other Jews for miles around.

So what *is* it about Tevye that makes him seem, as he puts it, *"a yid shebiyid,* a Jew's Jew"? Answer that question, solve that riddle, and we begin to understand what makes Yiddish literature seem so Jewish, and why even now the books we've found remain so compulsively readable and relevant.

The basic plot outline is well known. Each of Tevye's five daughters forces him to confront a different challenge of the modern world. The oldest, Tsaytl, forgoes an arranged match and marries for love. The second, Hodel, falls in love with a revolutionary and ends up following him into exile in Siberia. The fourth daughter, Shprintse, who along with her younger sister was omitted from *Fiddler,* becomes infatuated with the nephew of a rich man, apparently becomes pregnant, and when disavowed by her boyfriend's family, commits suicide by drowning herself in a pond outside Tevye's home. The last daughter, Beyle, rejects her older sisters' idealism and marries for money; her wealthy husband is as old as Tevye himself, and he tries to get his new father-in-law out of the way by giving him a one-way ticket to Palestine. There are two more stories at the end of the series, in which Tevye talks his way out of a pogrom, only to be expelled forever from his native home.

But it is the middle daughter, Chava, who presents Tevye with the greatest challenge by running off with a bookish peasant named Fyedka Galagan. The story is not so much about intermarriage (hardly a burning issue in the Ukrainian countryside in 1906) as it is about the lure of universalism: True to her name (Chava is Hebrew for Eve), she seeks to move beyond Jewish specificity and embrace the universality of all mankind. Her act not only breaks her parents' hearts, it also challenges the future of Yiddish literature itself: If all people really are one, then why continue living apart and writing in a provincial language such as Yiddish?

As Tevye knows full well, Chava is a highly intelligent and forceful young woman, and the logic of her position is not easily refuted. Consider, for example, this exchange, when Tevye catches Chava and Fyedka together for the first time:

I asked Chava, "What was Fyedka doing here?"

"Nothing," she said.

"What do you mean nothing?"

"We were just talking."

"What business have you got talking with Fyedka?"

"We've known each other for a long time," she said.

"Congratulations!" I said. "A fine friend you've picked for your-self. . . . His father," I said, "must have been either a shepherd or a janitor or else just a plain drunkard."

To this Chava answered, "Who his father was I don't know and don't care to know. All people are the same to me. . . . God cre-ated all men equal."

Tevye has no effective response. He begins quoting from Hebrew sources, as is his wont, but Chava, who can hold her own in an argu-ment, will have none of it:

"Marvelous!" she cried. "Unbelievable! You have a quotation for everything. Maybe you also have a quotation that explains why men have divided themselves up into Jews and Gentiles, into lords and slaves, noblemen and beggars?"

Interestingly, it's not Tevye with his highbrow Hebrew who breaks the impasse, but his wife, Golda, with her decidedly *heymish,* earth-bound Yiddish:

"Maybe you've done enough jabbering out there," my wife Golda called out from inside the house. "The borsht has been sitting on the table for an hour and he's still out there singing Sabbath hymns."

"Another province heard from! No wonder our sages have said, *The fool hath seven qualities* — A woman talks nine times as much as a man.' We are discussing important matters and she comes barging in with her *milkhiger* (dairy) borscht."

"My *milkhiger* borsht," said Golda, "may be just as important as all those important matters of yours."

"*Mazl-tov!* We have a new philosopher here, straight from behind the oven. It isn't enough that Tevye's daughters have become enlightened, now his wife has to start flying through the chimney right up into the sky."

"Since you mention the sky," said Golda, "I might as well tell you I hope you rot in the earth."

Tell me, Mr. Sholem Aleichem, what do you think of such crazy goings on on an empty stomach?

"*My* milkhige *borsht may be just as important as all those important matters of yours.*" When the rational, scholarly, masculine, Hebrew side of Jewish tradition fails, the *heymish,* workaday, down-to-earth, feminine, Yiddish side prevails. In the end, Golda suggests, it's borscht, more than Hebrew quotations, that will hold the Jewish people together.

Except that borscht alone is no more than ethnicity, and we soon see that it, too, is not enough to keep Chava at home. The next day she elopes. When Tevye finds out, from his nemesis, the local Russian Orthodox priest, he returns home, steps out to the barn, and blind with rage, beats his poor, tired horse. Why? "Because he was standing there with one foot on the other side of the slats," Tevye tells us. In other words, he beats his horse for doing the same thing he did: straddling the fence, trying to have it both ways, tradition and change, Hebrew quotations and Yiddish reinterpretations. The price of Tevye's homemade synthesis was too high to pay; his daughter is gone for good.

Eventually Tevye returns to work, to "*mayn bisl milkhigs,*" but he can't get Chava out of his mind. And then one day, as he rides alone through the woods, Chava runs out to meet him. In *Fiddler,* and even in Schwarz's film, she is wearing the bright costume of a Ukrainian peasant. In the story she's dressed just as she always was: "not her dress, not one hair on her head has changed"—meaning that she didn't need to leave Jewishness to embrace universalism. She begs her father to listen to her. Tevye is torn, he's tormented, but when she reaches for the horse's bridle he breaks free and leaves her alone by the side of the road.

> All the rest of the way, as I drove, I thought I could hear her running after me, calling, "Listen, father, listen to me." A thought crossed my mind, " . . . Will it hurt you to stop and listen to her? . . . I blamed myself . . . "Stubborn mule, turn your wagon around and go back and talk to her, she is your own child." And peculiar thoughts came into my mind. "What is the meaning of Jew and non-Jew? Why did God create Jews and non-Jews? And since God did create Jews and non-Jews, why should they be segregated from each other and hate each other, as though one were created by God and the other were not?" I regretted that I wasn't as learned as some men so that I could arrive at an answer to this riddle.

Then a remarkable thing happens. Tevye knows that Chava and Fyedke have left the village and moved to Kiev, a cosmopolitan city. After much soul-searching, he decides to join them. Since Kiev lies outside the Pale of Settlement and is thus off-limits to Jewish habitation, Jews refer to the city by the code name Yehupetz. After making Sholem Aleichem promise not to laugh at him, Tevye continues:

> I put on my Shabbos gabardine as though I were going away on the train, going to see them. I walk up to the ticket window and ask for a ticket. The ticket seller asks me where I want to go. "To Yehupetz," I tell him. And he says, "There is no such place." And I say, "Well, it's not my fault then." And I turn myself around and go home again, take off my Sabbath clothes and go back to work,

back to my own cows and my horse and wagon. As it is written, *"Each man to his labor*—The tailor to his shears and the shoemaker to his last."

Even when Tevye is finally ready to accept the logic of Chava's position—that all people really are equal and should not have to live separate one from the other—even when he's finally ready to join his daughter and son-in-law in Kiev, the non-Jews won't let him go, since Yehupetz is no more than a Jewish fiction and the real Kiev is a city where Jews are not allowed. So he gives up on the idea, returns home, hangs up his Shabbos clothes, and returns to his dairy business, to the everyday Jewish fold. But his lack of culpability is small comfort. His daughter has carried Jewish values to their logical extreme, she's left his home and gone where he can't follow, and he therefore regards himself as an abject failure. "I see that you are laughing at me," he tells Sholem Aleichem.

. . . Don't forget what I asked you. *Pasekh shin sha*—be silent as the grave concerning this. Don't put what I told you into a book. And if you should write, write about someone else, not about me. Forget about me. As it is written: *"V'yishkhakeyhu*—And he was forgotten." *Oys Tevye der milkhiger*—No more Tevye the Dairyman!

Of course, Sholem Aleichem *does* write about him. And although Tevye's personal tragedy is beyond recompense, in our eyes he is anything but a failure. If Jewishness was and is the product of a constant dialectic—between the holy and the everyday, male and female, Hebrew and Yiddish—then Tevye has the distinction of embodying these competing elements within himself. He may be too blind with grief to recognize the fact, but it is precisely that relentless interior debate that made him so quintessentially Jewish.

Much has changed in the hundred years since "Chava" appeared.

Most of the old legal restrictions on Jewish settlement are gone. Nowadays I can go to the train station or log onto the Internet and buy a ticket to pretty much anywhere. Which means there are no more excuses: If I want to move beyond the Jewish sphere, no non-Jew is likely to stand in my way.

Many Jews have left already. Assimilation is rampant. More often than not, those who remain tend to reduce Jewishness to religion alone. Few have the *kheyshek,* the inclination, to live as Tevye did. And why should they? If he managed, somehow, to keep his balance between old and new, he walked a tightrope across which his own daughters couldn't follow. How then are *we* supposed to keep our balance up there on the highwire, when our Jewish knowledge has grown so scant and the lure of the outside world so much more seductive than ever before?

Sometimes, at night, standing alone in our warehouse, looking at those rows upon rows of rescued books, I marvel at the wiles of history. How did it happen that we, arguably the most book-loving people on the planet, parted with an entire literature, without so much as a word of deliberation or regret? Even after twenty-four years of hauling and shelving and thinking about Yiddish books, I'm not sure I have an answer. On one level it's obvious: Jews gave up their parents' and grandparents' books because they couldn't read them, they didn't know what they were, and they figured no one else in their families ever would, either. But sometimes, when I'm feeling especially road-weary or discouraged, I wonder if maybe it's not more complicated than that. Maybe the reason Jews, the People of the Book, uncharacteristically discarded a literature was not because they didn't understand it, but rather because they understood it too well. After all, look how Yiddish literature ended up: its world in ruins, its writers murdered, its readers dying, its children estranged. Tevye's harsh judgment on himself could just as easily apply to every one of the one-and-a-half million books we've saved: *"V'yishkhakeyhu* (And they were forgotten). *Oys di yidishe literatur* (No more modern Yiddish literature)."

But then I remember that despite Tevye's certainty that his day is done, despite his insistence that Sholem Aleichem not write about him, the author does so anyway. And we, the readers, are glad he did.

Perhaps that's how it will be with the rest of Yiddish literature, too. Given the magnitude of the depredations Yiddish books endured — the Holocaust, Stalinist purges, displacement, assimilation — it's no wonder so many rational people concluded that their day was done. But just as Sholem Aleichem wrote about Tevye anyway, we have gone out and saved Yiddish books anyway.

"Un ver vet ibermishn gele bleter?" the poet Kadya Molodowsky asked: "And who will turn these yellowed pages?" She was referring to ancient Hebrew tomes, but today her words might apply just as aptly to Yiddish books, including her own. Who will read them?

According to the Midrash, the reason the Jews spent forty years in the wilderness after leaving Egypt was because only a new generation, unbent by slavery, could enter the promised land. Perhaps so it is with us. After six decades of recoiling from the memory of a world that was destroyed, a new generation is emerging, unbent and untrammeled, to recover the shards of a shattered past, to turn the yellowed pages, to discover just how hip Yiddish really is. "Yiddish has not yet said its last word," Isaac Bashevis Singer predicted.

It does have magic, and it is outwitting history after all.

NOTES

34   *"the wholly spontaneous questions"*   Ruth R. Wisse, *The Schlemiel as Modern Hero* (Chicago: University of Chicago Press, 1971), p. 3.

69   *A Brief History of Yiddish Literature*   This chapter is based in part, on A Portable Homeland, a permanent exhibitionat the National Yiddish Book Center. I want to acknowledge the contribution of my colleagues Neil Zagorin, Nansi Glick, and Nancy Sherman on that project.

74   *"The better Yiddish prose writers avoid writing about American Jewish life"* Isaac Bashevis Singer, "Problems of Yiddish Prose in America (1943)," translated by Robert H. Wolf, *Prooftexts: A Journal for Jewish Literary History* 9 (1989): p. 7.

75   *the Yiddish poet Mordecai Gebirtig wrote with blood-chilling prescience* Mordecai Gebirtig, "Es brent!" [It's Burning!] in Jerry Silverman, *The Yiddish Song Book* (New York: Stein and Day, 1983), p. 185.

108   *"Veyn nisht, Yishmeylikl tate"*   Itzik Manger, "Hagar farlozt Avrom's hoyz," in *Khumesh lider* (Warsaw: Farlag Aleynenyu, 1935), p. 29. English: Itzik Manger, "Hagar Leaves Abraham's House," in *The World According to Itzik: Selected Poetry and Prose,* translated and edited by Leonard Wolf, with an introduction by David G. Roskies and Leonard Wolf, The New Yiddish Library (New Haven and London: Yale University Press, 2002), p. 14.

119–20   *When I was growing up in Newark*   Reprinted in Philip Roth, *Reading Myself and Others* (New York: Farrar, Straus and Giroux, 1975), pp. 175–77.

129   *"In the eighteen minutes it took"*   In Irving Howe, *World of Our Fathers* (New York: Harcourt Brace Jovanovich, 1976), pp. 304–5.

129   *"Over whom shall we weep first"*   Ibid, p. 305.

131   *Yiddish in America became "a tin can"*   Michael Chabon, "Guidebook to a Land of Ghosts," *Civilization* (June/July, 1997).

159   *"No," replies the bookseller*   Isaac Bashevis Singer, *Enemies: A Love Story,* translated by Aliza Shevrin and Elizabeth Shub (New York: Farrar, Straus and Giroux, 1972), p. 261.

161   *"We fashioned our own little battle"*   Abbie Hoffman, *Soon to Be a Major Motion Picture* (New York: Putnam, 1980), p. 208.

162–63 *"They were utterly bewildered"*   Mendele Moykher Seforim, *Kitser masoes Benyomin Hashlishi; The Travels and Adventures of Bejamin the Third,* translated from the Yiddish by Joshe Spiegel (New York: Schocken Books, 1949), p. 116. Excerpts from the Yiddish original added by the author.

163   *" 'Your Honor,' Benjamin vociferated"*   Ibid., p. 123.

164   *"The high honor"*   Isaac Bashevis Singer, *Nobel Lecture* (New York: Farrar, Straus and Giroux, 1979), pp. 6–7.

164   *According to Max Weinreich*   See Max Weinreich, *History of the Yiddish Language,* translated by Shlomo Noble, with the assistance of Joshua A. Fishman (Chicago: University of Chicago Press, 1980).

166   *Consider, for example, Peretz's 1900 story*   See I. L. Peretz, "If Not Higher," translated by Marie Syrkin, in *The I. L. Peretz Reader,* edited and with an introduction by Ruth R. Wisse, The New Yiddish Library (New Haven and London: Yale University Press, 2002), pp. 178–81.

166   *Here's another of Peretz's stories*   I. L. Peretz, "Bontsha the Silent," translated by Hilde Abel, in *A Treasury of Yiddish Stories,* edited by Irving Howe and Eliezer Greenberg (New York: The Viking Press, 1954), pp. 225; 229–30.

167   *"want to see in the story a paean"*   Tzvi Howard Adelman, "Modern Jewish Short Stories and Diasporan Culture," course outline, A Cultural History of the Jews, Hebrew University. On the Web site of the Jewish Agency for Israel (http://www.jafi.org.il/education/juice/history1/week12.html).

168   *"Isaac Leib Peretz was arguably"*   Ruth R. Wisse, Introduction, *The I. L. Peretz Reader,* p. xvi.

206   *"Tell me, Rebbe"*   "Domestic Happiness," in *Stories and Pictures by Isaac Loeb Peretz*, translated from the Yiddish by Helena Frank (Philadelphia: The Jewish Publication Society of America, 1906), pp. 24–25.

207   *"'No Hannah'"*   Ibid., p. 25.

217   *It took months to sort and catalog all eighty-five thousand folios*   The National Yiddish Book Center published a complete catalog of the Metro Music Collection, under the auspices of the Mel and Shifra Gold Yiddish Music Project. The highlights cited here are taken in part from the work of our cataloger, Paula Parsky, in "Gleanings from the Garage," *Pakn Treger,* no. 8 (Winter, 1987).

219   *When Merriam-Webster*   *Webster's Third New International Dictionary of the English Language, Unabridged, with Seven-Language Dictionary,* 3 vols. (Chicago, London, Toronto, Geneva, Sydney, Tokyo, and Manila: William Benton, Publisher, 1966).

226   *"in hundreds of Jewish homes"*   Professor Novershtern's trenchant review of the Polish Jewry series appeared in both Yiddish and English (translated by Henia Lewin) in *Pakn Treger,* no. 15 (Summer 1991).

236   *"You are only ninety miles from the winking lighthouses"*   James Steele, *Cuban Sketches* (1881), cited in *Fodor's Exploring Cuba,* 2nd ed. (New York, Toronto, London, Sydney, and Auckland: Fodor's Travel Publications, n.d.), p. 58.

241   *Back in the U.S.S.R.*   This chapter is based in part on my two earlier accounts: "Yiddish in the Soviet Union: A First-Person Report by Aaron Lansky," *Pakn Treger,* no. 13 (Summer, 1990); and "Back in the U.S.S.R.: The Center's Summer Expedition Succeeds in Delivering 6,000 Yiddish Books to Baltic Jews," *Pakn Treger,* no. 14 (Winter, 1990-1991).

244   *"With what anguish"*   Chaim Beyder, "*Der Shayter*/Death Fire." Translated from the Yiddish by Leah Zasuyer, *Pakn Treger,* no. 13 (Summer, 1990).

245   *"For a time, life was sweet"*   Kenneth Turan, "The Last Widow," *Pakn Treger*, no. 13 (Summer, 1990).

266   *"It has nothing to do directly with defending our country"*   The exchange is recounted in Philip J. Hilts, *Scientific Temperaments: Three Lives in Contemporary Science* (New York: Simon and Schuster, 1982), pp. 98–99.

285   *"At the opening of the Center"*   Ruth R. Wisse, "Yiddish: Past, Present, Imperfect," *Commentary* (November, 1997).

286   *"He found them puerile"*   Cynthia Ozick, "Envy; or, Yiddish in America," in *A Cynthia Ozick Reader*, edited by Elaine M. Kauvar (Bloomington and Indianapolis: Indiana University Press, 1996), p. 20.

287   *"The new building"*   Ruth R. Wisse, "Yiddish: Past, Present, Imperfect."

293–94   *"a massive explosion ripped through"*   Nansi Glick, "Out of the Rubble," *Pakn Treger*, no. 20 (Fall, 1995).

299   *Forthcoming translations include*   The author gratefully acknowledges the assistance of Nancy Sherman in preparing these all-too-brief descriptions.

302   *In Philip Roth's 1969 novel* Portnoy's Complaint   Philip Roth, *Portnoy's Complaint* (New York: Random House, 1969), p. 224.

302–3   *"'Who'd you give the terfillin to?'"*   Philip Roth, *Patrimony* (New York: Simon and Schuster, 1991), pp. 94–96.

307   *"I asked Chava"*   Sholem Aleichem, "Chava," *Tevye's Daughters*, translated by Frances Butwin (New York: Crown Publishers, 1959), p. 97.

307–8   *"'Maybe you've done enough jabbering'"*   Ibid., p. 169. The adjective *milkhiger* (dairy) appears in the original Yiddish and was included here by the author.

309   *"All the rest of the way"*   Ibid., p. 177.

309–10   *"I put on my Shabbos gabardine"*   Ibid., p. 178.

310   *"Don't forget what I asked you"*   Ibid., p. 178. Excerpts from the original Yiddish included by the author.

ACKNOWLEDGMENTS

I DID NOT save Yiddish literature single-handedly. Tens of thousands of people helped, including staff, board, *zamlers* (book collectors), volunteers, donors, and members. It would take another book just to list them all, let alone adequately express my thanks.

But I do want to thank those who made this book possible. I began preliminary work thirteen years ago, with help from the John D. and Catherine T. MacArthur Foundation. Last year, when I returned to the task, the chairman of the National Yiddish Book Center, Lief Rosenblatt, offered his encouragement and made sure I had the time I needed to write. My remarkable colleague Nancy Sherman led the Center in my absence, with help from Eugene Driker, Penina Migdal Glazer, Mike Reiff, Sam Rotrosen, Lou Cove, Jack Fortier, and Paul Page. My loyal assistant, Kelley, guarded my solitude and helped with research, as did Anne Atherley, Catherine Madsen, and Aaron Rubinstein. Samuel Kassow, Nancy Sherman, and Kenneth Turan read the manuscript and provided invaluable advice. Ken Coplon and Noemi Schwarz are great friends who never wavered in their support. My agent, Carol Mann, matched me with the perfect publisher. Patty Williams gave of her time and talent in taking the author photo.

During the months I spent writing, my neighbors in Nova Scotia, Kenneth and Marlene Comeau, and my landlord in Holyoke, Fran O'Connell, showed me special kindness, and our dog, Sadie, never left my side.

My editor at Algonquin, Amy Gash, and my copy editor, Judit Bodnar, worked their magic above and beyond the call of duty. My awe and gratitude know no bounds.

Above all, I am grateful to my family: our daughters, Sasha and Chava, and my wife, Gail. "Just tell the story," Gail advised when I began. If only I had listened to her sooner, I could have finished in half the time.

Outwitting History

The Massachusetts
Book Award Winner in
Nonfiction for 2005

A Reading and
Discussion Guide

—w—

Prepared by
the Massachusetts Center for the Book
www.massbook.org

Wh=hen he was a twenty-three-year-old graduate student, Aaron Lansky stumbled upon an alarming fact: throughout North America, thousands of Yiddish books—books that had survived Hitler and Stalin—were being discarded and destroyed. As an older generation passed on, more often than not their precious Yiddish volumes were literally thrown in the trash by children and grandchildren unable to read the language. An entire literature was on the verge of extinction. So Lansky issued a public appeal for unwanted Yiddish books. The response was overwhelming.

When Lansky started out, it was believed that fewer than 70,000 Yiddish-language books existed. Lansky and a team of young volunteers hauled books from cellars, attics, synagogues, abandoned buildings, and even Dumpsters and recovered that number in six months. Twenty-five years and one and one-half million books later, the National Yiddish Book Center is one of the fastest-growing Jewish cultural organizations in the world.

Outwitting History is an inspiring adventure tale told with the exuberance of a man whose passion and persistence created a home for a precious legacy. And it confirms the prediction made by Isaac Bashevis Singer when he accepted the Nobel prize: "Yiddish has not yet said its last word."

DISCUSSION QUESTIONS

1. On their first trip to New York to look for Yiddish books, Lansky and his fellow students stop for lunch at the Garden Cafeteria (page 20). The humorous scene that follows highlights the central theme of difference and similarity developed throughout the book. How does difference yield to common cause at the physical level and the emotional level in this vignette? Where do you find these themes further developed in the book?

2. Characters in this story are dressed in particular and significant ways. How do the clothes help us to understand people, priorities, and cultures in *Outwitting History*?

3. Lansky describes himself as the man who saved Yiddish books (rather than Yiddish literature). What do books mean to Lansky and to the people who donate them? Look for examples on page 37 and page 45. What other passages about the meaning or importance of books did you notice? Do books bear meaning in your family or cultural history? And why did books take on such special importance for Jewish immigrants in America?

4. Why did so many older Jews consider their Yiddish books their *yerushe* or "inheritance"? How is this concept of inheritance different from or similar to your own?

5. Much is made of the differences between the Hebrew and Aramaic books that scholars read and the Yiddish books that Lansky too often finds heaped in dusty piles in attics and basements. The differences are those of classical and popular culture, of high and low art. How do those distinctions play out in the book? How do other distinctions between high and low culture affect your life?

6. Discuss some of the ways the next generation considered themselves to be "unlike" their immigrant grandparents. Is it unusual to find children more interested in the generation of their grandparents than that of their parents?

7. Lansky describes the National Yiddish Book Center as a "home" for Yiddish books. Where had these books been living before? Why did they need a home?

8. When Lansky wanted to start the National Yiddish Book Center, he came full circle, to Amherst, Massachusetts, where he first learned to read Yiddish. What motivated this choice?

9. What opposition to a National Yiddish Book Center did Lansky encounter and have to overcome? What were the political and fiscal reali-

ties with which he grappled? Do you think most start-up nonprofits face similar challenges?

10. Lansky describes the Canadian immigration experience as a "mosaic" rather than a melting pot (page 227). What does he mean by this? How did American Jewish culture and Canadian Jewish culture develop differently?

11. This is a story, finally, of local heroes, of individuals who make contributions to a larger good. Who is your favorite local hero or what is your favorite vignette from the book? How does this personal story fit into the larger historical context?

12. In the end, do you think Yiddish "outwits" history? Why or why not?

ACTIVITIES

1. Meals and food play a central role in *Outwitting History*. Plan a potluck for your discussion group using some of the dishes mentioned in the book.

2. Isaac Bashevis Singer—among other accomplished writers in Yiddish—is mentioned often in this account. Read aloud his short story "Gimpel the Fool." What makes this story relevant today?

3. Research other Yiddish authors at the website of the National Yiddish Book Center (www.yiddishbookcenter.org).

4. Place a long sheet of paper on a table. Using *Outwitting History* as a guide, draw a time line of the story of Yiddish.

5. The English language has been enriched by many Yiddish words. Discuss the meaning of words such as shmaltzy, kibitz, shmooze, chutzpah,

glitch, and mishmash. What other Yiddish words can you find in English use today? Create a list for your group.

6. Imagine that you are moving to a place with no knowledge of American culture or English language. What books would you select to reflect American culture, values, and language? If you can, gather those books together, and see if they will fit on a shelf, in a bag, in a box—or perhaps you will need a refrigerator packing crate! How can you preserve your selection of books? Who will inherit them?

MASSACHUSETTS
CENTER·FOR·THE·BOOK

The Massachusetts Book Awards are a program of the Massachusetts Center for the Book, an affiliate of the Center for the Book in the Library of Congress. We work with the national center and within a network of fifty state-center affiliates across the country to promote "books, reading, literacy, and libraries." The Massachusetts Center for the Book is supported by a partnership among the Boston Athenaeum, the Boston Public Library, Hampshire College, the Massachusetts Board of Library Commissioners, the Massachusetts Foundation for the Humanities, and Simmons College, with additional support from Five Colleges, Inc., and the Massachusetts Library Association.

"Incredible...Inspiring... Important." —*Library Journal,* starred review

"A marvelous yarn, loaded with near-calamitous adventures and characters as memorable as Singer creations." —*New York Post*

"What began as a quixotic journey was also a picaresque romp, a detective story, a profound history lesson, and a poignant evocation of a bygone world." —*The Boston Globe*

"Every now and again a book with near-universal appeal comes along: *Outwitting History* is just such a book." —*The Sunday Oregonian*

As a twenty-three-year-old graduate student, Aaron Lansky set out to save the world's abandoned Yiddish books before it was too late. Today, twenty-five years and one and a half million books later, he has accomplished what has been called "the greatest cultural rescue effort in Jewish history." In *Outwitting History*, Lansky shares his adventures as well as the poignant and often laugh-out-loud stories he heard as he traveled the country collecting books. Introducing us to a dazzling array of writers, he shows us how an almost-lost culture is the bridge between the old world and the future—and how the written word can unite everyone who believes in the power of great literature.

A *LIBRARY JOURNAL* BEST BOOK OF 2004
THE MASSACHUSETTS BOOK AWARD WINNER IN NONFICTION FOR 2005
AN ALA NOTABLE BOOK

AARON LANSKY is the founder and president of the National Yiddish Book Center (www.yiddishbookcenter.org) in Amherst, Massachusetts. The recipient of a MacArthur "genius" award, he has helped fuel the renaissance of Jewish literature in this country. He lives with his family in western Massachusetts.

MEMOIR/JEWISH INTEREST
ISBN-13: 978-1-56512-513-1 $13.95 in U.S.
Bookland EAN

Cover photograph: © by Bryan Regan

ALGONQUIN BOOKS
a division of Workman Publishing
www.algonquin.com